Tracing the Lines

Currents in Reformational Thought Series

Currents in Reformational Thought seeks to promote new scholarship emerging from the rich and dynamic tradition of reformational intellectual inquiry. Believing that all scholarly endeavour is rooted in and oriented by deep spiritual commitments of one kind or other, reformational scholarship seeks to add its unique Christian voice to discussions about leading questions of life and society. From this source, it seeks to contribute to the redemptive transformation and renewal of the various aspects of contemporary society, developing currents of thought that open human imagination to alternative future possibilities that may helpfully address the damage we find in present reality. As part of this work, *Currents in Reformational Thought* will bring to light the inter- and multi-disciplinary dimensions of this intellectual tradition, and promote reformational scholarship that intentionally invites dialogue with other traditions or streams of thought.

www.icscanada.edu/cprse

Robert Sweetman and Ronald A. Kuipers

SERIES EDITORS

Tracing the Lines

Spiritual Exercise and the Gesture of Christian Scholarship

Robert Sweetman

WIPF & STOCK · Eugene, Oregon

TRACING THE LINES
Spiritual Exercise and the Gesture of Christian Scholarship

Series: Currents in Reformational Thought

Wipf & Stock
An Imprint of Wipf and Stock Publishers
199 W. 8th Ave., Suite 3
Eugene, OR 97401

www.wipfandstock.com

PAPERBACK ISBN: 978-1-4982-9681-6
HARDCOVER ISBN: 978-1-4982-9683-0
EBOOK ISBN: 978-1-4982-9682-3

Manufactured in the U.S.A.

Contents

Acknowledgments

THIS VOLUME STARTED MODESTLY in 2001. It was then an attempt to read-with George Marsden's *The Outrageous Idea of Christian Scholarship* as part of a faculty research project dedicated to thinking through the case for "Christian Scholarship" again—a project furthered by a gift to the Institute for Christian Studies by Rimmer De Vries. The book review, however, next grew into ARIHE (Association of Reformed Institutions of Higher Education) Lectures given in one form or another at Dordt College, Trinity Christian College, and Calvin College during the academic years 2003 to 2004 and 2004 to 2005. The talks were subsequently rewritten and much improved by the feedback received at all three institutions of higher learning.

In the intervening years I began to assemble a scholarly apparatus to complete the project as I then conceived it (a small volume publishing the lectures in something like the form they had when I had given them). In the process, however, the manuscript inflated to book length. In its present form it has benefited from many generous readers. Nicholas Woltertorff, Hendrick Hart, Clarence Joldersma, Joseph Goering, and David Smith commented on early drafts of the opening chapters. Barbara Carvill read the whole manuscript and offered many wonderful suggestions from front to back. James Olthuis also improved the manuscript in crucial ways, particularly in the conclusions of the sixth chapter and then the conclusion of the manuscript as a whole. Allyson Carr and Ronald Kuipers bolstered my floundering efforts by putting their energy to editing (Allyson) and successfully getting a new publications series Currents in Reformational Thought on the institutional agenda (Ron) of the Institute for Christian Studies. Meanwhile, Isabella Guthrie-McNaughton worked quietly and steadily to negotiate our present arrangement with Wipf and Stock. I owe each of these people and institutions my sincerest gratitude; I am blessed. Academic production is a communal affair, no doubt about it. May this particular communal effort grace all the contributions of each of these my benefactors and prove a benefaction to each of its eventual readers.

Chapter One: Tracing Between the Lines

Imagining Scholarship as Christian

Some Christian scholars imagine their scholarship as markedly Christian. Or maybe they are more modest. Maybe they imagine in a general way that scholarship can be Christian and entertain the hope that people will see *their* scholarship as Christian too. Other Christian scholars with equal modesty and sincerity raise their eyebrows when they hear such talk. They cannot help wondering why anyone would think of their scholarship so. Their questions can become quite sharp: How does one dare think that? After all, history provides innumerable examples of destructive notions and actions baptized inappropriately as Christian, notions and actions that believers have learned to repudiate far too slowly and thus at cost to the integrity of their religion. In short, it is not obvious to all Christian scholars that a desire for scholarship that can properly be called Christian is itself proper.

Still, is the desire itself so hard to understand? Consider the following line of thought. Surely, Christians are called to live Christ-following lives? Unless we are satisfied that Christ-following remain ever a mysterious and invisible reality, we entertain a legitimate expectation that the lives Christians live will be marked in some visible way by that Christ-following. Moreover, if the Christ-following life in question is a scholarly life, it seems reasonable to expect that the scholarship itself will bear a correlatively Christ-following mark.

Of course, however understandable the desire for a Christian scholarship, it only raises more questions. What makes scholarship Christian? How would one know that a given instance of scholarship was Christian? Such questions are capable of more than one reasoned answer, and thinking about them can become an absorbing task. So it is that some Christians train their eyes on the scholarship Christians produce out of a conviction that it should and can bear an objectively Christ-following mark.

This book is written with just such an eye. It is written to explore the ways in which one can imagine *scholarship itself* as Christian. It does not, however, deny that many Christian scholars have other, equally legitimate emphases. One can, for example, concentrate on the character of a Christian scholar's scholarly faith. Such a focus would direct one's attention toward *faith claims* and toward the ways schooled thought can confirm, connect, or extend personal and communal grasp of those claims and their implications.[1] Alternatively, one can concentrate on the *character and calling* of the faithful scholar. That focus would entail exploring the sort of person it takes to live well as a Christian teacher, researcher, or writer, and on the ways of fostering just such persons in home, church, and school.[2]

Champions of these last two emphases sometimes struggle to understand or appreciate the perspective of those whose interest as Christians centers on the character of scholarship.[3] The reverse is also true. I think of this lack of mutual understanding and appreciation as a minor scandal. No matter what focus one chooses as primary, surely one must still struggle in the end to understand and account for all three of these foci: Christian faith, Christian scholar, and Christian scholarship.[4]

It is for this reason that the focus of this book is very broad: Christian scholarship thought of as a whole. From what vantage point can one have such a holistic conversation, however? Interest in discussions around Christian scholarship has largely been restricted to philosophers, theologians, and those scholars in other disciplines who have what can be termed a philosophical or theological interest in their disciplines. Nevertheless, if it is true that interest in questions surrounding Christian scholarship wanes the further one moves from the discussion's traditional home among

1. Sharon Daloz Parks trains her eyes on faith and the inculcation of a scholastically developed faith in Parks, *Big Questions, Worthy Dreams*.

2. Parker J. Palmer is particularly sensitive to the calling of the Christian teacher in one eloquent study after another; see for example Palmer, *To Know as We are Known*; see also Schwehn, *Exiles from Eden*.

3. See, in this regard, Jacobsen and Hustedt Jacobsen, ed., *Scholarship and Christian Faith*, above all, the editors' essay entitled "More Than the 'Integration' of Faith and Learning" found on 15–31.

4. This volume proves no exception to the "rule." Though the volume concentrates upon the Christian character of scholarship, that concentration leads by the sixth and final chapter to discussions both of the acquisition of scholarly faith and to the character of the Christian scholar.

philosophers and theologians, it is also true that the discussion invariably identifies Christian scholarship that has been produced in a wide range of academic disciplines.[5] That is a simple fact, of course, but it is also a challenge, for I can only speak most comfortably from my corner of the scholarly enterprise: the patristic and medieval chapters of the history of (you guessed it) philosophy and theology. A reader might well wonder, then, how I can hope to illumine the contours of so broad a multi- and transdisciplinary scholarly whole? I haul out my wares like any traveling tinker.

Spiritual Exercise as Imaginative Starting-Point

What I am selling here can be called thought exercises. Each of these exercises is designed to invite the reader to think about Christian scholarship in one fresh way or another. Some of these exercises take the form of arguments—or at least trains of thought like the one included above, that could form the basis for arguments proper. But many take other discursive forms: for example, stories, aphorisms, and turns of phrase. These latter exercises are designed to appeal to the mind in its intersection with imagination. In fact, the presentation of material in this book is more evocative and descriptive than argumentative. And that is a matter of intent, for it aims more to elicit recognition of something already inchoately sensed rather than to compel assent to something heretofore unthought-of.

The recognition I have in mind trades on and is simultaneously designed to stretch the reader's imaginative and conceptual elasticity. Such elasticity enables reader and writer together to negotiate a way around differences of vocabulary and disciplinary interlocutors. The hope is that a reader will encounter something in the text in such a way that he is minded to say, "Oh, I get it, except when you say '*x*,' I say '*y*.'" If all goes to plan, the reader will recognize in the text scholarly experiences that she "has always and wordlessly known" but can now "speak about," having been given words to express what had already been silently felt.

Having made this qualification, the exercises in this book remain properly scholarly acts. They are what the ancient philosophers called spiritual exercises—invitations to think again, but from newly imagined angles or starting points, about what one thought one always knew.[6] The ancient

5. A good example of the pattern is to be seen in Heie and Wolfe, ed., *The Reality of Christian Learning*.

6. In our day, the notion of spiritual exercise is associated with religious meditation,

philosophers invented this method because they had become convinced that the schooled love of wisdom would remain forever barren and ineffective as long as the social and cultural formation of its participants was distorted and unhelpful. And it was their judgment that the social and cultural formation of their day was profoundly distorted and unhelpful, right from the get-go. People were set on wrong paths by the very stories told in the nursery.[7] And the distortions only became more sophisticated as children were reared and received subsequent, formal training.[8] As a result, it was their judgment that if one were truly to learn the love of wisdom, one needed to learn to think outside of one's social and cultural formation (what the ancient Greeks called *paideia*). That is, one needed to learn to think what was, strictly speaking, unthinkable to a person of just that upbringing and training.[9] These philosophers appealed in their exercises to a principle of intelligibility in the cosmos that was deeper and truer than its articulation via social and cultural formation, a principle they called "nature." This principle could be accessed anew beyond that formation—provided one learned to feel, to imagine, and to think from starting points that put one at odds with one's formation, and so (it was assumed) in touch with the nature from which that formation had become alienated.

Limitations of the Current Conceptions

I assume a mode of presentation that has deliberate resonances with this pedagogy of the ancient philosopher because it is my sense that present discussions around Christian scholarship, even those discussions carried on by people committed to the project, run aground in certain ways. I give, for now, what I take to be three examples. First, I point again to the limited

if one thinks about it at all. Paul Rabbow, however, has helped historians of thought rediscover the philosophical origins of spiritual exercise. See in this regard, Rabbow *Seelenführung*. Pierre Hadot is the scholar most responsible for giving the ancient philosophical exercise some prominence along with its concomitant understanding of ancient philosophy as an art of right living. See Hadot, *Philosophy as a Way of Life*.

7. A fine example of this characteristically Hellenistic posture toward civic *paideia* is adumbrated by Plato in *Republic* 377a–392a.

8. Plato's account of *paideia*'s failing in formal as well as nursery formation is to be found in *Republic* 595a–607e and is commonly referred to as philosophy's quarrel with poetry.

9. On the notion of ancient philosophy, especially its Hellenistic representation, as a therapeutics, i.e., as medicine for the soul, see Nussbaum, *The Therapy of Desire*.

appeal of these discussions among scholars outside of the humanities. In other words, there is a *disciplinary narrowness* to the discussion as it presently exists that begs our attention; it is effectively restricted to disciplines in which a constructive role for perspective has been acknowledged as productive or at least as unavoidable.

Second is a matter of *dialogical situation.* Articulate concern for the discussion has overwhelmingly restricted itself to scholarly and institutional environments that are Christian-faith based—that is, largely, Catholic, Reformed, and Evangelical colleges and universities.[10] In being so restricted, the discussion occurs with little input from, (and indeed, can be inferred to be of little interest or benefit to) the largest group of Christian scholars: those who work at pluralist universities, whether public or private.

There are reasons for this state of affairs. A Christian scholar working in a pluralist academic environment is not likely to be rewarded institutionally for taking time and effort to think and write about the connection between her faith and her scholarship. Indeed, she might well be convinced that she will be punished, in that time and effort will be taken that would otherwise be used to publish articles and books necessary to secure and advance her academic position. Or it could just as often be the case that Christian scholars working in pluralist environments do so in part because they are uninterested in such effort. They may think of it as a kind of navel gazing, a diversion from the real business at hand. I suggest, however, that there is also something in the terms or way in which the present discussion is carried on that misses the mark for such scholars, that fails to touch or speak to their experience and goals as Christians and scholars. Not to seriously engage this largest group of Christian scholars in discussions about Christian scholarship seems a significant shortcoming that deserves careful consideration, for I want to say that in certain respects, these intellectuals are best positioned to insert Christian voices into the general scholarly discussion.

Third, there has been preference for *distinctions over connections*: conversation about Christian scholarship has been most attractive to discussants who are most at home in what might be thought of as the project of

10. There is, of course, a rich body of reflection upon the character of the Christian scholar to be found within Lutheran educational contexts and an interestingly mixed reflection upon scholarly faith, faithful scholar, and critical themes of Christian scholarship in Anabaptist contexts. They do not come in for primary analysis here because their entrée into discussions around Christian being and the scholarly enterprise comes via reflection upon scholarly faith or the character of the faithful scholar, first and foremost.

separating out one thing from another. As the old scholastic proverb would have it, *bene distinguere, bene philosophare*: good distinctions make for good philosophy. Now, I too want to make some distinctions, ones I hope will prove helpful, so it is not the making of distinctions per se that I am calling attention to. Rather, what I am getting at here is a tendency to make the kind of distinctions that so separate the things distinguished from each other that they must be thought of as mutually exclusive. When such habits are applied to positions about Christian scholarship, or between Christian scholarship and other scholarly types, the positions so distinguished come to seem incompatible in ways that cover over shared problematics I intend this book to bring to the surface, whether to celebrate or question. I have already alluded to the minor scandal in which discussions around Christian faith, scholars, and scholarship focus attention on only one of the terms and show little appreciation for the others. However, even within the subdiscussions developed in the context of one focus or another, distinctions are too often posited as exclusions.

Particularly in light of this last difficulty or problem, what is needed is a way of understanding Christian scholarship that acknowledges the many and legitimate differences that exist in the practice of scholarship and in accounts of the character of the scholarship so practiced. What is needed is an understanding that cultivates an eye for the unity equally expressed *in and through* those differences. We can limber up in preparation, so to speak, via the following exercise. What if Christian scholarship were thought of like a folk recipe? Folk recipes are famously different depending on the habits and predilections of each cook. I am suggesting that the diversity characteristic of a folk recipe as it lives in each separate kitchen applies equally to Christian scholarship. One must correlate the unity with the differences if one is to take the full measure of either folk recipes or Christian scholarship.

Catching the Unity of Christian Scholarship

In this light I invite the reader to turn, in my second chapter, to two ancient Christian scholars: Justin Martyr and Augustine of Hippo. Their examples serve to illustrate the unity-in-difference implied by the metaphor of folk recipe as it applies to Christian scholarship. We will see that each in their way intended to align their scholarship to the Christian scriptures. Alignment, however, was not first and foremost directed toward understanding those scriptures; it was not intended as a form of exegesis. Rather, alignment with the scriptures started from a prior immersion in them, an immersion that took place within their respective communities of faith and spiritual formation. The alignment they intended developed via study of God, self, and world in light of their religious formations so as to produce understanding consistent with deep hunches about the nature of things implicit in their formation.

I have chosen these two ancient Christians precisely because of their antiquity and consequent alien ethos. We might imagine it this way: these two early scholar-cooks allow us to pick up the whiff of a shared aroma to be enjoyed, or perhaps just sniffed at. Of course they cannot do this on their own. Readers must participate in the fun. We must be willing to follow the post-Platonic scholarly projects of these ancient examplars and compare them somehow with our own. This may pose an initial problem, for Justin Martyr's and Augustine's questions are quite narrowly theological and philosophical, so they cannot illustrate directly how alignment to the scriptures works for contemporary scholars in the many disciplines extant today. Nevertheless, they do raise the question of whether (and in what sense) one might think of diverse modern scholarly preoccupations in alignment with the scriptures. Indeed, the subsequent chapters of this book are an attempt to show how this might be done.

Acknowledging the Diversity of Conceptions of Integral Christian Scholarship

In chapter three, I go on to identify and illustrate three ways in which Christians interested in Christian scholarship have accounted for the intrinsic Christian unity or integrality of scholarship across the disciplines (what can also be termed its alignment with the scriptures). These accounts developed slowly over the centuries of Christian reflection subsequent to the patristic era of Justin and Augustine. As a result, I do not try to identify Justin or Augustine with one or another of these subsequent accounts; rather they can be legitimately claimed for the genealogy of all three. I examine these accounts in conversation with what I will call trustworthy guides to each way: for the first way, Bonaventure of Bagnoregio, Etienne Gilson and John Paul II; for the second, Alvin Plantinga and George Marsden; and for the third, Herman Dooyeweerd and H. Evan Runner.[11]

11. I use three examples of the first way because it is the way that has predominated within the Christian academy since the thirteenth-century flowering of Latin

The first of these ways speaks of the complementarity of faith and scholarship. Consequently, I refer to this way as a *complementarist account* of the integrality of Christian faith and scholarship. In this account, faith and scholarship are to be kept separate in all disciplines except theology, although faith should enable the scholar—following the lead of theologians—to judge claims and methods as believer rather than as scholar, with regard to their Christian appropriateness.

The second of these ways I call an *integrationist account*. It speaks of the possibility and desirability of the integration of faith and scholarship in all disciplines. In other words, it sees faith as a potentially intrinsic element in the scholarly disciplines, though not necessary in scholarly practice, strictly speaking.

The third of these ways I call a *holistic account*. It insists on the inseparability of faith and scholarship. In other words, it underlines that the scholar is a person, not a thinking substance, and that as a result all of our thinking emerges from a context that is already preformed. All scholars start from what they have received and put faith in, and these received starting points act in their lives as the gift of faith operates in the lives of Christian believers. Scholarship then is one way that these founding and hence religious convictions come to expression; faith and scholarship necessarily form an indivisible whole.

Each way has a recognizable provenance, and each carries with it a number of strengths and weaknesses. I end the third chapter by acknowledging the way (and its guides) that I have myself chosen to follow, but my intent is not to claim thereby that my choices are superior to the choices made by other Christ-followers. Rather, I am inviting the reader to think about how she understands the Christian integrality of academic work. Does her own way of thinking about this integrality recall one of the ways

scholasticism and hence has differentiated in the most complex ways. I use two examples of the second and third way because the first thinker in each way, while clearly the greater of the two thinkers at least from the philosophical and theological bias habitual in these sorts of discussion, is less easily accessible than the second. The second thinker then acts as a gloss on the first. I should say that one very prominent thinker whom I might have taken up within the framework of what I call the "holistic" position (below) is Nicholas Wolterstorff. He has done a great deal of thinking and writing about Christian scholarship. I will attempt to document my considerable debt to him in chapter three of this volume. I chose to use H. Evan Runner as my second example, in the end, because there is a more direct line between him and Herman Dooyeweerd, and as an act of filial piety since I presently hold the H. Evan Runner Chair in the History of Philosophy at the Institute for Christian Studies in Toronto, Canada.

described here? Who are her own guides, and what pattern of fidelity and inventiveness marks her own being-guided?

The Embarrassments of Christian Difference

In chapter four, I note that, despite the existence of different ways of accounting for the integrality of Christian scholarship across the disciplines, accounts of the distinctiveness of this scholarship sound strikingly the same. Whether one is considering accounts of Christian distinctiveness that emerge from complementarist, integrationist, or holist notions of Christian scholarly integrality, they all employ a common conceptual figure arising from a shared intellectual history and the deeply ingrained discursive habits that history inculcates. This is one place in which my own training and competence allows me to see something important: namely, that distinctiveness is almost always accounted for in an Aristotelian way. That is, scholarship is understood as a genus or general kind of human activity that encompasses many specific kinds, one of which is properly termed "Christian." These specific kinds are constituted by a stable "difference," to be identified with concrete scholarly methods and/or claims.

I proceed to explore certain embarrassments that seem to issue from this shared conceptual figure. These embarrassments circle around two issues. In the first place, embarrassment emerges from the contradictory impulse to simultaneously restrict and affirm the actuality of shared meaning in the claims one makes about the world. This is most obvious when different perspectives use the same words and phrases to articulate their claims about the world. In the second place, embarrassment arises around the difficulty Christian scholars have with identifying those concrete and available methods or claims that constitute once and for all the requisite "Christian difference."

I conclude from this exploration that the attempt to account for the distinctiveness of Christian scholarship on Aristotelian terms leads one to head in one of two directions. One is either forced to define difference at such a primary level that Christian and other forms of scholarship can only be termed "scholarship" if the word is used equivocally. In other words, an Aristotelian search for the Christian difference will tend to lead on the one hand to dissolution of the common genus. On the other hand, one can head in the opposite direction in one's searching. Such a search will come to an opposite but equally problematic solution. Emphasis upon unity at the level of genus leads to a potentially endless search for a stable Christian difference that tends to lead in turn to a denial of any significant difference at all.

I ask whether one might, in light of those embarrassments and the bifurcated pattern they indicate, experiment with other concepts, terms, and images. In asking this question, I take it that a way of speaking about the efficacy of Christian faith as scholarly resource will continue to be meaningful by virtue of the line of thought about Christ-following with which this chapter began. Of course, one needs to acknowledge how ingrained an Aristotelian way of accounting for difference is; it is embedded within Christian discourse in something like the way in which ancient Greek philosophers saw conventional understandings of say justice or love embedded within the *paideia* of their societies. What are needed are new ways of thinking that have the affective power to overcome the inertia of embedded understandings. I try to make a beginning toward such new ways of thinking at the conclusion of chapter four.

In general, I suggest that we identify the integrality of Christian scholarship with its animating spirit or ethos, rather than with delimited features intrinsic to its methods and claims. Moreover, we should do so in the context of a differently imagined root-metaphor: an image of scholarship as the work produced by scholars and scholarly communities self-consciously attuned to the shape of their hearts.

Of course, such a suggestion offers more than simple resistance to the more embarrassing conundrums flowing from a habitual "Aristotelianism;" it offers a different way of imagining the distinctiveness of Christian scholarship, one in which the integrality of Christian scholarship is more ongoing than established. It does so because of the nature of scholarship and its "public" character. That is, scholarly methods and claims are public and hence appropriable. As a result, no difference rooted in such claims and methods can have the exclusiveness and durability to count as "difference" in an Aristotelian sense. Nevertheless, such an alternative way of accounting for Christian difference may well call up its own resistance in the hearts and minds of readers.

Imagining the Spirit of Integral Christian Scholarship

Consequently, in chapter five, I examine certain impediments working against recognition of this alternatively imagined project, impediments that I will illustrate with reference to the religious culture of my own Protestant orthodoxy. I suggest that orthodox Protestant participants in the project of integral Christian scholarship struggle with a two-fold shadow side of their habitual character: a tendency toward what I will call "repristination" rooted in a conflation of holiness and purity, and in an "intellectualism" in which purity is further identified with its conceptual articulation.[12] These qualities, functioning in tandem, dispose such scholars to assume a cramped and fearful posture toward the diversity and provisionality manifested by Christian scholarship as it exists on the ground. Consequently, a certain conflation of "repristination" and "intellectualism" works against a truly heartfelt imagining of the constitutively diverse and provisional Christian scholarship that I am arguing for.

I conclude this section by suggesting an exercise particularly for those of us who recognize ourselves as orthodox Protestants. We might try viewing our constitutive orthodoxy itself as at its deepest a faith-enabled and Spirit-guided communal accrediting *process* rather than as a static, credible *essence* articulable in its core once and for all via propositions held as true "by all, at all times, and in all places."[13] In other words, here too we might be helped by the metaphor of the folk-recipe.

In chapter six, I trace some of the shapes that a re-imagined Christian scholarship might take. I propose in the first place that such scholarship requires a nose for the animating spirit of scholarship, and this in turn demands a particular kind of discipline: a scholarly discernment built up via what I have already called spiritual exercise. The ancient practice of philosophical spiritual exercise illustrates what I mean by scholarly discernment and provides a context in which I suggest exercises that can serve processes of discernment designed to attune the scholar to the shape of her Christian heart.

Thus I suggest as a first exercise of this section that we orient ourselves by constantly re-enforcing the notion that Christian scholarship takes place within a simultaneously created, fallen, and redeemed world. That ambiguous or un/trustworthy world marks out a common ground that Christian and non-Christian share. But to say that much is not yet to say enough, because while the world accessed by scholarship is always common, it is never neutral. Additionally, I suggest that imagining the scholar's world

12. For the historical location and meaning of Protestant orthodoxy used here see the first, second, and final chapters of Sweetman, ed., *In the Phrygian Mode*, 9–32; 287–309.

13. The formula or criterion of orthodoxy is famously associated with the figure of Irenaeus of Lyons in his polemics against the heresies of his day. A widely accessible edition of his *Adversus Haereses* is to be found in *Patrologia Graeca* VII: 433–1224.

as such a common but contested site should give rise to a certain posture toward non- and differently- Christian thought whereby all the features of our shared world can be counted on to be there in the products of serious thought. But the features of our world will be there in countlessly different orders or arrangements, and they will certainly travel under different names. Such a posture, as I imagine it, is enabled by a certain kind of eye that is sensitive to the play of unity and difference, and, above all, sensitive to unity manifest *in and through* difference. I think of that eye rather like a Cubist painter's eye for, delight in, and (where appropriate) lament of the multiple orders and "names" inherent within discourse about our shared world.

The Cubist painter's posture does not come naturally, however. Rather, it must itself be developed and exercised. Consequently, the reader is invited to consider yet another orienting exercise: namely, to recognize that in a world in which a deep creational goodness and an openness to redemption are ubiquitous, mistaken claims or understandings—whether made by a Christian or a non-Christian scholar—are more likely than not "almost right." In addition, they are invited to imagine that, because of the ubiquity of the Fall and its effects, true claims and understandings—again, whether made by a Christian or a non-Christian scholar—are more likely than not "almost mistaken."

Such exercises must understand that mistakes come in many grades and kinds, for it would be foolish to deny that some mistakes are malignant, in horrible and destructive ways, and must be resisted with might and main. Others are trivial and not worth attending to closely, but rather corrected with little comment. Still others turn out to be creative and should be embraced and indeed celebrated. Nor are the exercises intended to deny that some truths are so powerful that they can save the very damned, while others are too trivial to matter much, and the vast majority of truths fall somewhere in between these two moral extremes.

In short, these exercises are designed to orient the scholar's first impulse toward scholarship, fostering receptiveness even while acknowledging the reality and ubiquity of spiritual struggle. One might imagine it this way: One must be prepared to learn from one's scholarly friends and acquaintances, to be sure, but also from one's "enemies." It is a large part of how one loves them. That love involves really attending to what they too have seen in the world, their sensitivity to the good of the creation, their openness to and their feel for the workings of redemption, even in cases where one knows in one's bones that that sensitivity and openness becomes somehow skewed with harmful results. The point is not to read everyone as if they were Christians, but rather to allow scholars to be the sorts of scholar that each is, while assuming that the world we are all interpreting truly is a shared Creation. As such, it will be recognizable to us, too, however exotically and dangerously presented—though we must also acknowledge that this same world can be interpreted falsely even when presented in familiar and seemingly innocuous ways.

Scholarly discernment as I am imagining it connects scholarly activity and results with deep, "interior" and orienting impulses vis-à-vis scholarship and the world at large. As such it cannot be thought of as wholly restricted to the scholarly horizon. This admission however demands elaboration of our image of scholarly discernment in two directions.

In the first place, since "animating spirit" or "ethos" can easily seem to lack a sufficiently determinate conceptual shape and solidity to bear scholarly weight, scholarly discernment should also be thought of as translation, i.e., the translation of our deepest hunches and trajectories into principles and trajectories of scholarly production that we truly care about as persons. This is done by discerning within our founding hunches an appropriate discursive approximation (e.g., a root metaphor, axiom, aphorism, premise, etc.) that is capable of animating the process of scholarly inquiry in attunement with those hunches. I illustrate here what I take to be salient features of a pattern of discernment—though again, the point of using my own example is not to offer a normative paradigm but rather to provide a point for readerly comparison.

In the second place, understanding discernment as translation of "a prior ethos or spirit" enables that ethos or spirit to be fully at play in subsequent scholarly production and criticism. Otherwise, there is a legitimate fear that anchoring Christian scholarship in a prior spirit or ethos removes the scholarship's principles from the essential scholarly process of sifting or criticism. Such a removal would of course reduce the risk that scholarly criticism entails for the Christian scholar as Christian believer. Nevertheless, it would also impose upon that same scholar the isolation of the conceptual ghetto. In the ghetto, it becomes ever harder to benefit from scholarship produced beyond ghetto walls, for such scholarship comes to sound alien and so to attract suspicion. It becomes equally hard to benefit the wider scholarly community for an analogous reason: an ever more idiosyncratic voice becomes ever harder for outsiders to understand or credit.

And yet, the spirit or ethos of one's scholarship not only provides the principles and initial trajectories for scholarly production; it also represents one's very attunement to the shape of one's heart. Consequently, that spirit should not be put in play in such a way that it could be easily dispensed with or exchanged; it is the very stuff of one's scholarly principles and the animating direction of one's scholarly movements. While the principles and trajectories that translate it are to be put in play, it and the heart it is attuned to should be tended. I suggest then an image that can orient one to this difficult balance. Imagine Christian scholarship as oceanic and, as such, having a natural ebb and flow. Imputing such a flux and reflux to Christian scholarship helps to foster reciprocal engagement with the scholarship of other spiritual and ideological communities, while nurturing the Christian origins and dynamics at play in one's own scholarly contributions.

This ebb and flow is worth a closer look. One can think of the ebb side of Christian scholarship as attentive discernment of the shape of the heart and of the trajectories directive of scholarship attuned to that shape. Such discernment is properly communal. Christian academic communities committed to this type of scholarship should have an obvious interest in making space for, and giving prominence to, structured opportunities for discernment and the mutual support and correction such discernment entails. Christian scholarly institutions are natural centers for this side of the scholarly project.

Of course, even Christian scholarly institutions are not enough on their own to ensure the quality of the Christian hearts to be discerned; that is at bottom a matter of spiritual formation, and the ordinary contexts for that formation are the Christian home, Christian friendship, and the institutional church. Thus, the capacity of the Christian scholarly community to produce vibrant Christian scholarship will always be conditioned above all by the health or the effectiveness of spiritual formation among Christian families, friends, and churches. Consequently, it would seem that Christian scholarly institutions would also do well to attend to the patterns of spiritual formation within homes, friendship, and churches, and open themselves up to assist churches in thinking about and implementing healthy patterns of formation.

On its flow side Christian scholarship is well imagined as a joining of conversations that in our post-Christian world are nearly always already on the go. This joining too entails a proper orientation. Thus, I suggest as orienting exercise the thought that our joining must entail a valuing of the conversation as, on some fundamental level, right and important in that one is set in motion towards it by the very dynamic of one's Christian heart.

Such an approach contrasts perhaps with the insistence of some that Christian scholarship assume a *normatively* marginal status in the communities of scholarly discourse it inhabits. "Prophetic" hollering from the sidelines does, I admit, have a role to play in the community of faith's witness to a broken world.[14] Such hollering can be of high scholarly virtuosity.[15] But if that posture becomes the only one Christian scholars are allowed to assume as Christians, it becomes in its marginal way a centralizing of power around a narrow purity ideal. If all the world is simultaneously created, fallen, and subject to the operation of redemption, however, then purity is precluded. The dirt of the Fall is ubiquitous; Christian scholars must acknowledge "getting dirty," and can do so knowing that where there is fall there is also the operation of redemption. In other words, a central theme of Christian living allows one to acknowledge the ubiquity of the Fall within our own scholarly efforts without fear or despair. There is always *metanoia*, the equally ubiquitous opening to God's redemptive presence and call to turn the direction of one's thought and work in repentance.

On the other hand, the joining I have in mind will also involve in principle a Christian scholar's willingness and ability to assume a critical posture within post- and non-Christian conversations. That is, the Christian joiner will remain attentively open to the task of reinforcing all that is most attractive in the conversations she enters and to the possibility of nudging other less attractive dimensions in different and hopefully healthier directions, directions suggested to her by resources within her own Christian formation. Such formation includes, of course, the ongoing discipline of her devotion, the catechetics of her community of faith, within the determinate Christian theoretical trace that she assumes and develops in her interactions with other Christian scholars, and, finally, within what she encounters in the religiously heterogeneous conversations themselves.

The last phrase makes an important point. The religiously heterogeneous conversations we join are themselves to be imagined as a resource

14. See in this regard Walsh, *Subversive Christianity*.

15. The recent work of Brian Walsh and his collaborators in exploring a "biblical worldview and mode of living" illustrates the scholarly acumen attainable within scholarship from the margins of the world of biblical scholarship. See, Walsh and Middleton, *Truth is Stranger than it Used to Be*, and Walsh and Keesmaat, *Colossians Remixed*. One thinks as well of the work of Wendell Berry at the margins of environmental and sociological studies. See, for example Berry, *Sex, Economy, Freedom and Community*.

for the Christian scholar, for he should know, otherwise[16] and deep down, that the redemptively trustworthy is *as ubiquitous* as is the fallenly untrustworthy, and that redemption and fall exist only in relation to a creation judged "very good." It should never be forgotten that God never quite took back that initial judgment in the biblical stories of divine disappointment and wrath consequent upon human sin.

Throughout all of the following chapters, my remarks will maintain as expansive a focus as I can manage, though I will use examples to make matters more concrete. Such a focus cannot but flirt with abstraction, with being merely and vaguely general. Nevertheless, I do not intend to give in to the allure of the generic. Rather, I am aiming to foster sensitivity to the language we assume because it seems to us, for whatever reason, to express those deep secrets of the universe whispering subliminally of the creation's encounter with its lawful Maker.

16. The adverb "otherwise" is designed to indicate ways of knowing about God, self, and world that are trustworthy but are neither conceptualist nor intellectualist in structure. See in this regard Olthuis, ed., *Knowing* Other-*wise*. The "thing" this term "otherwise" points to is gotten at differently in other Christian discourses. If one looks at the lexicon of Abraham Kuyper, for example, he emphasized not the mode of knowing but what might be termed the organ of knowing. That he was yet speaking of the same "thing," can be inferred from his unwillingness to identify that organ with intellect. Rather he dipped into the insect world for his metaphor and spoke of antennae (*gevoelhorens*) by which we sense the religious charge and value of what we encounter in the world.

Chapter Two: Getting In Line with Justin Martyr and Saint Augustine[1]

The Challenge of the Concrete

To GIVE UP THE allure of the generic is a difficult renunciation. It means that one must dive into the lush excess of the concrete, of the sights and sounds of a neighbourhood, someone's neighbourhood. But such a locale cannot by definition be everyone's neighbourhood. If a place could be imagined somehow as a universally common place that belongs to all, it is no longer a neighbourhood, for it no longer exists in relation to the distinction between neighbours and strangers. A universally common place cannot then be concrete, for to be concretely human and humanly cultural is to be "neighbourhooded" as one of my most linguistically adventurous colleagues has put it.[2] We exist on location or in the concrete, among neighbours to whom we relate with greater and lesser degrees of intimacy. Beyond our neighbourhood we meet strangers with whom we are not intimate at all.

To renounce the generic, then, imposes a certain burden on oneself. More importantly, it also imposes a certain burden on one's reader. A mental elasticity and a listening patience is required. One must learn to take in the unfamiliar sights and sounds and remain receptive to their difference, expecting that there, precisely in all that is different, one will encounter an encompassing unity and so experience connection. These are, of course, the habits that a connoisseur takes with him or her when entering multiple kitchens in search of the variable taste of a beloved folk recipe.

This and subsequent chapters will require just such elasticity and patience of the reader. It will also exercise these virtues with malice

1. An earlier version that has undergone but modest revision was published in *Pro Rege* 33, 3 (2005): 26–36.

2. Cf. Seerveld, "Dooyeweerd's Idea of 'Historical Development,'" 41–61.

aforethought. So we will commence our search for the unity of Christian scholarship to be encountered in the most exotic of Christian scholars and texts by examining two of the earliest Christian writers on the topic to hand. We will take an unhurried look at the ancient neighbourhood they called their own precisely because it is alien. We will need to practice mental elasticity and listening patience. If we are successful, however, we will learn to see the lineaments of a shared project, even within the exotica of a long past world.

Justin Martyr and Christian Philosophy[3]

Christianity did not begin as the religion of philosophers, grammarians, experts in the law and forensic rhetoric, i.e., the religion most attractive to participants in the scholarly professions of the ancient Mediterranean world. But early on it did attract people of that sort. We know, for example, of some early converts who were interested in and gave themselves to philosophy or the love of wisdom. They asked questions about the relationship between the wisdom of their new-found faith and the schooled love of wisdom they took with them into it. The second century Christian Justin Martyr provides us an example in his *Dialogue with Trypho the Jew*.[4] Let us look over his shoulder.

As Justin tells the story, he is walking along one day when a man and his friends salute him. They address him as philosopher because he is dressed as such, bearing the pallium or philosopher's cloak. Justin asks the man what he wants and the man says that a renowned Cynic had taught him to engage philosophers in conversation at every opportunity; in doing so, he will either learn something of benefit, or the philosopher will, and either way it will be well for both.

3. Philosophy as Justin and later Augustine understand the term is not a scholarly discipline in our sense. Rather it is a schooled practice of right living, of life lived in accordance with our deepest nature (creatures in relation with their Maker). It is a conception of philosophy in continuity with the conceptions to be found in ancient philosophy generally. See for example Hadot, *What is Ancient Philosophy*.

4. An easily accessible edition of the Greek text is to be found in the *Patrologia Graeca* VI: 471–800. The English edition consulted here for the purposes of providing a translation is *The Writings of Justin Martyr*, trans. Thomas B. Walls, Fathers of the Christian Church Series (New York: Heritage Inc., 1948) 147–366. The work is divided into one hundred and forty-two chapters, the first ten of which set the scene for the dialogue or dispute proper and contain the biographical sketch used here. Henceforth with page # from Walls translation.

Justin next asks who the man is and he identifies himself as Trypho, a Jewish refugee. At this Justin's eyebrows raise and he asks why Trypho would think to benefit from a philosopher when he has Moses and the prophets. The question could equally be asked of Justin himself, as he well knows, adding or perhaps substituting Jesus Christ and the Apostles.

Trypho's answer begins by identifying common ground between philosophy and the revelation of Moses and the prophets: "do not the philosophers [too] speak always about God? Do they not constantly propose questions about his unity and providence? Is this not the task of philosophy, to inquire about the Divine?"[5]

Justin admits the common ground but then insists that it is not neutral ground. His admission and insistence are designed to point out that the philosopher's theological inquiry and the prophets' inspired reception of divine revelation do indeed share a common subject—the divine and its ways in the world—but that the philosopher's theological inquiry constitutes a grasping-for rather than a receiving-of knowledge, and this posture or attitude orients one's whole approach to the shared subject in ways that make a substantive difference. Justin gets at his point by emphasizing the relative fallibility of the philosophers' theological inquiry. "But," he says, "the majority of the philosophers have simply neglected to inquire whether there is one or even several gods, and whether or not a divine providence actually takes care of us, as if this knowledge were unnecessary to our happiness."[6] He goes on to list other important mistakes that are made even by those who do deal with these issues, mistakes that cut the ground out from under right, wrong, and the just relations between human beings and with respect to God.

Trypho plays out his role as straight man and asks Justin to explain where he stands on these central issues. He gladly tells his story. He begins by praising philosophy as "one's greatest possession," and as "most precious in the sight of God to whom it alone leads us and to whom it unites us." As a consequence he views those who apply themselves to philosophy as "in truth . . . holy men."[7] But there are many schools of philosophy and they bicker over how one is to love wisdom. Justin accounts for this in a story of gigantic beginnings whittled down to size. We who come after the larger-than-life founders mistake our giantish heroes for wisdom herself. Hence

5. Ibid., 1.148.

6. Ibid., 1.148.

7. Ibid., 2.149.

we parcel up their common enterprise, preserving the founders' opinions as if they were wisdom's, full stop.

Indeed, Justin's own biography as he tells it illustrates the point.[8] He had begun his pursuit of wisdom with a Stoic but learned nothing new about God. He then turned to an Aristotelian who insisted on tuition for his instruction. Justin judged this insistence to be evidence that the Aristotelian was not a philosopher, for one does not sell access to divine things. That is sophistry, and, as such, foolishness, the very antipode of wisdom. Justin next turned to a Pythagorean teacher who demanded he first study mathematics, geometry and astronomy. He had no stomach for such demanding preconditions and so turned to the Platonists. From his Platonic teacher he learned of incorporeal things. He named the effect of this learning in classically Platonic fashion: "it added wings to my mind."[9] But only folly resulted: "I fully expected immediately to gaze upon God, for this is the goal of Plato's philosophy."[10]

At this point Justin met an old man who introduced him via Socratic irony to the Christian religion. The old man began by asking after the purpose of Justin's earnest pursuit of wisdom. "Is it just about lingual facility as the sophists teach," he asked, "or is it about living well?"[11] Justin's response contested the disjunction: "To prove that reason rules all and [then] to rule it and be sustained by it is precisely to be enabled to live well."[12]

In short, philosophy for Justin, in these, his Platonic days, brought all other human pursuits into a unity and gave them value. And that means that philosophy produced (or at least aimed to produce) happiness, or the flourishing life—*eudaimonia*. Of course, he did not mean just any philosophy but the philosophy of Plato. And so the old man engaged this Platonic way of seeing philosophy and its connection to happiness, and exposed its vanity. His arguments came down to this: Even if Platonic claims are true, what good do they do? How do they increase our *eudaimonia*?

Justin's Christian Socrates was here exhibiting a fine sense of irony and knowledge of philosophical argument, for this argument is an adaptation of Aristotle's against Plato's account of the causal force of the Forms. Aristotle in the first book of his *Metaphysics* had granted to Forms their

8. Ibid., 2.149–151.

9. Ibid., 2.150–151.

10. Ibid., 2.151.

11. Ibid., 3.152.

12. Ibid., 3.152.

formal causality as the exemplars of things within our sensible world. In other words, he granted that Forms could be thought of as the principles of the intelligibility of things that we encounter in the world on the basis of which we can correctly answer the question as to what something is. Nevertheless, Aristotle denied that the formal causality of Forms could in any way account for the movement of bodies, and hence of the physical phenomena of continuity and change we experience in our day-to-day living. To put the matter in Aristotle's way, formal causes are not efficient causes, and it is efficient causes that act as movers in our world as we experience or perceive it.[13]

In this passage, Justin was slowly but unavoidably forced in the course of subsequent conversation to acknowledge that Platonic claims do not and cannot account for or increase our *eudaimonia*, our concretely flourishing living. And this left Justin asking where he was to go in his pursuit of wisdom if the philosophers, even the Platonic philosophers, did not know the truth? The old man turned him to the scriptures and the God revealed there as Father-Creator and Christ-Son.[14] The old man admonished him to "examine these writings with your philosopher's questions and you will learn at last the true answers to those questions."[15] Moreover, he insisted that Justin come to his examination in prayer: "beseech God to open to you the gates of light, for no one can perceive or understand these truths unless he has been enlightened by God and His Christ."[16]

Justin Martyr: Thinking in Alignment with the Scriptures

Here, we see already a pattern of thinking about Christian scholarship that will witness a dizzying number of variations throughout subsequent

13. Aristotle, *Metaphysics*, 991a8–33.

14. It is in this turning that our Christian Socrates also shows himself to be a master of Aristotelian rhetoric as it had come to be taken up into subsequent philosophical therapeutics. This gradual unmasking of the incoherence or unworthiness of intellectual competitors, capped by a final turning of the mind (*conversio*) toward that cognitive and conceptual regime that brings health of soul at last, is a classic example of the rhetorical form of protreptic. See, in this regard, Aristotle's *Protrepticus* published in the English translation of Barnes and Lawrence to be found in the second volume of *The Complete Works of Aristotle*. The Greek text is edited by W. D. Ross and is published in *Aristotelis Fragmenta Selecta*).

15. *Dialogue with Trypho*, 7.159.

16. Ibid., 7.160.

Christian experience. The deepest impulses of scholarly inquiry find, and can only find, their fulfillment in a lived relationship with the scriptures—or rather, the God they reveal. All Christian scholarship is in some sense scriptural scholarship, i.e., scholarship not so much about the scriptures as aligned to them. Though Justin's story brings the connection between scripture and his philosophical scholarship to the fore, it is worth noting that his questions were not about the meaning of scripture per se. Rather, they were about the meaning of truth and the shape of wisdom and justice as they were present in his life-walk. This sense of things marks out a common ground throughout the Christian era, and among all of the academies that Christian communities have cultivated.

Of course, common ground is not the same thing as neutral ground. One must ask, what precisely constitutes this alignment with the scriptures? In particular, what role do assumptions and data about life and knowing that come from outside of the scriptures play? What, for example, are we to make of Justin's old man's missionary playing on Platonic identification of knowing with illumination, and of sight with Truth?[17] How do we map this playing with Plato onto the datum of scriptural revelation that the Christ whom we meet in the Gospel of John is at one and the same time the Truth and the Light?[18] Where does Plato end and St. John begin? Can there be no St. John without Plato? And what of Plato himself? Can there be Plato without at least Moses and the prophets?[19] Such are the sorts of questions that have punctuated Christian debate in and since Justin's day.

Of course, it could be argued that Justin lets us see a second thing as well, another through-line that knits the hundred or so generations of Christian scholars and their scholarship together. When Justin looks to Scripture in order to align his own thinking about truth, wisdom, and justice, he does so as one already formed to a philosophical lexicon of Greek and pagan origin. When he meets homonyms in the scriptures, he assumes that they are in fact the same word. The examples of knowledge, light, truth, and sight as understood in Plato and John cited in the previous paragraph provide us a good case in point. Thus he can be said at times to have read

17. This is of course a way of speaking about knowing and Truth that recalls Plato's famous "Cave Analogy" from *Republic VII*, 514a–518c.

18. See John 9:5 (Light) and John 14:6 (Truth).

19. Justin includes a discussion of Plato's "dependence" on Moses in chapter twenty-nine of his *Exhortation to the Greeks*. The Greek text can be found in *Patrologia Graeca* VI. 241–312. An English version of the text can be found in *Writings of Saint Justin Martyr*, 373–423. (See especially pp. 411–412).

his antecedent Greek and pagan meanings into the words of scripture and then to have aligned his thinking with the sense of life, of right and wrong, of flourishing and failing, that emerged from this philosophically intinctured reading. The resultant pattern of eisegesis, followed by exegesis and subsequent application or mimesis, marks out a leitmotif in the history of subsequent Christian scholarly endeavor.[20]

Saint Augustine and Christian Philosophy

We next alight in Augustine of Hippo's works. We do so because Christian scholars in the Latin tradition (i.e., Catholic and Protestant) have made much of their Augustinian heritage, in particular his insight that human understanding of the central mysteries of life is built on a foundation of belief: what Augustine called "thinking with assent."[21] This enthusiasm is

20. One Christian philosopher of note, D. H. Th. Vollenhoven, saw this pattern (which he termed the eisegesis-exegesis method) as the very dynamic of a fatal synthesis of Christian understanding with the pagan spirit of Hellenic thought, which he understood to have dominated every era in the long story of Christian scholarly culture (with the exception of a brief interval in the heady first decades of the Protestant Reformation.) I view his analysis as both extremely helpful and as leading to an overly harsh conclusion. This eisegetical-exegetical pattern is indeed a principle way in which the Gospel became acculturated in the world of Late Antiquity. Moreover, this acculturation, like all acculturations, had ambiguous outcomes. It was able to express features of the Gospel with moving eloquence, while at the same time making other features almost impossible to express. It is this ambiguity, I would suggest, that Vollenhoven identified with the term "synthesis." His language gives the impression that a purely "thetical" (as opposed to "antithetical") alternative was available. I wonder about such a notion. Rather, I should think that the ambiguities to be noted in all our scholarly acculturations mean that we can continually expect such ambiguities to be present and so must remain ever self-critical. Of course, self-criticism involves an implicit awareness of normative sources by which criticism itself is possible. It may well be that such awareness is all Vollenhoven presupposed as well. For Vollenhoven's view, see Vollenhoven, *Kort overzicht*, 23, 32–33, now translated in *The Problem-Historical Method and the History of Philosophy*, 29–88. The passages cited in the Dutch edition of 1956 are translated on 61–62 and 74–75, respectively.

21. See, for example, the following passage of Augustine: *De praedestinatione sanctorum* 2.5: "For who does not see that to think is prior to the act of believing. Indeed, no one believes anything unless one first thinks that it is believable . . . For to believe is nothing other than to think with assent. For not all who think believe since there are many who think but do not believe. Nevertheless, all who believe think: each both thinks in believing and believes in thinking." (Quis enim non videat, prius esse cogitare quam credere? Nullus quippe credit aliquid, nisi prius cogitaverit esse credendum . . . Quanquam et ipsum credere, nihil aliud ist, quam cum assensione cogitare. Non enim omnis

unsurprising. If understanding were predicated on belief in so mechanical a way, then an understanding of the world that is predicated upon Christian belief would be easily imaginable and in fact inevitable. The plausibility of Christian scholarship would necessitate no stretching of the imagination. It would take its rightful place within the tournament of ideas alongside all other belief-based understandings of the world. And other such understandings there must be, for without belief, there is no understanding.

Augustine shares with Justin Martyr a sense that Christian faith exists in a world that is culturally older than it and hence in relation to two temporally antecedent sources of wisdom: Moses and the prophets on the one hand and the (pagan) philosophers on the other.[22] In the light of Christ, Christian scholars are able to bring each of these wisdoms to fulfillment. Moses and the prophets are fulfilled in the Gospel, in the person of Christ there revealed, and in Christ's communal presence in our world. The philosophers are fulfilled in the scriptural revelation of the absolute origin and end, and through the proper "middle things" that connect us to and move us from origin to end. Christianity's antecedent wisdoms, then, are realized anew by the faith of the Christian community and the revelation it extends its faith to even as it is made possible by it. That is, antecedent wisdom's aspirations to truth and happiness are taken up in the Christian religion and brought to a new perfection. Moreover, Augustine shares with Justin the sense that Platonic philosophy is superior to that of the other schools of philosophy, though its claims are equally vulnerable to Christian criticism. Indeed, Augustine pens just such a criticism in books eight through ten of his *City of God*.

What Augustine adds to Justin's enterprise is a deeper sense of what thinking in alignment with the scriptures amounts to. At several points in his early philosophical writings he meditates on a scriptural passage that he finds in the Old Latin version of the Book of Isaiah: 7:9—"Unless they will believe, they will not understand." In most of these citations he ties the relationship of belief and understanding to that which authority enjoys with

qui cogitat credit; cum ideo cogitent plerique, ne credant; sed cogitat omnis qui credit, et credendo cogitat, et cogitando credit.)

22. It was the burden of Augustine's relatively early *De vera religione* to make plain to Augustine's patron and fellow-traveler Romanianus the relationship of Christian faith to these older sources of wisdom. The Jews and their Scriptures are dealt with summarily in the context of the treatise but the pagans, and Plato in particular, receive extensive treatment in 1.1–5.9.

respect to reason.[23] In matters of faith, belief and authority lay claim to a priority that is proper to the Christian religion. To believe, says Augustine, is to hold something to be true (to think with assent), whether or not that truth can be demonstrated argumentatively. That is, to believe is to take something to be true on authority. Belief is a prior condition for the exercise of reason within the Christian religion. Subsequent use of reason leads to understanding. We Christians properly believe in order to understand.[24]

Later generations will capture this Augustinian inflection in a pseudonymous slogan: *credo ut intelligam*. But is this invocation of Augustine exhaustively Augustinian? Is he always thinking, when he invokes Isaiah 7:9, what, for example, Reformed or Thomist scholars are thinking when they intone *credo ut intelligam*?

On several occasions, Augustine's meditation on the priority of belief with respect to understanding, and of authority with respect to reason, is the first half of a conceptual diptych.[25] In these passages, Augustine be-

23. For the theme of authority and reason, see, for example, *De vera religione* 24.45. The crucial passage here reads "Therefore, the medicine of the soul that divine providence enacts out of its unspeakable favour, is beautifully ordered as to its constituent and discrete stages. For it is distinguished into authority and reason. Authority stokes up faith, and so prepares one for reason. Reason carries the person through to understanding and knowledge. Nevertheless, reason is never wholly absent from authority since one necessarily considers whom one is to believe. Moreover, the highest authority belongs to a truth that is always already known and permeating." (Quamobrem ipsa quoque animae medicina, quae divina providentia et ineffabili beneficentia geritur, gradatim distincteque pulcherrima est. Distribuitur enim in auctoritatem atque rationem. Auctoritas fidem flagitat, et ratione praeparat hominem. Ratio ad intellectum cognitionemque perducit. Quanquam neque auctoritatem ratio penitus deserit, cum consideratur cui sit credendum; et certe summa est ipsius jam cognitae atque perspicuae veritatis auctoritas.)

24. Augustine returns to Isaiah 7:9 time and again in the course of his writing career. Overwhelmingly he uses the verse to confirm the point that belief is prior to understanding. The claim that belief is prior to understanding, in turn, is put to different uses. He uses the claim to console fellow Christians who do not understand. Or, he will exhort them to stick with belief. He will use the same claim to mark out the future shape of his text; it will proceed from the claims of belief to an understanding of what is believed. Or, more darkly, he will use the claim in polemical contexts with Manichees and Donatists, for example, to discredit understandings that diverge from what he identifies as catholic. Since the heretics believe falsehoods they cannot be believed to understand truly; they are not credible. Examples of this usage can be found in *Enarrationes in Psalmos* 8.6, *Epistolae* 2.7; *De utilitate credendi* 1.2; *De libero arbitrio* 2.1.5 and 2.2.6; *Contra Faustum* 5.un., 12.46 and 22.53; *Sermones de quibusdam lectionibus evangeliorum* 39.1, 41.9, 68.1, 76.1, 89.1, 90.6; *De trinitate* 7.6.12 and 9.1.1; *Tractatus in evangelium sancti Joannis* 15.24, 27.7, 29.6, 45.7, 69.2; *De doctrina christiana* 2.12.17.

25. Examples of the kind of double-edged use I describe and analyze in what follows

gins by coming to a first and, I dare say, perfectly "Reformed" and also "Thomist" conclusion. But then he stops, as it were, and starts again. He muses that in order to hold something to be true, that is, to believe, one must already understand the terms in which that belief is expressed. Or rather, in order for the priority of faith to be reasonable, there must be some reason, however small, that precedes faith.[26] So it is simultaneously true that we must understand in order to believe.

In these latter passages, Augustine is affirming at one and the same time that we must believe in order to understand and that we must understand in order to believe. It appears, then, that a one-sided reading of this ancient North African bishop on belief and understanding would be inattentive. What are we to make of him and his viewpoint when we look at the entire diptych in which Isaiah 7:9 appears?

The Augustinian Aporia of Faith and Understanding

The juxtaposition of apparently opposite claims has a recognizable philosophical pedigree in Augustine's world, a pedigree that, as we will see, makes sense in his life. It is a philosophical strategy of the Late Academy, i.e. of ancient Platonic scepticism.[27] The sceptic of the Late Academy collected arguments of various kinds and logical forces, and practiced endlessly employing them against each other. The point was not to sift (à la Aristotelian philosophy) the things we say about the world so as to be able to judge which claims and arguments are first and most universal, most securely to be accounted as true, and consequently to order all other claims and arguments in relation to them. No, rather the point was to achieve a perfect cognitive equiposition in which every claim was balanced against a counterclaim of the exact same logical texture and force: an aporia (to give it its ancient and yet currently fashionable name). This was not to facilitate but to *impede* intellectual judgment and to suspend belief. What was to

(constituting parallels to the text from *De vera religione* cited above) are to be found in *Epistolae* 120.1.3; *Enarrationes in Psalmos* 118.18.3; and *De Trinitate* 15.2.2.

26. *Epistolae* 120.1.3. "But if it is reasonable that faith precede a certain great reason which cannot yet be grasped, there is no doubt that, however slight the reason which proves this, it does precede faith." (Si igitur rationabile est ut ad magna quaedam, quae capi nondum possunt, fides praecedat rationem, procul dubio quantulacumque ratio quae hoc persuadet, etiam ipsa antecedit fidem.)

27. See the chapter entitled "Skeptic Purgatives: Disturbance and Life without Belief" in Nussbaum, *The Therapy of Desire*, 280–315.

result from this cognitive labour was an affective state of mind, tranquillity, the very condition of a flourishing life under a sceptical description. So, what did Augustine think he was doing in playing with a scriptural pericope to create an apparently sceptical aporia or equiposition of claim and counterclaim?

Augustine was born into a North African Christian community that could not imagine either the world of day-to-day experience or the world encountered in the scriptures in any way other than in materialist terms.[28] That is, they assumed that for something to be real to their way of understanding it had to be like things that they encountered in their perceptual experience. North African Christians of Augustine's time were materialist not in the religiously impious sense of a Karl Marx. Rather, they were materialist in a religiously pious sense that was similar to the religious piety intrinsic to Stoic philosophy.[29] Like the Stoics, they affirmed that life was lived in the providence of God, and felt no need to understand the God they acknowledged and encountered in the scriptures in any other terms than the material. That is, they understood God as an unimaginably huge body so refined that it could exist everywhere—even where other and cruder creaturely bodies were present. And so they found, (to us), strangely imaginative ways to express their intrinsically Christian sense of the transcendence, immanence, and omnipresence of the provident Creator-God.[30]

Augustine grew up accepting what he would later view as this materialist and so impoverished or carnal Christianity. Thus, when he read Cicero's exhortation to the love of wisdom as an adolescent at school and felt a strange new longing within his breast, he took materialistic habits of thought and imagination with him on his new quest.[31] From within this materialist mindset, he concluded that if he did not know what wisdom was, and Cicero failed to inform him, he might yet ask after its opposite, folly. And indeed he received an answer to this question in stories artfully told by Faustus and his intrepid band of Latin Manichees. For them, folly or evil was substantial: a tangible and primary component of our every-day experience. As such, folly or evil was in principle intelligible to the inquir-

28. See the chapter "Martydom, Prophecy and Continence: Hermas to Tertullian," in Brown's *The Body and Society*, 65–82, esp. 77 on Tertullian.

29. See Armstrong, "Gnosis and Greek Philosophy," in Aland, ed. *Gnosis: Festschrift für Hans Jonas*, 87–124, especially 94.

30. See Augustine's account of one such way in his *Confessions* 7.1.1–2.

31. See Ibid., 3.4.7–8.

ing human mind. It stood to reason, then, that if one could but conceive the nature of folly-evil, one could move out toward wisdom by a process of conceptual inversion. This search by inversion is what Augustine was attempting in his nine questioning years as a Manichaean "auditor."[32]

Nevertheless, his gadfly efforts to explore the logical consequences of the stories of folly and evil to be heard among the Manichees met with Faustian resistance. Augustine became disenchanted but continued to hang on to what he was coming to suspect were fallacious beliefs. How else was he to move toward wisdom, since he did not know already what wisdom was?

The sceptics of the Late Academy eventually freed him from his Manichaean beliefs, and sent him inadvertently toward the books of the Platonists and the reality of the spiritual understood as other than material.[33] These books and their teaching in turn opened him to the preaching of Ambrose, bishop of Milan, and his eloquent, spiritual understandings of the scriptures.[34] All this coalesced in his mind to produce a mighty conundrum.

From the Platonists he learned of the philosophical power of introspection, of the great philosophical project captured in the Delphic slogan: "Know Yourself" and its coyly hidden codicil "to be divine." He was convinced that only via this inner way does one arrive at a knowledge that is sure; only so does one access the divine and see, as it were, what lies at the origin of the things of our experience and of what we say about the world.

From Ambrose he learned of the prior authority and luminous power of the scriptures spiritually understood. But they were external. One accessed them via an outer way—literary studies—and a grounding authority located outside oneself in the assembly of believers constituted as such an assembly by the apostolic succession of its overseer or bishop. How were these outer and inner sources of knowledge, these two loves of wisdom to be understood in relation to each other? The struggle to answer this question constitutes the dynamic animating much of Augustine's early philosophical writing, as a look at two early treatises, the *Soliloquia* and the *De Magistro*, makes clear.

32. See Ibid., 3.6.10–3.10.18. For Augustine's confrontation with Faustus, see Ibid., 5.3.3–5.9.17.

33. Augustine speaks of the importance of the skeptics of the Late Academy (presumably as mediated to him via Cicero's *Academica*) in Ibid., 5.10.19 and 5.14.25.

34. For the effect of Ambrose on Augustine, see Ibid., 5.13.23.

The Augustinian Aporia of Knowing and Reading

In the *Soliloquia* Augustine begins by examining our access to the divine within via a classically introspective and Platonic analysis of geometric figures: in relation to bodily figures, on the one hand, and in Truth, on the other.[35] He does so in response to a contingent conundrum or aporia. He wants to save up what he learns so as to pass it on to others. Thus, he must commit it to memory. But his memory is unable to contain all that he thinks about, and he is equally incapable of taking everything down onto papyrus, as his health is fragile. Neither should he employ a scribe, for what he is seeking demands solitude. This personal conundrum drives him to his knees in prayer—a prayer in which he explores the issue he faces by confessing the desires of his heart.[36] Indeed, in prayer he discovers what it is that he longs to know: God and himself and nothing more.[37]

But if he is to come to know God and self, he needs to know what form such knowledge is to take. Implicit is an adaptation of the Aristotelian sense that one comes to know what one does not know via what it is like among the things one does know. The Aristotelian principle is then employed in a Platonic project of introspection. What type of internal knowing will knowledge of God and self be like? What is knowing God to be like among the set of knowings I already contain in my memory? Does my memory have a capacity for God?

The initial segment of the *Soliloquia* represents a meditation on the types of knowing Augustine recognizes in his memory and their suitability as modes of knowing God. He considers, among other "knowings," his knowledge of friends,[38] of astronomical states of affair,[39] or of the every-day awareness of what he had for dinner the day before.[40] Each knowing proves insufficient to some belief that he holds about God. Each is insufficient either because of a disproportion between God as object and the creaturely

35. The resonance with Plato's *Meno* is undeniable, both in the *Soliloquies* and in the *De Magistro*.

36. *Soliloquia*, 1.1.1.

37. Ibid., 1.2.7.

38. Ibid., 1.2.7.

39. Ibid., 1.3.8.

40. Ibid., 1.3.8.

object being considered,[41] or because of a disproportion between the act of knowing and God as its potential object.[42]

At one point he comes to consider knowledge of geometrical states of affairs.[43] In the context of this inquiry he discovers that such knowledge is separable from corporeal things. Moreover it is stable or immutable. So, he asks himself, is such a knowing sufficient for knowing God? He thinks not, despite reason's urging,[44] for he cannot believe that God is like a line or a circle. On the other hand, our capacity for knowing things eternal allows us to understand ourselves as in some sense eternal.[45] Such an understanding does raise the possibility that we have an (as yet undiscovered) capacity for knowing God. Thus bolstered, he can continue the search for a knowing fitted to the reality of God.

In the course of continued inquiry, Augustine makes a pregnant move. He turns to literary science (*grammatica*) to see if such science also accesses the changeless divine.[46] He later expands this examination to include the liberal arts as a whole.[47] The assumption of literary focus is significant. If literary science in particular, and the textually and exegetically enclosed liberal arts in general, arrive at knowledge of Truth, and if the memory can contain them and the Truth they access, then the aporia of external and internal wisdom can be resolved, at least in principle. In other words, I take Augustine to be exploring whether we contain or can come to contain the written revelation of God within ourselves. The *Soliloquia* ends inconclusively. Platonic introspection and Christian thought in line with the exterior scriptures remain in antipathetic tension. They form a stubborn aporia.

In *De Magistro* Augustine takes up the great Platonic theme of the *Meno*: how do, or even can, you learn what you do not already know?

41. Ibid., 1.3.9.

42. Ibid., 1.6.12–13.

43. Ibid., 1.4.10–1.5.11.

44. Augustine responds to the pressure he feels from the voice of reason as follows: "Honestly, though you urge me forcefully and move to compel my assent, still I do not dare to say that I want to know God as I know these things [various geometrical figures—sw.]. For not only do the things themselves seem unlike each other, the knowing too seems dissimilar (Ibid., 1.5.11)." (Quaeso te, quamvis vehementer urgeas atque convincas, non audio tamen dicere ita me velle Deum scire, ut haec scio. Non solum enim res, sed ipsa scientia mihi videtur esse dissimilis.)

45. This discussion takes up most of the second book. See Ibid., 2.1.1–2.23.24.

46. Ibid., 2.11.19.

47. Ibid., 2.20.35.

Augustine asks whether a human teacher in fact teaches. It was in and through inquiring into the possibility of learning what one does not already know that Plato had developed his understanding of knowing as *anamnesis* or remembering. Augustine's conclusions in the *De Magistro* have strong family resemblances to this Platonic doctrine. Nevertheless, he makes important changes. In particular, he replaces Platonic remembrance of our divine pre-existence, with the regulative existence "within" of Christ our Inner Light and Teacher.[48] Moreover, he arrives at this Christ from literary studies, i.e., from an examination of a teacher's (or textbook's) words as signs.[49]

The *Soliloquia* and *De Magistro* can be understood then together to form a chiasm or A-B/B-A pattern. The *Soliloquia* start by considering and rejecting a variety of "knowings" until they arrive at what can be called the "internal divine" of geometrical figures understood in and of themselves rather than in terms of corporeal figures bearing their impress. They then move to literary studies. *De Magistro* starts from literary studies, or the science of signs both spoken and written and the things they signify, and moves to the "internal divine" of Christ the Inner Teacher. But even *De Magistro* leaves Augustine with the aporia brought to light in the *Soliloquia*. We are left asking the question: what is the relationship between the interior Christ caught sight of in philosophical introspection and the exterior Christ we encounter in the scriptures?

The Augustinian Aporia of Christ Within and Without

In the *Confessions*, Augustine wrestles with this aporia again along with—or better, in terms of—others. For example, already in the first chapter of the first book Augustine moves interrogatively from one conundrum to another until a circle has been circumscribed. He moves from praise to knowledge or understanding and back. He moves from invocation and confession to believing-in, and then back again to invocation and confession.[50] Logically, we could say that he circumscribes the circle implicit within any correlation; one cannot speak about the one correlate without recalling and hence returning to the other, and vice versa. What I mean is that the flow of Augustine's prose from one act to another and then back implies a logical

48. *De Magistro*, 11.38–14.46.

49. Ibid., 1.1–11.37.

50. *Confessions*, 1.1.1.

relation between them, a correlation. In a correlation the meaning of one term is dependent upon the meaning of the other. The term "double," for example, cannot be expressed without reference to its correlate, the term "half."

Having identified confession with invocation he moves on to ask where God and his Christ are to be called into since God is ubiquitous. This leads him to the conundrum of whether God is best understood as in the creature or the creature in God?[51] And this question leads in turn to a consideration of what containing might mean in this context: our containing God and God's containing us.[52] Augustine's meditation upon God prompts a plethora of further aporias. God is never new/never old; making all things new/working ever ancient of days, always acting/always at rest, seeking/though nothing is ever absent, loving/though never languishing, striving/though never anxious, wrathful/but at peace, changing works/not counsel, receiving what is found/though nothing is lost, never penurious/though taking joy in profit, never greedy/though demanding usury, taking on debt/though all others have only what is his, paying debt/owing nothing.[53] The mystery of a God who can only be invoked aporetically leads to questions of loving and being loved.[54] How is such a God to be loved? Why should such a God demand my love? Surely only such a God can peel back the shrouds that veil him in mystery?

The *Confessions* can be understood as Augustine's search for answers to the questions thrown upon his conscious mind by his opening prayer. In the context of this search, Augustine approaches again that Christ, the Word of God, who holds within his bosom the original secret of each and every creature. He is to be found introspectively in the darkest recesses of our deepest selves, our memory.[55] When we come upon him, however, we come to both be in and to gaze at the light of the Word through a gauzy firmament marking the boundary between our deepest within and the divine above.[56] And that which mediates the boundary between "the inside" of our deepest within and "the outside" of the divine above is the scriptures received in our memory through Christian formation—catechesis, preach-

51. Ibid., 1.2.2.
52. Ibid., 1.3.3.
53. Ibid., 1.4.4.
54. Ibid., 1.5.5–6.
55. Ibid., 10.17.26.
56. Ibid., 13.15.16–18.

ing, and disciplined meditation on scriptural phrasings.[57] In and through the internalized words of scripture we access the light of the Word above where the inspiring sun shines without limit. This supernal Word encountered introspectively is the ultimate source of all that is, and is the regulator or measure of our understanding of all that is.[58] Thus, the search of self for knowledge of the mysteries central to it, self, and God, holds out the promise of a primary knowing of God and a secondary knowing of self and the creation in God. But the knowing so received is a mediated knowing. It is mediated by the scriptures written on the heart; what is beyond moves within without thereby ceasing to be beyond. This mediation joins other analogous mediations of God's presence: kenosis, incarnation, sacrament.

Augustinian Aporias and the Practice of Christian Scholarship

What is made possible thereby is Augustinian Christian scholarship, what Augustine himself termed *philosophia christiana.* Again, we see Christian learning as a project of thinking in line with the scriptures, themselves understood as divine revelation. Moreover, in a much more reflective way than Justin Martyr, we see Augustine importing Platonic habits of thought into this scriptural learning. In general the process of importation occurs within the aporia of believing and understanding we observed in several of Augustine's treatments of Isaiah 7:9. We believe the claims of the scriptures in order to understand ourselves, our God and the world of creatures implicit in understanding our God. But we must first understand the words that the scriptures use in order to make their claims. And it is on this side of the aporia that Plato, Aristotle, the wisdom of Egypt or of the East could be of crucial, albeit limited service.

As with Justin we see Augustine working within a hermeneutic that has been termed the eisegesis-exegesis method of reading the scriptures. Some have seen this method as constitutive of the Christian community's mortally flawed first attempts to capture the conceptual clarity of pagan philosophical modes of expression and inquiry and put them at the service of the Christian community in its living with the scriptures.[59] The intent is clear and honorable: to think in line with the scriptures. The result is often far less happy. Forms of understanding are identified with the scriptures

57. Ibid., 13.12.13.

58. Ibid., 13.16.19.

59. See the reference to Vollenhoven's judgment as cited above.

themselves that produce discourse that makes it hard, if not absolutely impossible, to say what one knows in one's bones a Christian must say.

Augustine provides a particularly poignant example of the tension I am referring to in the first book of his *De doctrina Christiana*,[60] After using neo-Platonic and eudaimonistic notions to build up a sense of the proper mode of love encoded within the distinction between use (*uti*) and enjoyment (*frui*), Augustine struggles to say that and how God loves us in that fullest and most perfect way appropriate to Godhead. Indeed, a scriptural pericope such as John 3:16 becomes an anxiety-producing mystery, because human beings are not properly objects of the fullest and most perfect love. So Augustine is forced to explore how we can yet be assured within his framework of God's love for us. His solution is as ingenious as it is twisted and unlovely: God cannot be said to enjoy us, for only God is the proper object of enjoyment. Therefore, God must use us, for otherwise, as Augustine admits: "I cannot discover how He loves us." He uses us for his sake (indeed all use is ultimately for the user's sake), but such use is simultaneously productive of our own greatest good. Indeed, we are so accustomed to this Augustinian ingenuity that it might not even strike the reader as odd. But love, in that deepest and truest sense, a sense we would want to be able to ascribe to God who is deepest and truest, is, for Augustine, enjoyment, not use. It is love-as-enjoyment that entails a desiring the Other and his Good for the Other's sake. Augustine's move is to say that divine use does not desire the other and his or her good for the other's sake, but it does, nevertheless, desire and move to realize the other's good. So the effect of love-as-enjoyment vis-à-vis an other is present in divine love, even if the appropriate configuration of the divine intention is not.

This is very clever, but is it the highest love, in the end, at least as Augustine defines it? If it is not, how is it worthy of God? Moreover, does Augustine's ingenuity not force us to use God in our very enjoyment of him, since that enjoyment is at one and the same time our greatest good? Are our sakes and God's sake not indistinguishable in this way of understanding things? But then to be selfish and selfless become indistinguishable—as do manipulating the other, and trying to be truly and wholly for the other.

60. *De Doctrina Christiana*, 1.13.34. I owe a debt of gratitude for this example to Daniel Napier, doctoral candidate in the History of Philosophy at the Institute for Christian Studies, who recently defended a PhD in the Faculty of Theology of the VU University Amsterdam, entitled "From the Circular Soul to the Cracked Self: A History of Augustine's Anthropology from Cassiciacum to the *Confessiones*" now published as *En Route to The Confessions*.

In all of this, I have yet to address the role Augustine assigns to aporias, i.e., to equipositions of claim and counterclaim, in his *philosophia christiana*. As noted above, in the Late Academy, aporias were the conceptual means to a non-conceptual end, the tranquillity that resulted from the suspension of belief. Augustine's aporias serve an analogous function.

The seat of human personhood is identified in Augustinian parlance with "mind"[61] (*mens)* but Augustine does not mean thereby our cognitive powers, narrowly conceived. Rather, his is an altogether grander notion. Mind is the seat of all those capacities we have that allow us to be agents of our actions. In Augustinian shorthand, mind is the intrinsic principle of life and can be thought of in many ways: in its relation to our bodily living (then we name it soul); in relation to our spiritual living (then we name it spirit); in terms of our cognitive functions (then we call it reason or intellect); in relation to our affective functions (then we call it will or appetite); and finally, in relation to our perceptual functions (then we call it sense or sensuality).

By this understanding, when we think of mind in its depths we think of memory. And when we think of mind in its culminating height we call mind "heart" (*cor*).[62] The proper act of the heart, the seamless fusion of intellection and desire, is called love (*amor*); the very end of which is enjoyment (*fruitio/frui*).[63] But, Augustine points out, we properly enjoy only God. All else we relate to in our search for God; all else we merely use.[64] Intellection alone cannot attain to enjoyment, nor can desire alone. Only the concert of intellection and desire when directed toward its properly divine object achieves the enjoyment of love. So a cognitive or intellectual search for knowledge of self and God cannot succeed. Such a search must be wedded to desire if it is to meet the conditions of its end. In the love of God, you could say, love—true love—only begins in "the failure" of intellect.

This is the context in which aporias have a role to play. When our intellects encounter them, in all earnestness, the fires of longing are stoked. In those fires, affect is smelted together with an intellect that has learned to bow to its own "failure" with humility and without regret. As Augustine

61. See, in this regard, *De Trinitate* 9.4.7 and 9.12.18.

62. See, in this regard, the analysis of Edgardo De La Peza, *El significado de «cor» en San Agustín*; and Maxsein, *«Philosophia cordis»*.

63. For the connection between love and enjoyment see Augustine's *De doctrina christiana* 1.4.4.

64. For the distinction between use and enjoyment, see Ibid., 1.3.3.

puts the matter: "faith that works through love—let it exist in you and you will understand the teaching."[65] What is produced then by the heart's alchemy is love and love's knowledge: that cordial, you might say, that we enjoy by the grace and mercy of God.[66]

Ancient Christians and the Intentional Unity of Christian Scholarship

Justin Martyr's example illustrates one of the ingredients that are perennially present in Christian scholarship. Christian scholarship is thinking in line with the scriptures in their witness to divine revelation. Augustine agrees, if in his own and far more prolix way, and illustrates two other ingredients that are equally enduring elements of Christian scholarship. First, Christian scholarship is never the end; rather it is always but a means to non-scholastic ends, ultimately, the love of God (where the love of God entails the love of self, neighbour and all creation as the joyfully excessive gift of that first love). Second, because Christian scholarship is always a means, it is always understood, in some sense, as in the muddle of the middle; its results are always provisional. Scholarship occurs always too late to see the origin of what it would understand, and always too early to see the full results of the understanding it produces.

When I think about what more Augustine could allow one to see than he actually made explicit, particularly with respect to the second observation about the placement of scholarship in the middle of things, I arrive at three implications. First, *Christian scholarship always emerges out of what is prior and deeper than itself*. That prior fundament is made up of disparate sources; one's religious or ideological formation is a crucial source, but so too is the scholarly culture one enters and encounters in one's intellectual formation. To put it another way, scholarship flows from hunches, prejudices, or presuppositions; out of intuitions, circumspective conceptions, or ground-ideas; out of control-beliefs, principles, or articles of faith; there are many philosophically and religiously loaded ways of identifying the "what" from which it flows. Second, because it is made possible by what is prior

65. *Tractatus in evangelium sancti Joannis* 29.7.6: "fides quae per dilectionem operatur in te sit, et intelliges de doctrina."

66. Louis Mackey makes a very similar point about the "failure" of the *Confessions* as an intellectual inquiry and its success as a text in Mackey, "From Autobiography to Theology," 7–55.

and deeper—the distillate of one's individual and communal living with the scriptures (or rather the God revealed there)—*Christian scholarship is always an expression or better extension of what one understands that distillate to be* (remembering, of course, how fragmentary, misguided, or miscegenated such understanding can be). Third, the scholarship so produced because it is produced for an end that transcends itself, is to be judged in some measure by the outcomes it fosters. *Christian scholarship must be judged by its fruits,* for by its fruits we will know it. And when the fruits seem bitter and sterile, our critical search for the reason must take in the intrinsic elements of the scholarship produced, to be sure, but also one's prior sense of what it means to think in line with the scriptures or whatever else one thinks in line with, and the ways in which it is deployed toward human flourishing.

I am suggesting that all of what I have just been listing stakes out a common ground that all Christian scholars of whatever era and Christian academy share *at the level of deepest intention*—at least, when they insist on thinking about the Christian character of the scholarship they produce. We all intend our scholarship to be a seamless piece of our total living with the scriptures and our total worship of the God revealed therein. The strength of the claim is, of course, out of all proportion to the material used to illustrate it. It can only "make sense" if one recognizes in the alien examples of Justin Martyr and Augustine something true to one's own scholarly intentions and the scholarship they give rise to. But if one *does* recognize a shared hope or expectation, however oddly expressed, it becomes less outrageous to say that on some deep level the intent to align scholarship with the revelation of God in the scriptures marks out a unity that is expressed in all the differences that mark concrete Christian scholarly practice.

Differences there are aplenty. There are for example different ways in which Christian scholars and academies account for the unity or integrality of Christian scholarship, ways that divide persons and communities committed to the project of integral Christian scholarship. These differences and their ramifications call for and repay careful attention, which we will give in the following chapter. In light of these differences and their importance, however, it is good to begin with the spectre of what might strike the reader as a delightful surprise: a subterranean oneness precisely *in* those differences. Indeed, that is a unity well worth exploring and remembering.

Chapter Three: Lining up the Faces of Integrality

We have spent some time looking at two ancient authors in our previous chapter. The purpose of this chapter is to explore the ways in which individuals and communities have accounted for their scholarship's Christian integrality.

The term "integrality," as I am using it, marks out the unity of Christian scholarship across the disciplines and with respect to Christian faith. All who embrace the project of Christian scholarship seek to produce scholarship that has internal integrity, is in line with one's life as Christ follower, and is attuned to the God Scripture reveals. Consequently, individual scholars and communities of scholars who embrace the project of Christian scholarship must account for its integrality, either by generating such an account *de novo* or by appropriating an account already extant. This account allows scholars to be able to articulate for themselves how their scholarship benefits from the resources provided by their faith. In a secondary way it also allows them to show interested sceptics within the religiously heterogeneous academy how they understand faith and scholarship in unified form. Finally, they can use it to address fellow Christians who approach Christian faith, scholar and scholarship primarily from the point of view of the character of scholarly faith, or vocation of the Christian scholar, rather than of the scholarship itself.

The three basic accounts of integrality that have been developed heretofore among Christian scholars depend upon the relations one sees at play among religion, faith, and scholarly work. Before we go any further, I will outline them here. First, religion and scholarly work can be thought of as overwhelmingly separate phenomena with but a thin overlap. In this view, faith is inseparable from religion and so can only operate in scholarly work in that thin overlap between religion and scholarly work. Second, religion and scholarly work can also be thought of as overwhelmingly separate but in such a way that faith, as separable from religion, can also function positively within scholarship that is not directly in service of religion. Third, religion and scholarly work can be seen as inseparable in the sense that scholarly work is understood as a concrete field of expression for religion. Faith, in this account, is an aspect of religion that is present and active in all of religion's fields of expression, including scholarly work. Nevertheless, its presence within scholarship will be overshadowed by the logical quality foregrounded in scholarly work.[1]

In what follows, I will identify the general features of each of the three basic accounts before illustrating each via the particular language and vision of two or more of its exponents. Together, these three accounts can be thought of as integrality's three faces.

1. Complementarist Accounts

Complementarist accounts identify religion and scholarship as largely parallel and distinct fields of concrete socio-cultural endeavor. They identify faith by contrast as a primary, God-breathed power and mystery perfecting religion, first and foremost. As such, faith has its proper place within religion and extends as far as religion extends within human culture and society. Religion (and hence faith) extends some small way into the distinct field of scholarship insofar as there is one scholarly discipline that is properly religious (and hence carried on in and out of faith). That field is, of course, theology. What gives this way of thinking about religion, faith, and scholarship its integrality is the lead role assigned religion within socio-cultural endeavor, generally, and hence to theology within scholarly work. Religion sets the tone and parameters for the rest of socio-cultural life.

In the academy, religion's leadership is mediated by that scholarly discipline—theology— that is, at one and the same time, a mode of religion. This properly faith-filled scholarship sets the parameters for the other scholarly disciplines. Moreover, its relationship to the other disciplines can be typified by two terms: complementarity and finality. Complementarity names the structured fit of the unity formed by religion, faith and scholarship in this way of thinking. That is, faith-filled theology complements the

1. By logical quality I mean the predominance of logical concepts and chains of thought in scholarly work, i.e., at its most basic our capacity to distinguish "this" from "that" and then order their concepts validly in relation to each other.

other "merely" faith-directed and judged academic disciplines so as to form a harmoniously ordered scholarly whole. Finality, on the other hand, names the unifying purposive dynamic or direction that religion, scholarly faith and scholarship are together to take. That is, theology (religion's beachhead within the academy) relates to the other disciplines as a final cause relates to its "effects," in an Aristotelian way of understanding causality. "Final cause" names the purpose that a concrete being is imbued with, a direction-setting purpose that suffuses its motion and determines its development and perfection. As such it is the first of all the causes, and is presupposed from the very beginning, though it only really emerges in a palpable way in the perfection of the being in question. Since, in a complementarist account of integrality, theology has that purposive, direction-setting function with respect to the other disciplines, the scholarly whole that all the disciplines form is predicated upon the regulating virtue of theology and the faith that fills it and is a condition of its very possibility.

In order to see this account in one of its most pristine forms, we turn to the medieval Franciscan theologian Bonaventure of Bagnoregio or St. Bonaventure as he is more widely known. We turn in particular to his meditation upon scholarly study, *De reductione artium ad theologiam* (The Reduction of the Arts to Theology).[2] We will next turn to Etienne Gilson's account of the relationship between faith and philosophy in his understanding of what he called "Christian philosophy." We will then examine Pope John Paul II's recent encyclical, *Fides et ratio* (1998). We will see that in Gilson's discussion of faith and philosophy and in John Paul's encyclical on faith and reason, St. Bonaventure's central conceptual figure is preserved, albeit in languages shaped by very different scholarly formations to address different sets of founding circumstances. Together, they make a powerful case for this complementarist way of accounting for the integrality of Christian scholarship.

Bonaventure of Bagnoregio

St. Bonaventure was arguably one of the greatest Christian thinkers of the Middle Ages and perhaps of all time, although he is less well known in the

2. The edition used here is to be found in the *editio minor* published of Bonaventure's *Opera Omnia* published by the Collegium Sancti Bonaventurae, 219–228. An English translation is to be found in Heally, *De Reductione Artium ad Theologiam*. I use the editor's suggestion to translate the title idiosyncratically below.

Christian world at large than is his exact contemporary Thomas Aquinas. His most consequential theological work was accomplished in the years between 1253 to 1259, particularly the years 1257 to 1259, when he served as regent master in the faculty of theology at the University of Paris. After 1259, he was called to become the seventh Master-General of the Franciscan Order at which time, of necessity, the focus of his writing and thinking shifted to other matters than theology as a field of formal academic study.[3]

His modern editors speculate that his *De reductione* was meant as a companion to his spiritual classic, *Itinerarium mentis ad deum* (The Journey of the Mind to God).[4] They reach this conclusion because the two works most often travelled as a unit in extant medieval manuscripts. They also suggest that one could render the Latin title as "The Font of the Scholarly Disciplines." This rendering makes it clear that the discourse (*sermo*) as a whole was designed as a meditation upon what I am here calling the integrality of Christian scholarship. Moreover, it also makes clear that the disciplines were thought to constitute a whole endowed with a logical structure or intention that one can access via theoretical reflection.

Since the *Itinerarium* and the *De reductione* were read as a unit, we begin with the *Itinerarium* in order to place the project of the *De reductione* within its proper meditative whole. In other words, the *De reductione* was itself a part of a greater whole, namely, a program of meditation that was, in turn, designed to achieve the ends proper to meditation: availability to God (*vacare Deo*).[5]

3. For Bonaventure's life and philosophical theology, see, Bougerol, *Introduction à l'étude de saint Bonaventure*; Gilson, *La philosophie de Saint Bonaventure*; and Quinn, *The Historical Constitution of St. Bonaventure's Philosophy.*

4. See the editor's preface in *Opera Theologica Selecta*, 5–7. The *Itinerarium mentis ad deum* is to be found between 179–214 (hereafter cited as chapter #.paragraph #), whereas the *Sermo de reductione artium ad theologiam* is found between 217-228 (hereafter cited in terms of chapter #.paragraph #.page# from the edition used).

5. The claim is then that the *Itinerarium* (and the *De reductione* within the larger project of the *Itinerarium*) constitutes a Franciscan instance of the pattern of study and prayer classically described by Jean Leclercq, OSB in his *The Love of Learning and the Desire for God: A Study of Monastic Culture* (New York: Fordham University Press, 1974). As Franciscan, however, it participates in the pattern in its own idiosyncratic way, owing as much to a heremetical spiritual impetus as it does to the spirituality of Benedictine and Cistercian monasticism that Leclerqc had in his sights. Moreover, it was as influenced by the discourse of scholastic theology as by the *lectio divina* of monastic theology that Leclerqc contrasted with scholastic theology.

Bonaventure's Contemplative Itinerarium and the Scholarly Disciplines

In the prologue of the *Itinerarium*, Bonaventure lays out the contemplative ends of the treatise to follow. He begins with a recognizably Augustinian gesture: invoking the eternal Father through the Son. He does so because he understands the divine person of the Father to be the proper referent of the Apostle James's "Father of lights" and "the provider of all things given and of all perfect gifts."[6] That is, all that is creaturely (light is the first creation in Bonaventure's telling) is given, and perfectly so. Consequently, all creatures in their intelligibility (*illuminatio*) descend from the Father, and by implication can be understood to leave trails of light (*radios*) pointing back to that selfsame Father of lights.

Bonaventure invokes the Father through the Son because there is something he wants from the Giver of perfect gifts. What he wants is illumination. He is asking that his and his readers' minds' eyes be so illuminated that "we direct our feet upon the paths of the peace that passes all understanding."[7] Meditation, then, is to move through a process *of* understanding to an end, peace, that *exceeds* all understanding. This peace, says Bonaventure, is the peace that Saint Francis preached and received on Mount Alverna via his seraphic vision and its implicit christological and indeed cruciform gloss (the stigmata).[8] It was this peace that Bonaventure himself went to Mount Alverna to seek via what he terms "mental ascensions" (*aliquas mentales ascensiones*). By implication, the peace that passes all understanding exists above us. If we are to come into its presence, we must rise up. To seek is to ascend.[9]

6. *Itinerarium*, Prol. 1. 179.

7. Ibid., Prol. 1. 179.

8. St. Francis of Assisi was the founder of Bonaventure's religious order. Francis was known for many things in his day, things that were associated with the earthly ministry of Jesus recorded in the Gospels. His intent was simply to live as closely as possible to the life recorded in the Gospels. Contemporaries, above all Franciscans like Bonaventure, were convinced that his assimilation to Christ was as close as possible. He could justly be called *alter Christus* (another Christ), and the greatest sign of this assimilation was his reception of the five wounds that Christ had received on the cross, the stigmata. For the life of Francis, see Fortini, *Francis of Assisi*; and Habig, ed., *St. Francis of Assisi*. For Bonaventure's relationship to the figure of Francis, see Pegis, "Saint Bonaventure, St. Francis and Philosophy," 1–13.

9. Ibid., Prol. 2. 179–180.

Bonaventure understands this ascent to be a passing into excess in which we lose ourselves in what might be termed the taste (*sapor*) of Christian wisdom (*sapientia christiana*). He calls the way of ascent "the most burning love of the Crucified One." This is a love by which we are united—smelted, we might say—to the Crucified Christ who begins to live in us. With him, we ascend to God. This way of ascent is, fittingly, via desire: a desire evoked in the din of prayer (*per clamorem orationis*), in the resulting wail of the heart (*a gemitu cordis*) and the concomitant mirror-flash of sight (*per fulgorem speculationis*) whereby our attention is caught by rays of light leading back to the light's source.[10] The Augustinian provenance of this imagery should be obvious enough in the light of our prior discussion of Augustine and his conception of *philosophia christiana*. Like Augustine, Bonaventure conceives of a meditative path that leads back from the world of creatures to its divine Creator via a turn to the self in introspection.

Bonaventure's way demands of readers an appropriate purgation or cleansing of the mind and heart so that they are not blinded by the light of wisdom and cast into an even deeper pit of darkness.[11] He concludes his prologue by sketching out the seven chapters that mark the way the mind follows on its journey to God—but not the mind narrowly identified with the power of thinking. Rather, he is thinking of mind much as had Augustine before him; as our central identity and hence subject to many names, since we understand our personhood from different angles of approach.

As Bonaventure writes: "I ask, therefore, that the writer's intention be thought of more than the written work, that the meaning of what is said be impressed upon the mind more than the discourse by which it is said, that the treatise's truth be thought of more than its beauty, and that the stimulation of desire (*exercitatio affectus*) occur more than the sophistication of the intellect (*eruditio intellectus*)."[12] We see in this rhetoric a moving from lower to higher, from concrete thing to its intention, to what is meant from how it means, to its cognitive affect from its emotional affect, and finally, to the willed action it inspires from what it gives the intellect. Mind then moves centrally through, but is not limited to, intellect and its logical or analytic virtues. This should, however, be hardly surprising. After all, the peace that he is aiming for is that which passes (and passes through) all understanding.

10. Ibid., Prol. 3. 180.

11. Ibid., Prol. 4. 181.

12. Ibid., Prol. 5. 181.

The opening chapter of the *Itinerarium* outlines six steps that lead to the peace of contemplation in and through which we behold God in the deepest and most encompassing sense possible.[13] The chapter ends by discussing how we catch sight of God by looking out to the traces of his presence to be seen in the world of creatures.[14] The second chapter considers how we catch sight of God via our senses.[15] The third chapter considers how we catch sight of God via his image discerned within our souls' potencies and powers. This image is expressed in three acts: acts of memory, acts of understanding and acts of love. After examining each of these types of act,[16] Bonaventure turns to how it is that this tri-unity of powers and acts allows us to rise up to a sight of the Trinity of Father, Word, and Love. It is at this point that he summons the aid of what he terms the lights of the scholarly disciplines (*lumina scientiarum*). They perfect the image, inform it and represent the Trinity in a three-fold way.[17] As a result, Bonaventure's rehearsal of the disciplines of his day maps the disciplines and subdisciplines onto the sets of attributes considered first and foremost by theologians with respect to the persons of the Trinity. In doing so the separate (and also collective) theologically mediated godward drift of the philosophical disciplines is made apparent.

For Bonaventure, the constitutive unity of the scholarly disciplines was expressed by the single term philosophy. But he then divided philosophy into natural, rational, and moral philosophy. Natural philosophy related to the cause of being and so represented the Father as principle of the persons of the Trinity, who has himself no principle. Rational philosophy related to the nature of understanding and so represented the Son as Word in whom are contained all God's Ideas. Moral philosophy related to the order of living and so represented the Holy Spirit as Goodness, the ultimate end of every order, properly speaking.

Of course, when Bonaventure had named natural, rational, and moral philosophy, he had hardly exhausted the disciplines that made up the encyclopedia of the sciences of his day. Rather, each term of this first division represented a general class of philosophical discipline in which were contained three subdisciplines.

13. Ibid., Prol. 6–8. 182–184.
14. Ibid., Prol. 9–15. 184–187.
15. Ibid., 2.1–13. 187–193.
16. Ibid., 3. 1–5. 193–198.
17. Ibid., 6. 198.

Natural philosophy was divided into metaphysics, mathematics, and physics. Metaphysics related to essences, the first formal principles of things. As such it related to the Father as the first principle of the persons of the Trinity. Mathematics related to numbers and figures which together imaged the intelligible structures inherent in things. As such it related to the Son as the Image of the Father. Physics related to powers and actions, those dynamics in the world by which something could be given from one to another, and hence the Spirit as Gift par excellence.

Rational philosophy was divided into grammar, logic and rhetoric. Grammar related to the power of expression and Power was associated in a special way with the Father. Logic related to transparency of argument, and the Clarity by which transparency was achieved was associated in a special way with the Son. Rhetoric related to the capacity to move via persuasion and Charity, understood as the self-giving whereby the receiver was transformed in union with the giver. It was associated in a special way with the Spirit.

Finally, moral philosophy was divided into monastic, economic, and political philosophy. Monastic philosophy, by the indemonstrable primordiality of the individual subject it considered, represented the very "cannot-be-thought-to-have-come-to-be-ness" (*innascibilitas*) of the Father. Economic philosophy, because of the intimate filiality of the household, its subject, represented the filiality (*familiaritas*) of the Son. And political philosophy, because of the expansiveness of its subject, the city, i.e., the site in which all the possibilities for natural human flourishing are present, represented the generosity (*liberalitas*) of the Spirit.

The power of representation with which the scholarly disciplines are endowed is rooted in what Bonaventure calls the eternal law. Eternal law descends to us like lights and rays of light via the certain and infallible rules of the scholarly disciplines. When, in contemplation, our minds are irradiated by the splendour of these rules, we are led to contemplate the source of their luminescence. This image seems to be a way of understanding the conjunction of two Augustinian metaphors: first, Christ-as-sun, the source of light, in which we are able to see ourselves and the world of creatures; and second, Christ-as-Word, the rule or measure not only of the concrete being of each creature that is, but also of our knowledge of each creature. Each discipline, as a field and mode of knowing creatures, is ruled to the order established for it in the Word. This rule is itself a luminescence that comes to us like falling stars with rays of light going back to its divine source. The contemplation Bonaventure calls his reader to in this way will have a two-fold effect. It will produce wonder in the hearts of the wise, but it will disturb the hearts of the foolish.[18]

What Bonaventure explores in the last two paragraphs of the *Itinerarium*'s third chapter, then, are the ways in which the scholarly disciplines aid us in our leap from the created tri-unities of our conscious and subconscious awareness to the Trinity whom we would contemplate. In this treatise, the disciplines are themselves thought of as occasions for "mental ascension." Their upwardly directed unity is assumed, even made explicit, but is not itself the object of meditative enquiry. That enquiry is the function of the *De reductione artium ad theologiam* to which we now turn.

Bonaventure's Schooled Arts and Theology

The *De Reductione* begins, once again, by citing the Letter of James and its identification of "the best of what is given" and "the most perfect gifts" as descending to us from the Father of lights.[19] Consequently, Bonaventure claims that all illumination, by which he denotes the ground of our thinking about and knowing things, is profitably meditated upon as a free emanation from a single light source, the Father of lights. As in the *Itinerarium*, Bonaventure here presents the scholarly disciplines as they exist within us as internally perfective qualities of our minds—or better, of us *as* minds, for, as he puts it, "every illumination of knowledge is internal . . ." (*omnis illuminatio cognitionis interna sit*). Nevertheless, he will continue to exploit a contrast of inside and outside in its division of the disciplines as objects of meditative consideration. He divides the disciplinary lamps (*lumina scientiarum*) into groups under the rubrics: exterior, inferior, interior and superior. Each light illumines a distinct field of objects: cultural forms (*figurae artificiales*), natural forms (*formae naturales*), truth as intellectual (*veritas intellectualis*), truth as saving (*veritas salutaris*).

The first of these fields of light encompasses what Bonaventure calls the mechanical arts. Following Hugh of St. Victor, he names these as wool-making, arms-making, farming, hunting, sailing, medicine, and theatre. These arts exist to supply whatever the human body lacks, in and of itself. What they supply is one or another of two conditions: bodily comfort

18. Ibid., 3. 7. 199.

19. Bonaventure, *De Reductione*, 1. 217.

(*solatium*) and bodily ease (*commodum*).[20] These arts then constitute those "knowing" acts by which we operate bodily upon the world of other bodies on behalf of our body so as to provide for its various and relative needs.

The second of these fields of light encompasses what Bonaventure calls perceptual knowing; our relatively immediate perceptual engagement of the world of concrete material entities via our five external senses and the media appropriate to four of the five senses—light/fire (sight), moving air (hearing), vapour or the combination of air and water (smell), and water (taste).[21]

The third field of light encompasses intelligible truths. It is the light of philosophical knowing (*lumen cognitionis philosophicae*) dedicated to seeking the inner, hidden causes of things via those principles of the scholarly disciplines and of natural truth that every person has by nature. Bonaventure goes on to present much of the material about the disciplines that we looked at already in our discussion of the *Itinerarium*, beginning with the division of the disciplines into rational, natural, and moral philosophy.[22]

The fourth and final field of light encompasses saving truth. It is the light of sacred scripture. In this context, Bonaventure discusses the one literal and the three mystical or spiritual senses of scripture (the allegorical, the moral and the mystical). Indeed, it is in the context of the three spiritual senses that one is able to circumscribe the teaching of the scriptures as a whole. The scriptures teach the eternal generation and temporal incarnation of the Christ (allegorical sense), the right order of living (moral sense), and the union of God and the soul (mystical sense). This teaching then addresses itself to faith, morals, and the end of faith and morals, which are in turn the special prerogative of teachers (faith), preachers (morals) and contemplatives (the end of faith and morals). He ends this section by naming the requisite authorities for each of these subjects of scriptural teaching. Augustine was the teacher par excellence, Gregory the Great the preacher, and the pseudo-Dionysius the contemplative. Each has his successor among more contemporary thinkers. Anselm is Augustine's continuator, Bernard of Clairvaux is Gregory's, and Richard of St. Victor is that of the pseudo-Dionysius. Hugh of St. Victor is the successor of all three patristic greats (5.221).[23]

20. Ibid., 2. 217.

21. Ibid., 3. 219.

22. Ibid., 4.219–221.

23. Ibid., 5.221.

So, in the *De Reductione* there are four lights of which the third and fourth constitute the lights in which the scholarly disciplines participate. There are four lights but six illuminations, says Bonaventure; one illumination for every wing of the six-winged Seraph.[24] The disjunction is accounted for by insisting that the third light is constituted by three illuminations.[25]

These six illuminations correspond to the six-fold formation of the creation recorded in Genesis 1. Knowledge of sacred scripture corresponds to the initial formation of the creation account. Moreover, just as all the other formations or days of the creation account flow from that first formation, so the various modes of knowledge are ordered to the knowledge of sacred scripture and find their end and perfection in it.[26] Consequently, our knowledge has its stability in the knowledge of scripture, above all, as regards our understanding of the movement of mind upward by which the light of our knowing is referred to God in whom it has its ultimate origin.

We can see in Bonaventure's discourse that he is speaking of Christian scholarship as we described it in relation to Justin Martyr and Augustine. He too conceives the project as thinking in alignment with the Scriptures. Moreover, his view of Christian integrality is rooted in the role that knowledge of sacred scripture plays vis-à-vis the other scholarly disciplines. It is that to which they are ordered. They find their end and perfection in it. Theology, or the knowledge of sacred scripture, is to the other disciplines as a final cause is to its effects. It is presupposed by them in their whole and in each of their parts; in and through theology's final causality, scholarship

24. Bonaventure uses the image of the Seraph, the highest of the angels in thirteenth-century angelology, as an organizing image (and mnemonic aid) in the *De Reductione*. It was a Seraph that administered the stigmata to St. Francis and hence was associated in Bonaventure's mind with both revelation of knowledge on the one hand, and of being led by the hand contemplatively back to one's Origin, one's Creator, on the other.

25. Ibid., 6.221.

26. Ibid., 7.221–222. The passage I am paraphrasing is worth citing in full: "Whence it is that these six illuminations can be reduced to the six-fold formation or illumination in which the world was made, so that the knowledge of sacred scripture corresponds to the first formation, namely, the formation of light, and so on in order. And as all the illuminations find their origin in one light, so are all the ways of knowing ordered to the knowledge of sacred scripture, find their end and perfection in it, and via its mediation are ordered to the eternal illumination." (Unde valde apte possunt reduci sex istae illuminationes ad senarium formationum sive illuminationum, in quibus factus est mundus, ut cognitio sacrae Scripturae primae formationi, scilicet formationi lucis, repondeat; et sic deinceps per ordinem.—Et sicut omnes illae ab una luce habebant originem, sic omnes istae cognitiones ad cognitionem sacrae Scripturae ordinantur, in ea clauduntur et in illa perficiuntur, et mediante illa ad aeternam illuminationem ordinantur).

finds its integrality. On the other hand, theology fits with the other disciplines as their complement. This relationship is indicated by Bonaventure's placement of theology as a light that is distinct from that light distributed over the three illuminations of rational, natural and moral philosophy. What differentiates theology from the other disciplines is its *end*. It is what orders all that it is and all that it makes possible (as relative final cause) immediately to God—and the immediate ordering of created reality to God, including that reality that travels under the name of understanding, is precisely what religion is.

One last point needs to be made about Bonaventure's *De Reductione*. The *Itinerarium* makes the claim that there is an upward direction and movement to our journey to God, and the scholarly disciplines take a position in the middle of the vertical line formed by the treatise's elevating journey. From their middle position they survey the way that one has already come while plotting out where one must yet go; i.e., what is below, at, within, and above one's present, middle location. The close juxtaposition of the *Itinerarium* and the *De Reductione*, consequently, gives rise to the expectation that there is a similar verticality to the *De Reductione*. Moreover, when verticality is associated with religion, it is hard to avoid the assumption that the verticality is hierarchical. In a hierarchical verticality the superior relates to the inferior only via intermediaries. So one would expect the reduction of, for example, hunting to theology would occur only via the mediation of the knowledge of the senses and the philosophical sciences. The pattern of Bonaventure's meditation would appear to bear out the expectation.

Hierarchical verticality, however, is only one side of the *De Reductione*. The meditation does have another side. Though the opening citation from James and the circulation motif of paragraph seven (from God as origin to God as end) only re-enforces ascending and hierarchical expectations, there is another circularity, a relatively horizontal circularity, that must also be recognized. In the last half of the *De Reductione*, each of the lights and illuminations that together constitute the reduction of the arts to theology is itself a potential mode of theology, *in that it is itself potentially a way of knowing God*. Each leads to knowledge of God that is appropriate to the type of light or illumination that it is, but each also has an immediate issue in a presence of God. Bonaventure is elaborating here the representative function of the disciplines that he also spoke of in the *Intinerarium*. Thus, simultaneous to the circulation down from, and up to God, there is a meditative and horizontal circle formed by the contemplative movement from our knowing bodily actions to our contemplative or anagogical knowledge of Scripture. They can be said to circulate, relatively speaking, on the same creaturely plane, while each and every point of the circle they form is at the same time vertically connected to God as its immediate end and fulfillment. The figure thereby formed is a cone.

This means that our bodily knowledge is a way to God, as are our senses, our scholarly knowing, and our moral and contemplative knowing; *all our several capacities to know appear here as legitimate ways of knowing God.* But at the same time, the ways of knowing are not related to God in their own right. Rather, this work is accomplished via a contemplative or anagogical reading of our body-knowing, our perception, and our scholarly, as well as our moral and contemplative knowing—a reading that redirects them all to God. Thus, even here we see recapitulated (if from a different angle) the integrality provided by the final causality of the light of sacred scripture, since anagogical readings are precisely the contemplative's employment of the light of sacred scripture in the highest of its spiritual senses.

What becomes clear in all of this is that Bonaventure's is an account of the schooling of "right reason." As such, it brackets the concrete effects of sin in the world of scholarship. Moreover, it does not attend to the divide in the sedimented claims and methods of scholastic tradition between an overwhelmingly pagan legacy from Greco-Roman antiquity and the contribution of ancient and medieval Christian thinkers, whom he would have named the "saints" and the "teachers" respectively.[27] It is not that he did not acknowledge the divide or did not think it important. His critical treatment of the philosophers—by which he meant the pagan and Islamic philosophical traditions—speaks eloquently of his critical posture.[28] Nevertheless, such concerns proved surmountable via the unifying effect of final causality. "Right reason" was at work even in the needlessly flawed efforts of "the philosophers."

27. Cf. *Breviloquium*.Prol.6.5 in *Opera Theological Selecta*, 16.

28. Joseph Quinn cites and discusses the major texts in which Bonaventure deals with the philosophers, both pagan and Arabic, and their doctrines in Quinn, *Historical Constitution*, 590–663.

Etienne Gilson

Bonaventure's articulation of a complementarist account of Christian scholarly integrality is very clear. Nevertheless, it sounds quaintly antiquated. We gain a sense of the tenacity and adaptability of the account, however, when we examine versions that have been developed in close proximity to our own day. Thus, we turn to examine a second (and eventually a third) example. Our second example draws on a philosopher of the twentieth-century; our third on an ecclesiastical prelate with a lively interest in questions of Catholic scholarly integrity.

Etienne Gilson (1884 to 1978) grew up in a devout Catholic family of Burgundy in France.[29] As a boy he was sent to Catholic schools throughout his primary and secondary education. He did not, however, proceed to study philosophy at one of the Catholic centers of neo-scholasticism in France or in French-speaking Belgium. Rather, his university study took place at the Sorbonne in Paris under the direction of a historically and sociologically inclined Jewish thinker, Lucien Levy-Bruhl. Moreover, his thesis work addressed itself to early modern, not medieval thought; it was Descartes rather than Thomas Aquinas who cast the longest shadow. Nevertheless, the historical emphasis of his mentor led him to examine medieval scholasticism, for it was considered the immediate context for the Cartesian achievement. It was here, and particularly among the works of Thomas Aquinas, that Gilson found his philosophical home.

The point of this biographical rehearsal is this: Gilson did not approach Aquinas and medieval scholasticism from the same angle and with the same concerns as the neo-scholastic thinkers who in his day dominated study of the thought of Thomas Aquinas. His Thomas and his medieval scholasticism looked different from theirs, and seemed indeed suspicious to them. Whereas neo-scholastic scholars were anxious to establish scholastic thought, and Thomism in particular, as a legitimate philosophical voice by the criteria of present-day "rationalist" philosophies,[30] Gilson was by contrast keenly aware of the ways in which the Christian commitments of medieval scholastic thinkers had pushed them toward certain philosophical

29. See. Shook, *Etienne Gilson*, especially the first four chapters, 1–65.

30. I adopt here the historiographical nomenclature of Gilson in lieu of a common vocabulary to appeal to. He is I think speaking here of all forms of philosophy that are founded upon the *cogito* as first principle and basis, rather than on some narrower construal of the word.

possibilities and away from others.[31] This contrast in angle of approach and consequent judgment about the relationship of medieval scholasticism and Christian faith led to a short-lived but animated debate surrounding the possibility and nature of "Christian philosophy."[32] Gilson's Gifford Lectures given at the University of Aberdeen in 1931 to 1932, published in 1936, allow us to see his contribution to the debate.[33] It is here and in his later meditation on the spirituality intrinsically related to his Thomist philosophy that one can see his continuity with the complementarist account of Christian integrality across the disciplines.

Gilson on the Possibility of Christian Philosophy

In his preface to the published volume of his lectures Gilson claimed to have taken on the challenge of the Gifford organizers to "define the spirit of mediaeval philosophy" (vii).[34] He did so because of the widespread academic judgment that, in contrast to the fields of art and literature, the Middle Ages lacked "a philosophy that could be called their own."[35] Gilson went on to transpose the term "spirit of medieval philosophy" (with its German and idealist overtones) as the "essence of medieval philosophy" (a notion much more Latin and Aristotelian). The latter philosophical vocabulary could then lie behind and give meaning to the former. In this way he could call the desired essence "the Christian philosophy *par excellence*."[36] At the same time, he could without contradiction sum up the working hypothesis of the book in the German style as follows: "As understood here, then, the spirit of mediaeval philosophy is the spirit of Christianity penetrating the Greek tradition, working within it, drawing out of it a certain view of the world, a

31. For neo-scholasticism and its concerns see, McCool, *The Neo-Thomists*; McCool, *From Unity to Pluralism*, and also McCool, *Nineteenth-Century Scholasticism*.

32. For the debate on the possibility and nature of Christian Philosophy see Maritain, *An Essay on Christian Philosophy*; Nédoncelle, *Is There a Christian Philosophy?*; Coreth et al, ed., *Christliche Philosophie im katholischen Denken* and Owens, ed., *Christian Philosophy*, a special issue of *The Monist* 75.3 (July 1992).

33 Gilson, *The Spirit of Mediaeval Philosophy*. All references to the text however will follow the pagination of the reprint published by University of Notre Dame Press in 1991.

34. Ibid., vii.

35. Ibid., vii.

36. Ibid., vii.

Weltanschauung, specifically Christian."[37] The body of the book attempted to prove the truth of this hypothesis.

Gilson thought that on a very naïve level it would seem impossible to deny that there was Christian philosophy in the Middle Ages. Christians of all kinds produced philosophy during these centuries. But such an angle of approach was, to his mind, historical and therefore was bound by the strictures of the discipline, in particular its restriction to what was factually the case in the period in question. But, as a matter of fact, Christian scholastics worked in association with Jewish and Muslim counterparts. There were no distinctions made by the medieval thinkers themselves that divided scholastic thought into religiously distinct subspecies. Thus there were no properly historical reasons in this line of thought for treating the Christian contribution to medieval scholasticism in abstraction from Jewish and Muslim contributions.

This fact provided Gilson an opportunity to step back and ask whether the reason medieval scholastics made no distinction between religiously identified philosophies was because the notion lacked any internal coherence. In fact, he said, one can cite two arguments against the term's coherence. One is historical and involves proving the assertion that Christians have never in fact had a philosophy and have never made a creative contribution to philosophy. Such a position identifies all philosophical arguments and claims that one finds in the Middle Ages as philosophically eclectic appropriations by theologians to shore up with logical heft their intrinsically irrational (because theological) concerns. The second argument against the coherence of the notion of Christian philosophy is philosophical, and trades on a similarly dichotomous opposition of religion and philosophy. The latter is in the order of reason (A) and the former is irrational (not A). Since they must be understood as related as some "A" with respect to its negation, collaboration is inconceivable and thus the notion of Christian philosophy absurd.

Gilson's formulation of the philosophical objection is closest to that of what Gilson calls "pure rationalists" or secularist philosophers. But the formulation is also structurally the same for neo-scholastic thinkers. True, they would deny that philosophers who happen to be Christians have had no creative impact on the philosophical tradition; Thomas Aquinas is a glaring and perhaps lonely counter-example, at least until the neo-scholastic revival of the nineteenth century. But it was not as a Christian, in

37. Ibid., viii.

their view, that Thomas contributed to philosophy. Rather, his considerable contribution was "constructed on a purely rational basis."[38] Neo-scholastics did understand theology to assume its rightful place at the head of the hierarchy of the sciences. Moreover they recognized that if there were to arise a conflict between one's faith and one's philosophy the presumption would have to be that there had been some philosophical error. As such, philosophy and the other disciplines could be said to be subordinate to theology. But philosophy could not be said to depend on anything but "its own proper method; based on human reason, owing all its truth to the self-evidence of its principles and the accuracy of its deductions."[39]

Gilson went on to imply that neo-scholastic resistance to the notion of Christian philosophy arose in response to its association in their minds with a certain kind of Augustinianism. That is, they were worried about the conflation of faith and reason that they perceived in the thought of many Augustinian theologians. But, said Gilson, Christian philosophy need not be associated with an improper conflation of faith and reason. Rather, one can acknowledge a proper distinction between faith and reason that holds even for Christians, as did Augustine himself.[40] Moreover, even Thomas Aquinas explicitly recognized that reason is not "to be divorced from faith in the sphere of its exercise."[41] So there could be no reason in principle to foreclose on the possibility of a Christian philosophy. Moreover, a comparison of early modern and ancient philosophy demonstrated that medieval Christian scholasticism had a recognizably Christian effect upon the development of philosophy in Europe.[42] Indeed, the cosmos as contingent creation and the Creator as transcendent Origin of creation *ex nihilo* dominated the work of Descartes, Malebranche, and Leibnitz. This was an orientation to the world that was absent among the ancient Greek philosophers but was shared by medieval scholastics of all three religions of the Book. However, the theme of Grace and freewill was a parochially Christian theme and it was also widely operative in philosophical texts of the same seventeenth century. All this allowed Gilson to conclude his first chapter rather grandly: "If pure philosophy took any of its ideas from the Christian revelation, if anything of the Bible and the Gospel has passed into

38. Ibid., 4.
39. Ibid., 6.
40. Ibid., 12.
41. Ibid., 12.
42. Ibid., 13–17.

metaphysics, if, in short, it is inconceivable that the systems of Descartes, Malebranche and Leibnitz would be what in fact they are had they been altogether withdrawn from Christian influence, then it becomes highly probable that since the influence of Christianity on philosophy was a reality, the concept of Christian philosophy is not without real meaning."[43] What is important to see at this point is that Gilson too was thinking of Christian scholarly endeavor as at bottom an alignment of scholarly thought and production with the Christian scriptures.

Gilson on the Nature of Christian Philosophy

When he moved in the next chapter of *The Spirit of Mediaeval Philosophy* to examine the concept of Christian philosophy appropriate to medieval scholasticism, he did so under the following enquiry: "what intellectual advantages were to be gained by turning to the Bible and the Gospel as sources of philosophic inspiration?"[44] The question sent him to St. Paul and the Pauline contrast of the wisdom of the world with the wisdom of God. Gilson glossed the contrast in such a way that philosophy could be substituted for "the wisdom of the world," whereas salvation could be substituted for "the wisdom of God." Put this way the two wisdoms were mutually exclusive. The hard distinction of the "pure rationalists" with respect to religion and philosophy thus could be seen to find its echo in Paul's rhetoric. As a result what counted as wisdom for the one pole counted as foolishness for the other and vice versa. They related as a positive phenomenon relates to its privation, as sight, for example, relates to blindness. In Gilson's telling, it was Paul's intent to substitute the one wisdom (salvation) for the other (philosophy). True wisdom superseded the wisdom of the world and could be thought to do so because it fulfilled it or brought it to perfection; it embodied what its opposite lacked but aspired to. By implication, it was by possessing salvation that one possessed philosophy and "all the rest."[45] One could affirm this claim in faith, but one could also try to prove it. The attempt at proof marked out the very dynamic and direction of Christian philosophy.

Gilson went on to confirm the picture using the witness of Christianity's early philosophical converts. Two are already familiar to readers of this

43. Ibid., 18.

44. Ibid., 19.

45. Ibid., 23.

book, Justin Martyr and St. Augustine, but he added two others, Tatian and Lactantius. Their philosophical experience before and after their conversion confirmed the picture Gilson drew from St. Paul. This historical confirmation allowed him to articulate a first concept of Christian philosophy: "[the] effort of truth believed to transform itself into truth known is truly the life of Christian wisdom, and the body of rational truths resulting from the effort is Christian philosophy itself."[46] More formally then he was prepared to "call Christian, *every philosophy which, although keeping the two orders* [of revelation and reason—sw] *distinct, nevertheless considers the Christian revelation as an indispensable auxiliary to reason* [italics his]."[47]

Since Christianity was at bottom a religious way of salvation, the Christian philosopher would be interested primarily in those philosophical matters that affected the conduct of religious life. Gilson listed these matters as "the existence and nature of God, and the origin, nature, and destiny of the soul."[48] In short, the orientation of Christian philosophy was ever with respect to the relation of humankind and its persons to God. Everything was examined from this focus. The dynamic, direction, and focus so identified constituted together the concept of Christian philosophy as he had arrived at it by 1931. It presented philosophy largely as a system-building activity. When one bore in mind Gilson's concept of Christian philosophy one could identify any number of Christian philosophers doing Christian philosophy in the history of medieval and early modern thought. Gilson made the point in a rhetorical question of Christian philosophers: "in spite of the purely rational texture of their systems, can we not still today discern the mark of the influence of their faith on the conduct of their thought."[49]

By the end of his life and active career, Gilson had become ever more aware of the fact that Thomas Aquinas had never, ever thought of himself as a philosopher. Rather, his philosophizing took place within the context of his work as a theologian. He was, in fact, a theologian. The theological context of his practice of philosophy proved paradigmatic for the aging Gilson. The inner connection between Christian philosophical thinking and the deep dynamics of the Christian spirit mediated by theology became a matter of meditative concern.

46. Ibid., 34–35.

47. Ibid., 37.

48. Ibid., 38.

49. Ibid., 41.

One sees this all come together in a slim but profound meditation upon the spirituality native to philosophical Thomism as he understood it.[50] In it he illustrated the relationship between religion and scholarship on the one hand and between theology and philosophy on the other. Religion and scholarship could be thought to share an orientation to wisdom. Faith opens up and makes the supernatural wisdom of religion available while reason makes the natural wisdom of scholarship available. But in the end these available wisdoms flow from the source and end of all wisdoms: Wisdom herself. This unity must be respected if the wisdoms available to us in this life are not to wither. Gilson put the matter this way: "For all wisdoms draw life from the highest among them, and if religion is eliminated, metaphysics dies with it, and philosophy in its turn dies along with metaphysics."[51] One can illustrate the point via his account of the proper relationship between scripture, theological principle and metaphysical doctrine. It is worth citing in full:

> We do not say: Since scripture says so, the philosophical notions of being and God are in the last analysis identical with that of the act of being. In fact, scripture itself does not say this; but it does say that the proper name of God is He Who Is. Because it says this I believe it. While I thus cling to the object of faith, the intellect, made fruitful by this contact, makes deeper progress in the understanding of the primary notion of being. With one and the same movement it discovers an unforeseen depth in the philosophical meaning of the first principle and gains a kind of imperfect but true knowledge of the object of his faith.[52]

All of the subjects examined by the scholarly disciplines, what Thomas Aquinas had called the philosophical sciences (*scientiae philosophicae*), could be examined theologically inasmuch as those subjects could also serve as divine revelations themselves. Gilson referred to this insight as the very keystone of Christian philosophy or by extension (since we are speaking of all the subjects) Christian scholarship.[53]

By now, it is clear that Gilson thought of the integrity of Christian scholarship in ways that are remarkably similar to Bonaventure. Moreover,

50. Gilson, *Introduction à la philosophie chrétienne*, published in English as *Christian Philosophy*. All citations and references will be to the English translation.

51 Gilson, *Christian Philosophy*, 67.

52. Ibid., 31–32.

53. Ibid., 76.

he did so despite choosing self-consciously for the thought of Thomas Aquinas where it differed from that of Bonaventure.[54] For Gilson too, Christian scholarship was at bottom an alignment of thought with the scriptures in which theology was at one and the same time the complement of the rest of the scholarly disciplines *and* the principle of their unity as it mediated the spiritual dynamic of religion in the way that a final cause mediates perfection to its effects.

John Paul II[55]

When we turn to John Paul II's *Fides et ratio*, we take note of a very different language and set of founding circumstances.[56] John Paul II was not (like Bonaventure) a thirteenth-century theologian with the soul of a contemplative. He was not attempting to place the study of theology within the spiritual and sanctifying *askesis* of a new and internally divided order of friars.[57] He was not formed to the fluid cadences of Latin Augustinianism, starched by the technical rigour of Aristotelian philosophy. Nor was he (like Gilson) a professional philosopher or academic of any kind. Rather, John Paul II wrote *Fides et Ratio* as a late twentieth-century bishop of Rome to his fellow bishops. He wrote out of an intellectual formation that emerged from the phenomenologically intinctured personalism of his Polish Catholic training, which contrasts both with the historical and sociological cast of Gilson's Sorbonne training and the existential Thomism Gilson co-founded with others.[58] Of course, John Paul II had more in mind in this encyclical than the instruction of his fellow ordinaries. He used the opportunity to speak through them to Catholic theologians; but also, and especially, to philosophers of whatever stripe as they and their discipline were, in his

54. See Gilson's *La philosophie de Saint Bonaventure*.

55. An earlier version of this section was previously published as Sweetman, "John Paul II's Account of the Unity of Scholarship," in Goheen and O'Gara, eds., *That the World May Believe*, 203–214.

56. John Paul II, *Fides et Ratio*. Hereafter cited as chapter.paragraph.page of present edition.

57. For the history of the Franciscan Order and Bonaventure's role in the order's discovery of a constitutive academic calling, see the pertinent chapters of Moorman, *A History of the Franciscan Order*.

58. For the philosophical and theological formation of John Paul II, see, for example, Kupczak, *Destined for Liberty*.

view, the key to the culture of the academy at large, and through the culture of the academy to the human community.

This desire to appeal to philosophers has a striking effect on the encyclical that follows. When one thinks of an encyclical one rightly thinks of the church's magisterium—its teaching authority as understood in a Catholic context. Moreover, whether rightly or wrongly, many think of magisterial interventions as designed to end rather than enable thought and discussion, and it is not inconceivable that some encyclicals have discussion stopping as one side of their intent. Strictly speaking, however, the intent is more positive than that. An encyclical *precisely as authoritative* is meant to enable thought and discussion, by identifying the right starting points for healthy thought and discussion. Of course, where the starting points of discussions already on the go are unhelpful an encyclical will admonish those who start there to start rather at a better place. And when such admonition directly effects discussions about the verbal formulae used to indicate the faith at its core, such admonition will take on a compelling force.

In *Fides et Ratio*, however, the tone is one of entreaty rather than command. To the degree that John Paul II addressed philosophers he was not addressing persons who are interested, at least, in their role as philosophers, to articulate the faith correctly. He thought, as we shall see, that what philosophers are thinking and discussing has an impact on faith and its articulation—though that impact is mediated and therefore muffled: easy for busy ecclesiastics to overlook. The philosophers as philosophers fall outside his direct province and so he addressed them as one would an outsider, with a discourse of persuasion, not compulsion. He wanted to insert the voice of religion into their philosophical discussions, to be sure, but was required to do so on their disputative and mutually critical terms.[59]

Philosophy as Symbol of Rational Enquiry

John Paul II felt the need to address philosophers because he viewed the academy of our day to have lost its way. Indeed, at "the present time," he

59. This paragraph is my attempt to adjust to the responses I received to a draft of this section given at Sacred Heart University of Fairfield CT on 25 October 2006. My public thanks to Professor John Roney of the History Department for his kind invitation to speak about *Fides et Ratio* to faculty and students at Sacred Heart. Thanks are also due to the several departments that sponsored the talk. It was clear at the time that the encyclical was being heard as a discussion stopper. As I have said above, I understand the nature of encyclicals, or at least this encyclical, differently.

says, "the search for ultimate truth seems often to be neglected."[60] Such a search, in his view, is founded in human nature itself.[61] It is constitutive of our humanity, and hence is an important and privileged vehicle for the human encounter with God—who says of himself, among other things, that he is the Truth. Since philosophy most clearly and universally brings this purposive structure of the human life of reason into the open, philosophy can and does stand for the life of rational enquiry as a whole, and it is this life that the academy institutionalizes in its service of the human community.[62] Thus philosophy is, as said, a valuable and irreplaceable feature in the human landscape, one that can and does guide the human community as it moves toward or away from its proper and ultimate end. Precisely because it is a valuable and irreplaceable feature, however, when philosophy fails to serve the human community in its allotted function, there are potentially dramatic consequences for the community of believers, as well as the human community as a whole.

Despite its high role within the academy, philosophy, in distinction from faith, is not a truly elemental component of human life and flourishing. While faith marks out a basic starting point in our reflection upon the human condition, philosophy expresses something deeper and more elemental than itself: namely, reason. Philosophy is a mode, perhaps the primary mode, of human reason—at least if one speaks, as John Paul II did, of the "philosophy" that all people fashion from the resources available to them. This "philosophy" is sometimes called a "worldview."[63]

Thus it is faith and reason, not faith and philosophy, that occur in the first sentence of the encyclical. Faith and reason are described in relation to each other to be "like two wings on which the human spirit rises to the contemplation of truth."[64] Both faith and reason direct the human spirit toward the Truth. Indeed, the desire for truth, to which they respond, is implanted by God *qua* Truth so that, by knowing Him, human beings come to "the fullness of truth about themselves."[65]

In the beginning, philosophy, as a formalization of the life of rational enquiry, responds to a whispered and divine voice ("Know Thyself!") that

60. John Paul II, *Fides et Ratio*, 1.5.9.

61. Ibid., 1.3.6.

62. Ibid., 1.5.8–9.

63. Ibid., 3.27.44.

64. Ibid., 1.1.3.

65. Ibid., 1.1.3.

awakens desire.[66] That desire in turn sets in motion the twin capacity in the human spirit of faith and reason. From the point of view of philosophy, then, the Delphic Oracle speaks to the human spirit as a revelation, coming to philosophy from before its very birth. Using Kantian language, one could say that it is a condition of philosophy's very possibility. What John Paul II was saying is that the Delphic Oracle is not a revelation of Apollo but rather of the God of Abraham, Isaac and Jacob. Moreover, the Delphic Oracle is no airy principle hovering over the void; it is present, concretely, in the hurl-burly of the human story, in what might be called the Genesis 1–11 of the history of philosophy, i.e., in the roughly simultaneous emergence in both East and West of explicit concern with "fundamental questions."[67]

The Hebrew Bible or Old Testament of Jew and Christian, the Veda and Avesta of Hinduism, Confucius and Lao Tze of Chinese wisdom, Gautama of Buddhism, and the Greek tragedies can be said to sing, each in their own way, of the separation of conceptual light from dark, of the exile of ignorance, but also of the scandal of a mythopoetic discourse capable of entertaining the most monstrous ideas. The fundamental questions asked by each of these sources of wisdom share something in common. They are all motivated by the desire for the truth, by which John Paul II denoted the very meaning of our lives.

While human cultures have developed a number of ways of seeking this truth and meaning, philosophy is the most transparent of these modes. For it "is directly concerned with asking the question of life's meaning and sketching an answer to it."[68] By its very nature, philosophy is that search for truth that asks directly after the meaning of life.

For John Paul II, philosophy asks its proper questions in its own peculiar way, and in so doing, it builds up a body of knowledge.[69] For all this corporeality, however, philosophy must be seen for what it is: primarily a mode of human enquiry. Philosophical systems—that is, bodies of claims arranged in coherent and validly connected concepts—are worthy of respect. Nevertheless, in the long run, they are less important than the philosophical enquiry that gave them rise. Philosophy is then a *critical* discipline, in the original Greek sense of a sifting of what "we" say about

66. Ibid., 1.1.4.

67. Ibid., 1.1.4.

68. Ibid., 1.3.5–6.

69. Ibid., 1.4.7–8.

the world.[70] But once we acknowledge this, we must also acknowledge that there are themes that are intrinsic to properly philosophical enquiry. These themes mark out "an implicit philosophy" or "reference point for the different philosophical schools", i.e., a *philosophia perennis*, but one of enquiry rather than systematic result. One can call this form or mode of philosophical enquiry right reason (*recta ratio*).[71]

In John Paul II's view, then, philosophy has recently turned away from its proper end and nature. Instead of searching for ultimate truth, "modern philosophy has preferred to accentuate the ways in which [the human capacity to know the truth] is limited and conditioned."[72] Present preference has encouraged forms of "agnosticism and relativism" which have "led philosophical research to lose its way in the shifting sands of widespread scepticism."[73]

So, to recapitulate briefly, philosophy is a mode of reason: namely, that mode by which the human spirit enquires directly after the meaning of human life. Philosophy can stand for reason. Reason is in turn an elemental phenomenon of the human condition and stands in primary relation to faith. But, reason is not faith. In that sense, it can be opposed to faith. John Paul II's way of opposing reason and faith begs our attention.

The Correlation of Faith and Rational Enquiry

The rhetoric of the encyclical leaves no doubt about John Paul II's way; he opposed faith and reason (and hence philosophy) via an opposition of correlation. In a correlation, things are properly distinguished even though the one pole of the distinction is intrinsic to the other. I can illustrate what I mean with the same example that Aristotle once used. The concepts "double" and "half" are correlates. Though "double" is not the same as "half", "double" has no meaning except in relation to "half," and vice versa. As John Paul II put the matter with respect to reason and faith, "There is thus no reason for competition of any kind between reason and faith: each contains

70. For this ancient Greek and philosophical sense of criticism and its relation to "what we say about the world," see Nussbaum, *The Fragility of Goodness*, especially 240–263.

71. John Paul II, *Fides et Ratio*, 1.4.8.

72. Ibid., 1.5.10.

73. Ibid., 1.5.10.

the other, and each has its own scope for action."[74] Faith incorporates reason in its progressive self-understanding, whereas reason incorporates faith in its assumption of the accessibility of the truth of human life and in its acknowledgement that it needs the [superadded] light of faith in order to achieve its end.[75]

Of course, once the correlativity of faith and reason has been established, it needs to be illustrated. Looking at faith and reason in their opposition, one to the other, their correlativity is indicated by the notion of their intrinsic harmony. As John Paul II described it, "The fundamental harmony between the knowledge of faith and the knowledge of philosophy is once again confirmed. Faith asks that its object be understood with the help of reason, and at the summit of its searching reason acknowledges that it cannot do without what faith presents."[76]

The harmony is accounted for (using Thomas Aquinas) by an appeal to their single origin from God. Moreover, their fittedness (harmony) is indicated by analogy. "Just as grace builds on nature and brings it to fulfillment, so faith builds upon and perfects reason."[77] Because each of the correlata (faith and reason) are presupposed in the other, all thinking about one leads to the other and vice versa. Consequently, the shape of their harmony is best thought of as a circle.[78]

On the other hand, if one is looking at faith and reason, not as opposed (albeit correlatively) but as fitted to each other, one indicates this fittedness by the term unity. This unity of faith and reason is to be seen in their shared theme. Indeed, said John Paul II, "The ultimate purpose of personal existence . . . is the theme of philosophy and theology, alike."[79] Moreover, they also share a single end, the unity of truth.[80] Faith and reason work as a team to realize the destiny of both and the human spirit in virtue of which they exist.

This unity of truth, as it rules both faith and reason, is to be seen and learned, in turn, from the history of human culture. The lesson is this: "It is faith which stirs reason to move beyond all isolation and willingly to run

74. Ibid., 2.17.29.

75. Ibid., 1.17.30 but especially 4.42.64.

76. Ibid., 4.42.64.

77. Ibid., 4.43.65.

78. Ibid., 6.73.107–108.

79. Ibid., 1.15.26.

80. Ibid., 3.34.51.

risks so that it may attain whatever is beautiful, good and true. Faith thus becomes the convinced and convincing advocate of reason."[81] From faith's perspective, in its orientation to truth as revealed rather than as intelligibly created, all of history, including the history of philosophy, is centered on the Christ event.[82] Revelation calls reason forth; it stirs reason to ceaseless effort. It does so from its fullness and center in the Christ-event. From Jesus Christ the voice of revelation whispers its call to self-knowledge. And reason, said John Paul II, does achieve such knowledge in measure.[83]

In its very structure, then, reason is a response (fittedness) to faith. Revelation calls reason to itself and the mediating structure of that revelation is faith. This is the overarching analytic framework that John Paul II used to understand the relationship between faith and reason, and between faith and rational enquiry into the truth of our existence (i.e., philosophy). The structure should be recognizable enough and is well expressed in Aristotelian terms: faith is to philosophy as a final cause is to its effect. Revelation, the instrument of which is faith, calls forth reason. Grace is the end and perfection of nature, of which reason is the instrument. As final cause, grace—and its created instrument faith—is first in the order of causes. Grace is operative as rule and condition from the very beginning of nature and its instrument reason.

Faith and the Misdirection of Rational Enquiry

On the other hand, the correlation of faith and reason means that any rational turning away from the truth and meaning of life has implications for faith and its self-understanding. By John Paul II's account, this is because reason, in its search for truth, is called forth by revelation. But it also provides a rational platform or foundation for faith in its drive to understand itself. Reason is faith's correlate; it is an intrinsic presupposition in what faith in fact is. Consequently, reason's turn from truth puts the understanding of faith at risk. And that is where the magisterium, i.e., the teaching authority of the Catholic Church, becomes interested and intervenes in the development of reason, philosophy, and the academy at large.

In John Paul II's understanding, for the sake of faith's understanding and the health of the Catholic church, the magisterium, (the voice, we

81. Ibid., 5.56.86–87.

82. Ibid., 1.14.23.

83. Ibid., 2.23.37.

might say, of right religion under a Catholic description,) must speak to the academy, and especially to philosophers, to recall them to their proper end and focus. As he puts the matter, "With its enduring appeal to the search for truth, philosophy has the great responsibility of forming thought and culture; and now it must strive resolutely to recover its original vocation."[84] Such renewal will allow the human race to sense the greatness of its endowment and so to enact, whether it wills to or not, "the plan of salvation of which its history is a part."[85]

We see in *Fides et Ratio*, then, the language of finality and end as the ground of unity across the encyclopedia of the academic disciplines. It is the language that we have identified as characteristic of complementarist accounts of the integrality of Christian scholarship. But, of course, we also see the language of complementarity—the metaphor of the two wings, the movement of circling between two points, the logic of correlation, and the aesthetic sensibility encoded in the term harmony. Such language points ever to a unity constituted by irreducible constituents. Thus, faith and reason constitute the two wings of the human spirit. Faith and reason contain each other and yet each "has its own scope for action."[86]

On this account, philosophy (and by extension all the non-theological disciplines) has its own questions, methods, and objects. Each has an intrinsic autonomy vis-à-vis both the church's magisterium and the discipline of theology—that discipline which emerges from the attempt to understand what one believes (*intellectus fidei*)—though autonomy should never be mistaken for self-sufficiency.[87] Thus, philosophy has a sphere that is its own in that it is neither the sphere of theology nor that of magisterial pronouncement. Nevertheless, the unity of truth and of the ultimate end of human living precludes philosophy's self-sufficiency such that it would escape both the theologian's scholastic interest and the ecclesiastical magisterium's religious interest. The two (or three) form a unity. Their irreducible complementarity is unified by the finality of the one with respect to the being of the other(s). And of course, what holds for philosophy in relation to theology and ultimately to the church's magisterium, also holds *a fortiori* for all the other academic disciplines.

84. Ibid., 1.6.13.
85. Ibid., 1.6.13.
86. Ibid., 2.17.29.
87. Ibid., 6.75.109–110.

As said, Bonaventure of Bagnoregio, Etienne Gilson and John Paul II show how tenacious and adaptable a complementarist account of the integrality of Christian scholarship has been over time. It has been able to leave the medieval discourses that gave it rise and adapt itself to the post-Enlightenment languages of existential Thomism on the one hand and phenomenological personalism on the other. It has made itself as at home within the Catholic magisterium as among the far-flung community of Catholic scholars. Indeed it is the default position, one might almost say, for Christian scholars asked to account for the Christian integrity of their labour as scholars. Still, it is not the only account developed by Christian scholars and so we turn to the second account we introduced briefly at the beginning of this chapter.

2. Integrationist Accounts

Integrationist accounts of the integrality of Christian scholarship accept the complementarist identification of religion and scholarship as concretely distinct socio-cultural endeavors and faith as a God-breathed power and mystery perfecting religion. Where integrationist accounts sound their distinctive note is in their uncoupling of faith from religion. For them faith is crucial to our participation in religion, but religion does not exhaustively mediate the presence of faith in the rest of our lives. Rather, faith is properly (and hence immediately) present in all the dimensions of our lives, and our lives and endeavors are the richer for it.

Here too religion overlaps with scholarship in the discipline of theology. Nevertheless, though the rest of scholarship need not give a place to faith, in the sense that the rest can develop in relatively healthy ways without it, faith need not be excluded from the non-theological scholarly disciplines either. Rather, faith can play a proper and generative role across the encyclopedia of the sciences. In such a view, it is crucial for the integrality of Christian scholarship that Christian scholars acknowledge and define the role faith can play in scholarly practice, i.e., to integrate faith and scholarship into a productive unity. We identify this approach as an integrationist one.

We illustrate this position using two exemplars. The first is a philosopher, and is perhaps the most sophisticated thinker to use and develop the potential of this account in the world today. The second is a prominent historian of American religious experience whose recent apology for

Christian scholarship arose in the context of a well-publicized scholarly flap. This second version of the account, which places it within the disciplinary frame of history rather than philosophy or theology, contextualizes the account within a sense of contemporary North American society and what makes for cultural viability within society.

Alvin Plantinga

Alvin Plantinga (1932–) is without doubt one of the most important theistic Christian philosophers working in the analytic style and tradition of philosophy today.[88] From 1963 to 1982 he taught philosophy at Calvin College in Grand Rapids, Michigan, and has since come to serve as the John A. O'Brien Professor of Philosophy and the director of the Center for the Philosophy of Religion at the University of Notre Dame in Notre Dame, Indiana. Consequently he serves as the perfect bridge figure from the Catholic milieu of Etienne Gilson and John Paul II to the Evangelical and Reformed contexts in which integrationist and holist accounts of Christian integrality have flourished.

There are several small but important papers within his oeuvre in which Plantinga has addressed himself to the problem and nature of Christian philosophy and of Christian scholarship generally. We will begin with his "Advice to Christian Philosophers" (1984) and his "Christian Philosophy at the End of the 20th Century" (1995) in order to examine his sense of the integrality of Christian faith and his own discipline before moving on to his consideration of Christian scholarship as a whole in the Stob Lectures he gave at Calvin College and Seminary (1989).[89]

88. I take Plantinga and others who identify themselves as theistic philosophers to mean that they are philosophers who include the proposition that God exists and others like it among those basic propositions that lie at the base of or as principles of subsequent philosophical enquiry.

89. The first two of the pieces were first published in *Faith and Philosophy*, 253–271; and in Griffioen and Balk, eds., *Christian Philosophy at the Close of the Twentieth Century*, 29–53. They were republished together in Sennet, ed., *The Analytic Theist*, 296–315 and 328–352, respectively. The third essay first appeared as a Calvin College pamphlet, and was, as said, eventually published as Plantinga, "The Twin Pillars of Christian Scholarship," 121–161. All citations from "Advice" and "Christian Philosophy" will be from *The Analytic Theist* and thus will reflect its pagination; the third essay will be drawn from the Eerdman's publication and will use its pagination.

Plantinga on the Tasks of the Christian Philosopher

In his inaugural address, "Advice to Christian Philosophers," delivered upon assuming the John A. O'Brien professorship at the University of Notre Dame, Plantinga identified philosophy as a complex social practice. Just because it is so, it was important on his view for philosophers and especially Christian philosophers to acknowledge the implications.[90] Contemporary Western societies are of course culturally plural and that plurality can be mapped from a number of angles of approach. One way of understanding that plurality is to see within Western societies a number of cultural communities, one of which is the Christian cultural community. Christian philosophers naturally make up a part of the Christian cultural community, but they are also just as naturally a part of the community of philosophers within their society at large. Thus they participate in at least one other community inasmuch as the community of philosophers is properly distinct from the Christian community.

Christian philosophers in Plantinga's view participate in more than one cultural plurality as well as community. This is so because they participate in more than one community within the societies they inhabit and these communities are themselves culturally plural. Plantinga grudgingly admitted, for example, that the Christian community is culturally plural. The contrast he drew between the perspective of a Christian theologian such as David Tracy and of a Christian philosophical theist such as Plantinga himself illustrates what was in his mind an unfortunate plurality at play within the Christian community.[91] Moreover, there was at least a second culturally plural community to which the Christian philosophers of whom Plantinga was thinking belong: the community of largely Anglo-American analytic philosophers. In the latter case, however, the perspectival plurality implicit within and representative of cultural plurality throughout this essay was by Plantinga's lights barely acknowledged by the community itself. He described the situation as follows: "most of the major philosophy departments in America have next to nothing to offer the student intent on coming to see how to be a Christian in philosophy—how to assess and develop the bearing of Christianity on matters of current philosophical concern, and how to think about those philosophical matters of interest to the

90 Plantinga, "Advice," 298.

91. Ibid., 306–307.

Christian community."[92] Indeed, he went so far as to identify the present ethos of the community as a whole as "non-theistic," even "anti-theistic." As a result, the Christian philosopher faced a situation in which she must be willing "to reject widely acknowledged assumptions as to what are the proper starting points and procedures for philosophical endeavor,"[93] if she was to philosophize in a manner that was consistent with and so of service to her Christian community and faith. Consequently, what was called for, said Plantinga, was a measure of autonomy from the currently dominant assumptions and concerns among Anglo-American analytic philosophers. This measure of autonomy included of necessity a sensitivity to the Christian integrality of one's own assumptions and concerns in philosophy, and the courage to maintain such a posture even at cost to reputation, self, and career.[94] In this setting and with the intent to encourage this posture, Plantinga described a two-fold communal task for philosophers.

In the first place, Plantinga identified the task of logical criticism. This is a task shared by any and all who engage in philosophy. It amounts to "a clarification, systematization, articulation, relating and deepening of pre-philosophical opinion."[95] The task is remarkably similar to the Aristotelian understanding of the philosopher's social function as I detailed above. Such criticism is not just about adding philosophical heft to pre-philosophical opinion, nor is it just about ever deepened continuity. Rather, it can lead to startling turns in a person's thought. Logical sifting of pre-philosophical opinion can lead to disillusioning "incompatibilities or other infelicities," as the philosopher examines opinions and makes "unanticipated interconnections" or answers "unexpected questions."[96] But while logical criticism of pre-philosophical opinion is the common task of all philosophers, this does not entail the simultaneous canonization of a shared and secular body of opinions that all or almost all philosophers agree with—nor the consequent exclusion of idiosyncratic, particularly religious opinions that only a few share. Rather, pre-philosophical opinion is just that: pre-philosophical opinion. "And," as Plantinga put the matter, "the point is: the Christian

92. Ibid., 297.

93. Ibid., 299.

94. Ibid., 297.

95. Ibid., 312.

96. Ibid., 312.

has as much right to his pre-philosophical opinions as the others have to theirs."[97]

In the second place, however, philosophy has a perspectival task. In other words, in addition to being a socio-cultural site for logical criticism about what "we" say about the world, it is also "an arena for the articulation and interplay of commitments and allegiances fundamentally religious in nature."[98] Philosophy as just such an arena is "an expression of deep and fundamental perspectives, ways of viewing ourselves and the world and God."[99] It is here that we see Christian philosophers operate at one and the same time as members of society's community of philosophers and as servants of society's Christian community. In this capacity, Christian philosophers sift what Christians say about themselves, God, and the world. They do so to systematize, deepen, explore, and articulate what Christians say, so that their saying is internally consistent and its valid implications fully developed. It is this second task above all that demands of Christian philosophers autonomy, integrality, and confidence, for it is here that they must swim against the dominant cultural current of the community of philosophers to which they also belong.

A decade latter, Plantinga addressed the business of Christian philosophy again and with a view to the coming millennial turn in "Christian Philosophy at the End of the Twentieth Century." There, he articulated how the two tasks identified in the earlier essay—logical sifting of what "we" say and the articulation of religious views—have come together in the concrete outworking of twentieth-century Christian philosophy. The two tasks were to remain conceptually distinguishable, to be sure, but together they were to forge a unitary, if complex, practice. It is here that one begins to see an implicitly integrationist account of the Christian integrality of Christian philosophy.

Plantinga on the Present Dis-integration of Faith and Philosophy

To see this, however, we need to back up slightly. The Christian philosopher belongs to at least two communities, each of which is culturally plural: the Christian community, and the community of philosophers, represented by one of its subcommunities, the community of analytic philosophers.

97. Ibid., 312.

98. Ibid., 315.

99. Ibid., 315.

At present, the cultures of these two communities do not mesh well. The community of analytic philosophers is dominated by a culture that is non-theistic and indeed anti-theistic in orientation. Plantinga used the first section of this essay to describe the ethos in some detail.[100] The ethos emanates from the dominant role assumed by two conceptual step-children of positivism: orienting conceptions that he titled "perennial naturalism" and "creative anti-realism." Both conceptions produce opinions antithetical to central pre-philosophical opinions that Christian philosophers bring to philosophy as a result of their membership within the Christian community. Perennial naturalism, in Plantinga's telling, denies the opinion that the God of Christian revelation or any other deity exists. Creative anti-realism by contrast does not deny that that God exists so much as it affirms that such a God exists, strictly speaking (i.e., as representable and represented conceptually), only with respect to a set of claims that are generated within our human discourse. But philosophical members of the Christian community, provided they have the requisite autonomy, integrality, and courage, affirm antithetical opinions, namely, that the God revealed in the Christian scriptures does indeed exist and that that existence transcends absolutely all human discourse about it. Indeed, Christian philosophers who hope to serve the Christian community philosophically will take such opinions with them into their philosophical work. And this "taking-with" sets up a difficulty, a disjunction between the pre-philosophical opinions that Christian philosophers take with them into philosophy from the Christian community and the philosophical opinions and assumptions that dominate the culture of philosophy that they enter. This is not a structural matter, to be sure. It is not that the assumptions and methods of the community of philosophers are *necessarily* antithetical to the Christian pre-philosophical opinions of Christian philosophers. But this *is* the practical state of affairs on the ground.

The Five Divisions of Christian Philosophy

In "Advice . . .," Plantinga claimed that philosophy had as its most encompassing task logical criticism of what "we" say about the world. But Christian philosophers, by virtue of their dual communal belonging, include both Christians and anti-theistic philosophers within the "we" who by rights say things to them about the world. Consequently, given the antithesis at

100. Plantinga, "Christian Philosophy," 329–335.

play between what these two groups in fact say about the world, there is a terrible and corrosive tension at play for Christian philosophers in what for them "we" say. Christian philosophers, then, start from a situation of factical dis-integration. In this light, Christian philosophy can be seen as an attempt to integrate pre-philosophical Christian opinions with philosophical claims and arguments about the world. And this integrative effort can be divided into five tasks: negative apologetics, positive apologetics, philosophical theology, Christian cultural criticism, and positive Christian philosophy.

Both constitutive voices of the "we" are accounted for in this division. Negative apologetics and Christian cultural criticism are directed primarily at the anti-theistic elements of the "we" the Christian philosopher encounters as dominant within the community of philosophers. In particular it is directed at the anti-theistic things they say about the world. By contrast, positive apologetics, philosophical theology, and positive Christian philosophy are directed primarily at that part of the Christian philosopher's "we" constituted by the Christian community. They are directed in particular at developing and validly ordering Christian pre-philosophical opinions about God, self, and world.

Negative apologetics deals with anti-theistic sayings *as sayings* particularly as they impact the capacity of saying-as-such to bear religious identity and meaning. Christian cultural criticism deals with anti-theistic sayings as themselves bearers of religious identity and meaning. In other words, negative apologetics refutes the denial of meaning and validity to theistic sayings, whereas Christian cultural criticism identifies the implications of positive anti-theistic sayings when viewed in terms of the implications of positive Christian sayings. Positive apologetics, philosophical theology, and positive Christian philosophy, on the other hand, all address the meaningfulness and validity of Christian philosophical, theological, and (by extension) other Christian sayings about the world.

Throughout these two essays Plantinga contrasts membership in two societal communities: the Christian or religious community, and the scholarly community of philosophers. By implication we see here acceptance of the distinction between religion and scholarship as distinct spheres of concrete societal living.[101] Christian faith on the other hand, is a distillate

101. Even the occasional coloring of the distinction using the eschatological categories, *civitas Dei* and *civitas terrena*, does not obviate the identification, for in Augustine's *City of God* the distinction between the two cities is not at bottom mutually exclusive, although there is an important sense in which they give concrete existence to the two

of divine revelation and Grace. In philosophy, that faith takes on the form of distinct pre-philosophical claims about the world that the Christian philosopher is to assume in his philosophical work. Such claims can form the very material that the Christian philosopher subjects to logical criticism. More importantly, it forms the basic premises from which the philosopher begins in order to subject other claims to logical criticism. Indeed, they should be accorded a certain privilege by the Christian philosopher.[102] The more seamlessly and philosophically active the Christian philosopher is able to make basic Christian beliefs within her philosophical work (and that presupposes the more successfully she is able to defend those claims from philosophical attack), the more integral the Christian philosophy she produces. The opposite is also true.

Philosophical attack can come from a variety of angles. It can come from philosophers working with the resources of other religious perspectives, whether or not those perspectives are theistic or atheistic. It can also come from non-religious angles; the perspective of Willard van Orman Quine is cited as a prominent example,[103] as is much of the work being done in contemporary philosophy of mind.[104] In other words, philosophy can be carried on in faith and the things faith-filled people say about the world, but it need not. Philosophy will be the richer for the presence of faith-filled philosophers, however, perhaps especially Christian philosophers. Plantinga shrugs shyly before citing his own work in epistemology as an obvious example.[105]

Moreover, he holds out the possibility that this work will be of interest to philosophers who are not Christians because it formulates an account of knowing and of coming to know that is superior to other accounts available. And this can happen because there is much in the world that the Christian philosopher shares with others. All inhabit the same world, an ordered world that exists to be investigated and known. And indeed it is this shared world that gives warrant to his hope, for it is a world in which a ubiquitous inkling of the divine, or an inkling oriented towards truth

---

sides in that penultimate division of the human race into two warring communities. Still, the division is penultimate; the earthly city remains for all that, at bottom, a temporal precinct of the heavenly city, and that despite the evil resident within it as a result of the Fall. See, in this regard, Augustine, *De civitate Dei* XIX.12–17.

102. Plantinga, "Christian Philosophy," 347–348.

103. Plantinga, "Advice," 299.

104. Plantinga, "Christian Philosophy," 342.

105. Ibid., 345–346.

and knowledge, or Lord knows what more, stretches across religious and philosophical divides, inklings that can only be denied with enormous and sustained effort.[106] This optimism, even in the face of antitheistic prejudice, is quite remarkable and underlies Plantinga's clear sense that the antithesis between theistic and antitheistic belief is not at all operative at the level of the proposition, i.e., of logical conception and its protocols. True propositions simply reflect the way things are and can together constitute what John Paul II called *recta ratio*. While philosophy can develop without the benefit of faith, then, it can also be furthered by the presence of faith in the form of pre-philosophical opinions worked into philosophical criticism by the Christian philosopher.

The Integration of Faith and the Deliverances of Reason in Christian Scholarship

Of course, one might think of the integrality of faith and philosophy as unique. Given the presence of a theological subdiscipline within the work of the Christian philosopher (philosophical theology) as Plantinga describes it, one might see here the sort of Augustinian conflation of theology and philosophy that Gilson presented as problematic to neo-scholastic philosophers. Such a conflation allows the extension of the complementarist relationship of theology to faith and religion on the one hand and to rest of the scholarly disciplines on the other to include philosophy (or at least Christian philosophy) *as if it too were theology*. However, Plantinga does not leave us to these speculations. Rather, we see how he construes the matter of theology, faith, and Christian scholarship as a whole in the second of the Stob Lectures he gave at Calvin College and Seminary in 1989.

The last section of the second lecture brings to the fore precisely the relationship between theology, faith, and scholarship. Furthermore, it does so against the backdrop of a version of Thomism that sounds like Gilson's portrait of neo-scholasticism. Plantinga identifies his own position as Augustinian.[107] The question is this: How ought the Christian scholar to participate in his or her discipline? Ought she to take "the deliverances of faith" into her discipline? Or ought she to restrict herself to "the deliverances of reason?" In Plantinga's view the Thomist insists on the latter course, if she is to pursue any discipline other than theology. That is, only in theology is

106. Ibid., 347.

107. Plantinga, *Seeking Understanding*, 159.

faith allowed to be intrinsically operative. Plantinga much prefers the Augustinian alternative in which the Christian scholar takes all that he knows, from whatever source, into his study in order to arrive at the most complete understanding we can get.[108]

So, faith is restricted to theology in the Thomist view, with which he constrasts his own Augustinian view, whereas in his view faith can also function within the other scholarly disciplines. That is, faith can provide non-scholarly opinions that are translatable into a scholarly form and thereby become theological. The Augustinian scholar seeking to understand the part of the world that the sociologist studies should not hesitate to bring these theologically reworked deliverances of faith to bear on understanding of the part of the world that he would understand as sociologist. Moreover, when he does this, says Plantinga, he is engaged in an exercise that produces a deliverance of reason not of faith. His argument is ingenious, so I cite it in full.

> There are the deliverances of faith: call them 'F'; there is also the result of thinking about the subject matter of science, appealing to the deliverances of faith as well as to the deliverances of reason: call that 'FS.' Thomist and Augustinian concur that we need FS; but the Thomist adds that FS is really theology rather than sociology or psychology of whatever. But now consider the conditional or hypothetical proposition *if F then FS*: the proposition that says what the implications of the faith *are* for the discipline in question. Perhaps this proposition *if F then FS* is best thought of as a large number of propositions, each explicating the bearing of the faith on some part of the discipline in question—or perhaps we should think of it as one enormously long proposition. Either way, both parties to the discussion will agree that this proposition is not *itself* among the deliverances of faith; we learn it, or know it, by reason, not by faith. It is by reason rather than faith that we see what the bearing of the faith is on psychology; it is by reason rather than faith that we see how the scriptural teaching on love, or sin, or morality bears on what we study in psychology or anthropology or sociology.[109]

The discovery of just what the conditional *if F then FS* is constitutes a scholarly activity he identifies with reason and the relevant discipline, not as a deliverance of faith. The type of scholar best placed to do this work is

108. Ibid., 157.

109. Ibid., 159.

not the theologian, for he has not been trained in the requisite discipline. Rather, it is the Christian scholar trained in the non-theological disciplines who is most qualified to carry on this work. It is in working out the implications or asserting the consequents of the conditional *if F then FS* that integration of faith and scholarship occurs, one discipline at a time. What results from this assertion is a Christian understanding of that part or dimension of the world that the discipline studies.

George Marsden[110]

George Marsden (1939–) served from 1992 until his retirement as the Francis A. McAnaney Professor of History at the University of Notre Dame. Before that he served in the History Department of Calvin College, and later at the Divinity School of Duke University. In 1994, he published his acclaimed *The Soul of the American University*, a study which he ended in a reflective and confessional mode.[111] This prompted a searching critical response from Stanley Fish.[112] Fish's criticism prompted Marsden to respond in turn by publishing an extended apology for Christian scholarship in which he articulated and defended an integrationist account of the integrality of Christian scholarship.[113]

The thesis of his apology was that the mainstream secular academy should be open to explicitly faith-inflected learning and that faith-informed scholars should spend time and energy on the integration of faith and scholarship.[114] Marsden used the book to address two sets of readers. In the first place, he addressed mainstream or secular university scholars who are sceptical of the notion of "Christian scholarship." In the second place, he appealed to Christian scholars who are confused about what Christian

110. An earlier version of this section was previously published as Sweetman, "Christian Scholarship: Two Reformed Perspectives," 14–19. At that time I did not see the three accounts as separate accounts of integrality, rather, I only thought of what I here call a holist account as such. Marsden's response published as Marsden, "Reformed Strategies in Christian Scholarship," 20–23 was instrumental in helping me to see that all three accounts are accounts of the integrality of faith and scholarship. I am grateful for his gentle admonitions.

111. Marsden, *The Soul of the American University*.

112. Fish, "Why We Can't All Just Get Along," 18–26.

113. Marsden, *Outrageous Idea*.

114. Ibid., 3–4.

scholarship might be, either because they have not thought much about it or because they are unaware that instances of the species already exist.[115]

Marsden and the Liberal Exclusion of Faith from Scholarship

Marsden grounded Christian scholarship in a universal application of what he called the Augustinian principle, *credo ut intelligam*. The scholarship generated out of this epistemological orientation, said Marsden, is distinguishable from both "dogmatism" and "moralism." Why did he choose to distinguish Christian scholarship from these two qualities? He acknowledged thereby the twin judgments of secularist academics upon any scholarship produced by mixing faith and learning. Marsden argued in contradistinction that Christian faith is relevant to contemporary scholarship *of the highest standard*.[116] Since this is so, Marsden suggested that the secular liberal academy expand itself to include explicitly faith-inflected scholarship.[117] Moreover, it could do so with minimal disruption of the scholarly patterns secularists hold dear. Thus, it is legitimate to argue, as Marsden in fact argued, for a temporary and relatively harmonious co-existence between faith-inflected learning and secular, even secularist learning, within an overarchingly liberal academy.

In addition, Marsden's project must be placed within his primary cultural judgment or prophecy: "So long as the very idea of Christian scholarship is questioned, the cultural forces encouraging abandonment of distinctive religious outlooks will almost certainly prevail. If on the other hand scholars . . . can embrace the vision of the positive contribution faith can make to learning, then, perhaps we can enter a creative era . . . ."[118] Marsden wanted to restore the cultural plausibility of faith-inflected scholarship. Drawing on *The Soul of the American University*, he located this loss of plausibility in the twentieth-century movement to accommodate increasing diversity within the academy by dissolving the old privilege of Protestantism and its ethical emphases. Marsden contrasted his understanding of the academy in the twentieth century with both the secularist story of learning's emancipation from religious constraints and the conspiracy theory put forth by many conservative Protestants that the academy has

115. Ibid., 8.

116. Ibid., 9.

117. Ibid., 10–11.

118. Ibid., 12.

been taken over by souls eager to use higher education and the scholarship produced in its course to propagate a secularist cultural ethos throughout American society.[119]

Marsden listed three types of arguments against the inclusion of faith-inflected scholarship in the mainstream academy. First, there were the familiar Enlightenment arguments about the intrinsic antagonism between religion and science. A second argument rested on the cultural and social diversity within the academy and the need for multicultural openness, to which faith-inflected scholars and scholarship were presumed to be antithetical. Finally, in the United States, a third argument derived from the constitutional principle of the separation of Church and State. Marsden showed how each of these arguments is either "dogmatic" (arguments 1 and 3) or "moralistic" (argument 2). In doing so, Marsden achieved a clever turning of the tables on his secularist liberal interlocutors, for, as already noted, the negative qualities denoted by the terms "dogmatism" and "moralism" were precisely those qualities predicated of Christian scholarship from within their discourse.

Marsden marshalled a number of arguments against the presumed antagonism of science and religion. These arguments effectively employed the philosophically realist assumptions implicit within the Christian philosophical orientation called Reformed Epistemology associated, among others, with Alvin Plantinga.[120] His arguments centered in addition upon that philosophy's demonstrations of the legitimacy of prior commitment in the structure of theoretical analysis.

Marsden made equally interesting moves in combating the cultural diversity arguments against the academy's inclusion of explicitly faith-inflected scholarship. He acknowledged the historic role of Protestants in American oppression of Jews, gays and lesbians, and Marxists; hence, he insisted that these groups' sensitivities to the inclusion of Christian scholars and scholarship into the mainstream secular academy must be treated respectfully. Moreover, he thought that these groups have a point when they spoke of the imperial pretensions of some conservative Christian viewpoints. Nevertheless, he maintained that most Christians, including Catholics and Fundamentalist Protestants, have reconciled themselves to

119. Ibid., 29.

120. For an introduction to Reformed Epistemology, see Hoitenga, *Faith and Reason from Plato to Plantinga*.

the existence of both a liberal polity and academy.[121] Thus, he distanced himself from a powerful stream within his own Christian world without capitulating to the disenfranchisement of a Christian voice in the American academy.

Marsden was striking a fine and delicate balance here. On the one hand, he assured secularist scholars that Christian scholars have every intention of playing by the existing rules of the secular and liberal academy. On the other hand, he insisted that what Christian scholars produce is Christian in some meaningful and specifiable ways. The nub of his argument was that there are no compelling *liberal* reasons for excluding what he sometimes called "supernaturalist" viewpoints from public discourse. After all, in his view, Christian convictions ought to have little transformative impact on the *techniques* used in academic work. Nor need the Christian's subjection to revelation obviate Marsden's claim. While worldviews or background beliefs may be shaped by faith, revelation-enabled claims must be defended in a pluralistic setting with arguments and evidence that are publicly accessible.[122] In short, faith-inflected scholars can produce scholarship compatible with a secularist scholarly ethos, since the technical forms of scholarship, because they constitute an implicit historically conditioned *recta ratio* available to believer and unbelievable alike, are unchanged by faith.

Marsden and Faith-Inflected Scholarship

Marsden's position here must be seen in terms of his cultural concern with the plausibility of faith-inflected scholarship. What is at stake is the freedom to make one's background beliefs explicit. Not to be able to do so diminishes those beliefs, by suppressing the rigorous development of their connections to scholarly production.[123] In the end, of course, Marsden affirmed an antithesis between Christian faith and secularist learning. He admitted that at an ultimate level, a rejectionist attitude to human reason, *when that reason is held up as final criterion,* is correct.[124] But he appealed to Augustine, his *City of God* and its identification of overlapping, though

121. Marsden, *Outrageous Idea*, 31–33.

122. Ibid., 45–48.

123. Ibid., 51–52.

124. Ibid., 58–59.

distinct spheres to argue for a significant shared terrain in which secularists and "supernaturalists" can cooperate productively.[125]

The last three chapters of Marsden's book addressed the second of his intended audiences: Christians unsure of what Christian scholarship might look like. Marsden identified how and where faith makes a difference in Christian scholarship, locating areas in which the Christian scholarly voice will take on a characteristic timbre. He mentioned a critical eye for reductionism, a nose for religious motive and agency, and an intuitive opposition to all scholarship predicated on one or another version of the humanistic, transcendent self. The most explicit and obvious contexts in which this Christian difference comes to expression are to be found, said Marsden, in the interpretive or hermeneutical disciplines such as philosophy. In the empirical disciplines, such as the natural sciences, Marsden allowed that faith shows up most obviously on either end of the scholarly process. There, it motivates the scholar and determines appropriate applications for the scholar's work.

All the elements of an integrationist account of the integrality of Christian scholarship are here in Marsden's apologia. Religion and the academy are understood to mark out concretely distinct spheres of socio-cultural endeavor. Faith is that power and mystery perfective of human beings as religious. Faith comes to expression in a manner adapted to the needs of the academy in the form of theological claims about God, self, and world.[126] But, unlike parallel accounts of scholarly integrality of the complementarist type, Marsden does not distinguish between the immediate role of faith in the constitution of theology on the one hand, and the mediated and indirect role that faith plays in the constitution of the other disciplines on the other. Rather, Christian faith can and often does play an immediate and intrinsic role in the constitution of all academic disciplines. It is the task of academics participating in those disciplines to explore the lineaments of that role. While formal ecclesiastical overseers and the community of theologians can aid in their explorations, chiefly by their contributions to the Christian formation (e.g. biblical literacy) of the Christian community to which disciplinary experts belong, they cannot replace disciplinary experts in the process of discerning the implications of faith for the non-

125. Ibid., 55–56 and 97–99.

126. This is especially clear in the chapters of Marsden's book entitled "What Difference Could it Possibly Make" and "The Positive Contributions of Theological Context" (59–82 and 83–100, respectively).

theological disciplines. It is the Christian scholar working in one or another of the disciplines who is best placed to discern the difference that Christian faith makes.[127]

3. Holist Accounts

Complementarist and integrationist accounts of the integrality of Christian scholarship do not exhaust the basic accounts generated by Christian scholars. There is a third type we must yet examine. This third basic account of the integrality of Christian scholarship rejects the identification of religion as a concretely delimited socio-cultural endeavor. At the same time, it acknowledges that socio-cultural endeavor can be religious; indeed, it denies that socio-cultural endeavor can ever be *irreligious*. The question is never whether some bit of human culture-making is religious but rather what religion or religions does it bear witness to.

So, for these scholars, the contrast between religion and scholarship as distinct forms of socio-cultural endeavor is transformed. Religion, in these accounts, is that deepest integrating dynamic of human living that comes to concrete expression in a wide range of socio-cultural endeavors, one of which is scholarship. Scholarship, then, is an expression of religion.

In this account, scholarship is a concrete socio-cultural practice. This practice is based on our human capacity to distinguish and conceptualize various patterns scholarly activity brings to the surface within our ordinary involvements with creatures, as part of cultures, and with events. While scholarship is a social and cultural practice, faith is not. Rather, faith is better seen as something closer to a quality of creaturely life.

Creaturely life knows many such qualities, and these qualities are thought to imbue all our life practices. One could say, perhaps, that the qualities variously present in all human living give a distinctive color to the many practices that make up such living. For example, a logical quality is thought to be particularly prominent in the practice of scholarship. Faith by contrast is held to be particularly prominent in the practice of cultic life carried on in churches, mosques, synagogues and temples.

Faith does not stand out in the practice of scholarship the way that the capacity to conceive things as distinct but interrelated does. It is not

127. This is indeed the implicit assumption of the chapters entitled "Building Academic Communities" and "Getting Specific: A Readable Appendix" (101–111 and 113–119, respectively).

that faith or any of the other qualities at play in the practices of human living are absent from scholarship. It is, however, that it and they remain in the background, so much so that they can easily be taken for granted or overlooked, and so be assumed to be absent altogether.

Consequently, in this account, faith and logical thought are to be distinguished one from another as separate qualities present within the practices of human living. In addition, faith can be opposed to scholarship as any quality can be opposed to a concrete human practice. Nevertheless, neither faith and worship nor logic and scholarship can be separated from religion. Rather, in this account, all the qualities and practices of human living are expressions of religion. Christian scholarship, then, is scholarship that gives expression to the Christian religion as opposed to any of the other (including the gamut of secularist) possibilities. Christian scholarship is that practical expression of Christian religion characterized by its logical or discursive or theoretical quality. Because, in this account, religion is the whole (integrating dynamic[128]) of which practices like scholarship and qualities like logical thought and faith are parts, we name the account itself as holistic.[129]

128. The dynamic I am naming as religion, while it is integrating, is not necessarily, and indeed is very seldom, unitary. It is most often a complex in which the parts stand in tension vis-à-vis each other in a dizzying variety of ways.

129. As stated in chapter one, I could easily have taken up Nicholas Wolterstorff as a thinker working out of a holist account of the integrality of Christian scholarship or learning as he prefers to name it. His holism is evident in his "Public Theology or Christian Learning?" 65–87; the essays that make up *Educating for Shalom*; and the published version of an address given to commemorate the fiftieth anniversary of the founding of Dordt College, in Sioux Center Iowa; Wolterstorff, "Fifty Years Later," 26–30. It must be said that to have included him would have entailed a number of alterations in the generic account as presented here. For, though I suspect he could live (if only wryly) with the account of logicality and its role in scholarly activity, he would perhaps take issue with the distinction between faith and religion included in this description as the best or even a good way to make the point the distinction is used by its defenders to make: namely, if one is a Christian and understands that as the deepest unifying dynamic in one's life, then one brings that with one in all one does, even when it remains merely but properly implicit in one activity or another. He would, I am sure, say that the generic account presented here is tailored too much to the philosophical peculiarities of the figures who are cited in what follows as its "trustworthy guides." I would concede the point.

Herman Dooyeweerd

Herman Dooyeweerd (1894 to 1977) spent nearly all of his adult life closely associated with the then self-consciously "Calvinistic" Free University (Vrije Universiteit) in Amsterdam, first as student and from 1926 as professor in the Faculty of Law.[130] Together with his brother-in-law, D. H. Th. Vollenhoven, he elaborated a distinctively Reformed orientation to European philosophy, and above all to those texts and philosophical movements now often identified as continental philosophy. In the process, they founded the Society for Calvinistic Philosophy and served as early editors of its trade journal *Philosophia Reformata*.[131] His philosophy, which he called *de wijsbegeerte der wetsidee*, (inelegantly translated as the "philosophy of the cosmonomic idea,") forms the historical and philosophical basis of our third account of Christian integrality across the curriculum.[132]

In 1958 and 1959 Dooyeweerd traveled widely to various centers of Presbyterian and Reformed thought in Canada and the United States. The lectures he developed for that tour were collected, edited and published.[133] They were meant to communicate the gist of his philosophy to a North American audience, and they make for as good an entree as any into Dooyeweerd's holistic approach to and account of the integrality of Christian scholarship.[134]

130. For an intellectual biography of Dooyeweerd, see Verburg, *Herman Dooyeweerd*. For an English language study of the crucial years in the formation of Dooyeweerd see Henderson, *Illuminating Law*. For the cultural and historical context of Dooyeweerd and his project see the two volumes of Johannes Stellingwerff dedicated to the history of the Vrije Universiteit te Amsterdam: Stellingwerff, *Dr. Abraham Kuyper en de Vrije Unversiteit*.

131. For the thought of D. H. Th. Vollenhoven see Stellingwerff, *D. H. Th. Vollenhoven,*. In English, see, Kok, *Vollenhoven: His Early Development* and Tol, *Philosophy in the Making*. The Society for Calvinistic Philosophy now known as the Association for Reformational (Protestant) Philosophy has published since 1935 the trade journal *Philosophia Reformata* and maintains a Centre for Reformational Philosophy and it is linked to an electronic library that can be accessed via its website. For a memoire/history of the "school" of philosophy see Stellingwerff, *Geschiedenis van de Reformatorische*.

132. I think one could even say this of Wolterstorff, though in a less direct way than for others. Dooyeweerd has been an important interlocutor for him over the years. He has learned from him matters of mutual agreement but has also profited from formulating his philosophical differences, for Dooyeweerd is a worthy adversary as well as a source of inspiration.

133. Dooyeweerd, *Twilight of Western Thought*.

134. One of the best introductions to philosophy in the spirit of Herman Dooyeweerd

Dooyeweerd and the Religious Root of Theoretical Thought

Central to Dooyeweerd's account is what he called a truly radical, transcendental critique of theoretical thought. Such a starting point for his account was both enabled and necessitated by what he perceived to be the deepening of a fundamental crisis in the Western academy.[135] This crisis enabled his starting point because, in Dooyeweerd's view, the scholarly world had come to organize itself around the fundamental assumption that theoretical thought is and ought to be the very acme and core of civilization, marking out and enabling the fulfillment of human living.[136] That assumption had attached to it a corollary, namely, that theoretical thought is and ought to be autonomous vis-à-vis other sources of cultural understanding, and that, as such, it properly recognized nothing as authoritative that it could not account for from *within* its own principles and resources. In Dooyeweerd's view, the present crisis threw into skeptical relief all the landmarks and reflexes of the culture it threatened to split open, even the most secure of these reflexes, e.g., the autonomy of theoretical or scholarly thought.[137]

The crisis then suggested new possibilities for a radical or transcendental critique of theoretical thought that would expose as contestable any claim made for the autonomy of that thought. In addition, arguments for the claim's inversion, the necessarily religious root of theoretical thought, could be used to ground an equally radical account of the integrality of Christian scholarship across the curriculum. Nevertheless, if crisis enabled such a critique, it did not do the critique's work for it. Rather, the ethos of the Western academy in crisis still called for such a critique because the assumption of theoretical thought's fundamental autonomy had become so woven into the fabric of the Western academy that it threatened to survive the very crisis itself as ungrounded prejudice rather than as considered principle. And the assumption, it had to be admitted, rendered the very idea of a Christian scholarly integrality implausible, for Christian faith is not generated by theoretical thought and, as a result, its authority must be considered part of that with respect to which theoretical thought is autonomous.

is van Woudenberg's *Gelovend Denken*. For an English language introduction see Kaalsbeek, *Contours of a Christian Philosophy*. For a critical appraisal see A. L. Conradie, *The Neo-Calvinist Concept of Philosophy*.

135. Dooyeweerd, *Twilight of Western Thought*, 1.

136. Ibid., 2.

137. Ibid., 2.

To insist as Dooyeweerd did on a *transcendental* critique of theoretical thought is to position oneself vis-à-vis Kant and in particular his daunting critique of "pure reason." This is not surprising given the prominence of self-consciously Kantian modes of philosophizing regnant in the Dutch and German universities of Dooyeweerd's intellectual formation.[138] If a Christian of Dooyeweerd's world was to get a philosophical word in edgewise, if he was to be able to challenge the assumption of the autonomy of theoretical thought, he would do well to start where Kant had started: self-consciously reflecting upon theoretical thought, that is, upon the common basis of all scholarship, by asking the question: what are the conditions that make this kind of thought possible?

Dooyeweerd's own critique, then, started where Kant started, but he was aware of his starting point as a strategic choice. It was not that a Kantian starting point was correct, absolutely. Rather, he wished to push the philosophers and philosophies of his world (Kantians and post-Kantian phenomenologists) to recognize a religious dynamic at the very root of theoretical thought itself.[139] Such pressure could in principle be applied using other philosophical frameworks and tools. To be able to show how all thought is subject to the formative dynamism of a religious root—that was the philosophical task that Dooyeweerd named "a truly radical transcendental critique of theoretical thought."[140]

Dooyeweerd's own critique would remain deeply Kant-inflected. In its telling, theoretical thought bore a relationship to the world it is used to understand that contrasts with that of our every-day thinkings and doings. Dooyeweerd claimed that ordinary interactions in the world, or what he called "naïve experience," do not occur in a posture of separation from it. Rather, we ordinarily experience ourselves as participating in a shared world with the creatures and events we experience. Moreover, we experience those creatures as concrete wholes.[141] Such naïve interactions, however, contrast with those of the scholar investigating the same world theoretically. It is true that the scholar acknowledges or should acknowledge the existence of the entities and events that are the stuff of ordinary

138. For an account of the neo-Kantian schools in late nineteenth and early twentieth century Europe, see T. Willey, *Back to Kant: The Revival of Kantianism in German Social and Historical Thought, 1860–1914* (Detroit: Wayne State University, 1987).

139. Dooyeweerd, *Twilight of Western Thought*, 5.

140. See, in this regard, Geertsema, "Inner Reformation of Philosophy," 11–28.

141. Dooyeweerd, *Twilight of Western Thought*, 12–17.

or naïve experience. Those wholes and that experience lie at the basis of all theoretical enquiry. Nevertheless, the scholar's acknowledgement occurs from the point of view of one or another aspect of those wholes and that experience. In other words, the scholar abstracts an aspect from naïve experience of the world and works to represent the abstracted aspect of that world in a logical concept.[142] A zoologist studies pigs as to the phenomena that account for or flow from their existence as living organisms; a geometer might study the same creatures, but as to their particular existence in space, while a jurist, or at any rate a medieval jurist, could study them as to their existence as subjects in law, in fact, as defendants in a homicide trial.[143] One could go on.

A theoretical perspective, then, views the things of our world in terms of abstracted aspects that are not and cannot be things in themselves. Dooyeweerd indicated this by calling each abstracted aspect not a "what" but a "how."[144] I illustrate. The zoologist (though probably not the same one mentioned above) studies hippos first and foremost as living organisms, not as impacts upon the economies of central Africa, nor as components of the aesthetic realism of the movie "The African Queen." To mistake a zoologist's perspective on the hippo as if it exhausted what we can know (theoretically) about hippos and the meaning of their existence would be akin to the tragi-comic scenario once told me by a friend. She knew an ophthalmologist who was once dragooned by the desperate administrators of the British hospital to which his practice was attached to help out in the emergency room. At one point he was asked to treat a victim of a work-related accident. The victim had (among other injuries) gotten glass fragments in his eye. The ophthalmologist saw this immediately and went right to work. When he was satisfied with the job he had done removing the glass and making sure the eye would be all right, he looked at the patient and said, "Right then, that's done. You can go home now." To which the patient responded by asking, "But what about me broken leg?"

Dooyeweerd on the Character of Theoretical Thought

Theoretical thought, then, is for Dooyeweerd—as it was for Kant—a schooled and abstractive way of thinking about the world. As such, it breaks

142. Ibid., 6–12.

143. Cf., Evans, *Criminal Prosecution.*

144. Dooyeweerd, *Twilight of Western Thought*, 6.

the inner coherence of our ordinary experience in two ways. First it relates the theorist to the world of experience *as if* the theorist were opposed to that world and not a part of it. Secondly, it distills from whole entities and events of ordinary experience a number of aspects, so as to subject one or more of those aspects to the theorist's antithetical regard. This theoretical antithesis, however, while it characterizes the quality of theoretical thought, does not account for theoretical understanding, since theoretical understanding does not result merely from breaking apart experience of the world. Rather, it results from connecting what has been broken apart and representing what results within the unity of a logical concept.

Here is an analogy that may help to give Dooyeweerd's point concrete shape. You don't understand a car's transmission by taking it apart until each separable piece lies lonely on the garage floor. You only really understand a transmission if you can take the separate pieces and reconnect them in such a way that the transmission works properly when reassembled. But how is this reconnecting to be understood? If theoretical thought has as its characteristic pose the opposition of the thinker's logical functioning and the non-logical aspects of her experience, what can account for the synthesis by which what has been so opposed comes together fittingly within a theoretical concept so as to produce (theoretical) understanding of the world?

This is where one must remember, as indeed Kant remembered, that it is not thought that thinks but a *thinker*, a "thinking I" as Dooyeweerd put it.[145] It is the human person that thinks. But that realization immediately raises the anthropological question of what this human person *is* that thinks. And here, said Dooyeweerd, is where Kant ran into a problem that compromised the radicality of his transcendental criticism; that is, that diverted him from the very root he was seeking. This problem is that the "I" that thinks is not a thing in and of itself.[146] One can think about *thought* because it is not the source or agent of the thinking. But the "I" that thinks is prior to, and so presupposed by, any act of thought—even thought about the "I" that thinks. To think about something is to translate it into thought. But one cannot translate the "I" that thinks into thought since it is always prior to, and hence transcendent with respect to, the thought that it produces even when thinking about itself. And that means that it is not a thing; it is not a proper and available object of theoretical thought. So

145. Ibid., 21.

146. Ibid., 28.

how is one to gain a purchase on the "I" that thinks in such a way as to be able to account for the synthesis that leads to theoretical understanding and that occurs subsequent to the theoretical antithesis of the thinker's logical functioning and the non-logical aspects of the thinker's experience?

Dooyeweerd insisted that, abstractly conceived, one could strive to understand the "I" that thinks in only one of three ways. It could be that the "I" receives its identity or meaning from its relationship to the world of experienced wholes and the aspects of those wholes opened up to view via theoretical thought.[147] But such a search is self-contradictory. It implies that the "I" is at one and the same time prior and transcendent with respect to its act of theoretical thought and posterior and so available to that same thought.

Secondly, it could be that the human "I" that thinks receives its identity or meaning from its relationship to all other human I's.[148] But if the human "I" that thinks always escapes its own thought about itself (because it is ever prior and transcendent with respect to it), surely that same situation will apply to all other human I's; they too will transcend and so escape any attempt to comprehend them theoretically. Moreover they, via the theoretical or antithetical attitude of their thought, will stand in opposition to the world of experience they seek to understand. Consequently, all human I's thought of in relation to each other will presuppose and so not offer a ground for the resolution of the theoretical antithesis within a theoretical synthesis.

And that leaves a third and last possibility. It could be that the human "I" that thinks receives its identity from an Origin transcendent both with respect to the human "I" and indeed the world it experiences.[149] The affinity constituted by a single, transcendent Origin would seem to re-establish the continuity of the theoretical thinker and the world thought: they would belong together by virtue of the comprehensive order constituted by their common Origin. In this way, one could account for the conceptual syntheses that lead to theoretical understanding.

Again, one must acknowledge that Dooyeweerd is still working with the Kantian framework—though here one begins to see him diverge from his interlocutor, especially terminologically.[150] For Dooyeweerd does not

147. Ibid., 28.

148. Ibid., 28–30.

149. Ibid., 30–33.

150. Kant for example does not use the language of Origin at this point of his critique.

see in his Origin what Kant saw, namely, a transcendental and logical Origin of our theoretical syntheses, always already operative in any act of theoretical antithesis, one and the same for all concrete "I's" that think and their thought inasmuch as it is the very condition of possibility of their thinking at all. If thinking was an internal and constituting capacity of the "I" that thinks, its transcendental and universal condition of possibility will simultaneously be the transcendental and universal condition for the possibility of an "I" that thinks, not just its thought.

By contrast, Dooyeweerd insisted that what he saw was not bounded by theoretical discourse or anything finally available to theoretical thought itself. His Origin was in fact transcendent (in contradistinction to transcendental) and in fact divine. Consequently, Dooyeweerd knew that his account of theoretical synthesis was not itself a theoretical account. Rather, it was a properly religious and supra-theoretical account, adapted in such a way as to become meaningful with respect to and so transcendentally illuminative of theoretical thought in its transcendent root. We will return to this divergence between Dooyeweerd and Kant shortly.

Dooyeweerd on the Human Person as Intrinsically Religious

In Dooyeweerd's view, the "I" that thinks becomes aware of its identity in relation to its Origin, a divine Origin. This formulation ascribes agency to the "I" that thinks, but Dooyeweerd insisted that the relation is one in which the "I" is passive. That is, when the "I" is oriented to its Origin, it receives its identity from the meaning-constituting dynamic of that Origin's revealing Word; a dynamic that Dooyeweerd indicated using the formula: creation, fall, redemption by Jesus Christ in communion with the Holy Spirit. For Dooyweerd, only those who so acknowledged their identity in relationship to their divine Origin as that relationship is revealed in the dynamic of Word-revelation, only those whose whole living, including their theoretical thinking, have been infused by that dynamic—only they will produce scholarship that is integrally Christian. Moreover, this being infused by

Rather, he speaks of the Transcendental Ego or I that accounts for the empirical I-that-thinks. In other words, he sees a repetition of the theoretical antithesis between knowing subject and known object occur between the concrete I and its thought that can itself be brought into synthesis via the idea of the Transcendental I. That this simultaneously accounts for the possibility of a synthesis at the level of the concrete ego as knowing subject and the object it knows implies that the object as known is reducible to the concrete ego's thought about it.

the spiritual dynamic signified by the formula creation, fall, redemption by Jesus Christ in communion with the Holy Spirit is not a lonely act of contemplative encounter. Rather it is communal; the dynamic is present within a community and inculcated in and through its modes of religious formation (33–34).[151]

Finally, the Christian scholar will be one whose life and scholarship is suffused by the revealed dynamic of Word-revelation set in motion in the scholar's relationship to the divine Origin. All other scholars will be forced in the end to define the "I" that thinks in terms of some aspect of the world opened up by theoretical thought. That aspect will be held as absolutely basic, as that from which everything else, including the thinking "I" itself, is derived. It will never be just one aspect, however, but always two so that thought remains ever suspended between irreconcilable poles. Indeed, the dynamic set up by the dialectical tension between the aspects of the world posited as absolute basis for all else mimics the constituting dynamic of Word-revelation for the "I's" self-understanding and for its enquiries into the nature of the world.[152] Of course, these alternative dynamics will also be communal and inculcated by a spiritual formation whether or not that formation is understood to be religious. Consequently, one will be able to plot their historical appearance and development in human culture. In addition to the Christian dynamic, what he called "the biblical ground-motive," Dooyeweerd identified a spiritual dynamic of the ancient Mediterranean world (form-matter), of the medieval Latin world (nature-grace) and the modern Western world (nature-freedom).[153]

So why did Dooyeweerd think that Kant ran into a problem when he sought to understand and account for theoretical synthesis in terms of a transcendental, still theoretical Origin of thought's relationship to the "I" that thinks? Dooyeweerd noticed that when Kant came to speak of the relationship of his Origin to the concrete "I" that thinks and its thought,[154] he used language and relational patterns that he had already used when describing the antithetical relationship between logical subject and non-logical object. This is how Dooyeweerd summarizes Kant's position:

> [The universal-transcendental I] does not belong to empirical reality. It is much rather the general condition of any possible act

151. Ibid., 33–34.

152. Ibid., 35–39.

153. Ibid., 39–52

154. See the preceding note for a summary of Kant's position.

> of thought; and as such it has no individuality of any kind. It is the theoretical-logical subject to which all empirical reality can be opposed as its objective counter-pole, its object of knowledge and experience.[155]

What Dooyeweerd saw in Kant's account, then, was a doubling of the relationship of thought to the world in the relationship of a universal-transcendental "I" to the concrete "I" and its thought. The universal-transcendental "I" is to the concrete "I" and its thought as thought is to the world perceived in experience. Dooyeweerd concluded from this doubling that Kant had turned back to the world of experience to define the universal-transcendental "I" in terms of the logical capacity of the concrete "I" that is foregrounded in theoretical thought. Indeed, the empirical ego, the concrete "I" who can be experienced in perception, was constituted by its relationship or access to and participation in a universal transcendental logical unity. That unity was for Kant the ground of the synthetic logical concepts by which we gain theoretical understanding of the world of our experience. If one asks why he would turn back in this way, Dooyeweerd responded that he was blocked from any other move by a controlling assumption, namely, the autonomy of theoretical thought.

Dooyeweerd's radical transcendental critique of theoretical thought then led him to affirm that all theoretical thinking is rooted in a religious dynamism that has its origin either in the Word revelation of the God of Christian faith or in some substitute drawn from the world of theoretical thought and experience. Since all scholarly disciplines are forms of theoretical thought, all scholarly thought is rooted in the same religious dynamism. Christian scholarship then is at bottom theoretical thought that has been set in motion by the dynamism let loose by the self-revelation of God inherent in the formula creation, fall, and redemption by Jesus Christ in the communion of the Holy Spirit when that dynamism has come to suffuse theoretical enquiry into the world of our experience.

Dooyeweerd on Scholarly Traditions and Religious Dynamics

The scholarly disciplines were, for Dooyeweerd, all grounded in the various aspects of the world of experience brought to the fore by theoretical thought. Dooyeweerd provisionally listed fifteen such aspects or modes he

155. Ibid., 23–24.

was prepared to defend: the numerical, spatial, kenetic, physico-chemical, biotic, psychical, logical, historical, lingual, social, economic, aesthetic, juridical, moral, and faith modes.[156] Dooyeweerd saw the scholarly disciplines as ways of analyzing the world that focused enquiry upon some delimited configuration of these elementary modes of theoretical experience. The disciplines and their methods then developed in accordance with the specific meaning displayed within each of the disciplines' constitutive aspects.

The scholar, of course, functioned in all fifteen modes all of the time, including when she was engaged in scholarly work. But it was the characteristically distinguishing role of her logical functioning that gave her theoretical or scholarly work its determinate quality. While faith was certainly present in the scholarship produced by the Christian scholar it was not by virtue of the presence of faith in the scholar that the scholarship he produced was to be thought of as integrally Christian. Rather, it was the religious dynamism at play in the scholar's logically qualified scholarly work that determined the Christian integrity of the scholarship. And, on this score, the theologian was in no different position vis-à-vis his discipline than was any other scholar vis-à-vis his.[157] That is, theology was not identified with religion in a way that differed fundamentally from that of any other discipline. As a result, as with integrationist accounts, it was not, for Dooyeweerd, the theologian who was best placed to identify what it means to be busy at Christian scholarship in any of the other disciplines. Rather, it was the Christian scholar trained to work within the discipline, the Christian scholar whose sense of self and work have been forged by the dynamism revealed as creation, fall, redemption by Jesus Christ in communion with the Holy Spirit. Indeed, this last point was brought forcibly home in Dooyeweerd's assertion that what it meant for the theologian to be Christian in her theological scholarship was perhaps best identified by the transcendental criticism of the Christian philosopher.[158]

Indeed, here was another move reminiscent of Kant. To philosophy belonged the task of conceptualizing the proper ontological object (*Gegenstand*) of the scholarly disciplines and of establishing their valid interrelations. If theology was a discipline then the conception of its proper object and its relationship to the objects of the other disciplines was part and parcel

156. Ibid., 7.

157. Dooyeweerd, *Twilight of Western Thought*, 135–140.

158. Ibid., 5.

of philosophy's proper task. Moreover, if theology was a scholarly discipline, then, one could not maintain continuity with the age-old scholastic identification of the proper subject of theology as God. Rather, any and all encounter with God who addresses us in Word-revelation, must necessarily occur at the level of the "I," what in the Old Testament is referred to as "the heart" prior to or beyond the scholarly field per se. In Dooyeweerd's view, what the theologian studies by contrast is the faith aspect, that dimension of experience that is manifest to theoretical thought. Faith in this restricted sense is the trace within the world available to theoretical thought of the "I" *in its orientation to its self-revealing divine Origin*. It bears witness to, but is distinct from, the "I" and its constituting orientation.

It is clear how important the hegemony of Kantian and post-Kantian thought was in the crucial decades in which Dooyeweerd developed his philosophy and orientation to Christian scholarship. His philosophy was built up as a constant challenge to that great philosophical tradition. His fundamentally holistic account of Christian integrality across the curriculum, however, would be taken up by many thinkers who were far less attuned to transcendental modes of philosophizing. While Dooyeweerd's thought and manner of philosophizing has exerted a powerful influence on subsequent versions of the account, Kant has rarely been as materially significant. This can be seen in a second and last example of the account, the thought of a thinker whose interaction with thought owed as much to orthodox Presbyterian theological formation and its deeply vertical and theocentric angle of approach as to his philosophical connection to the transcendental, anthropocentric angle of approach of Herman Dooyeweerd.

H. Evan Runner

H. Evan Runner (1916 to 2002) studied at the Free University of Herman Dooyeweerd, though with Dooyeweerd's brother-in-law, D. H. Th. Vollenhoven. He received his doctorate in 1951 for a thesis on Aristotle's *Physics* and the evidence internal to it of a number of distinct philosophical conceptions reflective of different stages in Aristotle's philosophical development.[159] It was also in 1951 that Runner began his North American teaching career at Calvin College in Grand Rapids, Michigan, where he would teach until his retirement in 1981. During his tenure, he would work tirelessly to promote in Reformed and Presbyterian settings through-

159. Runner, *The Development of Aristotle*.

out North America the worldview or spiritual orientation that lay behind the philosophical work of Dooyeweerd, Vollenhoven, and their associates within the Society for Calvinistic Philosophy. He was particularly effective among the communities of Reformed immigrants from The Netherlands in Canada. It was in the context of this latter work that in 1959, and then again in 1960, Runner travelled to Unionville, Ontario to address a conference sponsored by the Association for Reformed Scientific Studies (later called the Association for the Advancement of Christian Scholarship). These addresses were collected and published in 1972 under the title *The Relation of the Bible to Learning* by the Toronto-based Wedge Publishing Foundation. Its "holist" account is forcefully put from its first page:

> These lectures spring forth from the conviction that the Word of God as "Orderer" of all creation addresses itself to the totality of human experience, as the supremely authoritative condition for all meaningful experience, as both the limit and the source of all meaning. The place of scholarly activity as one human task among many in the integral unity of life presupposes that all things academic depend on subjection to the Word for their meaning.[160]

Throughout these lectures, Runner insisted on seeing academic work as of a piece with all "life-in-the-world" and all such life as an indissoluble unity. As a consequence, life-in-the-world flows from a single source or principle, and does so, willy-nilly. That source is "the Word of God." Since "the Word of the living God *has come* with its revealing light into our life," said Runner, "*all human life*, whether [humans] are aware of it or not, *is some kind of response to that Word.*"[161] And this means that a Christian scholar should account for the unity of Christian scholarship in terms of the intrinsic connection that obtains between the Word of God and the world of learning.[162] That is, Christian scholarship is unified by its intrinsic connection to the Word of God. And that means, in turn, that Christian scholarship is scholarship that scholars produce when the problems of their field of study are "seen" in the "revealing light of the Word of God."[163] It is paramount, then, to understand what "the Word of God" is to which the scholar is to respond in her scholarship.

160. Runner, *The Relation of the Bible to Learning*, 5.

161. Ibid., 14.

162. Ibid., 15.

163. Ibid., 16

Runner on the Word of God and World Orientation

In Runner's view, the Word of God is best understood as "the POWER of God, that comes to our hearts and opens our eyes so that we may understand the singleness of meaning of all the Scriptures."[164] This understanding is not theological. Nor is it exegetical. Rather it is personal, and as such is always already operative in any theological or exegetical act. When the Word opens our eyes we see Christ; Christ is the meaning and unity of the Scriptures. In and through Christ we are brought to a true vision and knowledge of God, self, and world. Such knowledge is of the heart, i.e., "the religious concentration point of our existence." It comes "in a single flash of insight" that "brings us world-orientation, and thus sets our lives going in the right direction."[165] In the grip of this power, we become existentially aware of the integral Creation-Order, radical Fall, and the Restoration in Christ.[166] It is, in turn, within the awareness of Creation Order, radical Fall, and Restoration in Christ that the great diversity of our world's states of affairs speak to us and have their meaning. If one lacks this awareness, one will have to invent an Order of one's own devising to act as the structuring principle of the cosmos of which we seek understanding.[167]

Time and again, Runner emphasized that we cannot get our hands on the unity of the Word of God and the Order present to our awareness in the grip of that Word. That is, the unity remains ever beyond our logical grasp.[168] Nevertheless, religiously, we have it in our sights. That religiously available unity or Order holds for the whole creation and the spectrum of irreducible, though relative, moments it manifests.[169] The unity itself is religious; the life lived with respect to that Order or whatever is substituted for it is religion. Consequently, Christian scholarship is—like all other endeavors of human living—an act of religion, whether that religion is in accord with or discordant from the God-ordained Order we are made aware of by the power of the Word of God.[170]

164. Ibid., 23.
165. Ibid., 32.
166. Ibid., 33.
167. Ibid.. 33.
168. Ibid., 36.
169. Ibid., 46.
170. Ibid., 46–47.

The mystery of the Word of God is matched by the mystery of the receiving selfhood: "We can never quite reach the unity [of the Word of God—sw.], cannot put our fingers solidly on it, as is also the case with our thinking about our own selfhood. The unity is just beyond our logical grasp; yet *religiously* we are aware that the unity is there."[171] Christian scholarship in this view, as said, is scholarship done out of an awareness of the "intrinsic connection between [the] Word and the world of learning."[172] It is this awareness that puts the scholar in the truth. As a result, a clear distinction must be drawn between "a more or less correct description of . . . limited states of affairs that immediately press upon us all and the truth about those states of affairs. The *truth* of them cannot be seen in isolation from the whole coherence of meaning of the creation-order."[173]

As a result, one ought not to seek this deep unity of things in any body of scholarly knowledge.[174] Life in its wholeness is only accessed pre-scientifically in a mode of knowing or engagement that can be called naïve experience. It is here, says Runner, that "we experience not only persons and things, events and institutions in their wholeness, but also the *given* interwoven-ness of all these in their . . . relations."[175] Of course, naïve experience too is not the place in which we find the unity and meaning of existence. It is to be found, again as said, only when in the grip of the Word on our hearts we are united to Christ and so know the Truth. And this is religion, the concentration-point of all the "sides" or "aspects" of created meaning.[176]

Runner on the Word of God and Scholarly Office

The life of scholarship then is an expression of religion or of heart-service of God.[177] And scholarship entails the existence of a scholarly office that responds to a divine Word for it, i.e., a structuring order that conditions the healthy performance of scholarly functions.[178] Crucial to the scholarly

171. Ibid., 36.
172. Ibid., 35.
173. Ibid., 37.
174. Ibid., 126.
175. Ibid., 126.
176. Ibid., 127.
177. Ibid., 145.
178. Ibid., 145–148.

office is the self-conscious act of abstraction whereby persons and things, events and institutions, can be analyzed in terms of their various functional aspects. Such analysis depends upon the capacity for logical distinction. These aspects can be listed as the numerical, spatial, physical/kinematic, energetic, organic, psychical, analytical, historical/technical, lingual, social, economic, aesthetic, jural, ethical, and pistical/believing.[179] In scholarship it is the scholar's logical function that lends its peculiar quality to scholarly practice, for it is the capacity to distinguish and relate these various functional aspects that lies at the basis of our scholarly disciplines when they are viewed as fields of investigation. But always this office is carried on out of one's religious stance, whether in relation to the transcendent Origin of things or in relation to one or another functional aspect of persons, things, events or institutions viewed as original.[180]

4. Provenance, Strengths and Weaknesses

Each of the basic accounts of the integrality of Christian scholarship that we have been examining—the complementarist account of Bonaventure, Gilson and John Paul II, the integrationist account of Plantinga and Marsden, and the holist account of Dooyeweerd and Runner—has its own history, its own philosophical and theological provenance within the Christian tradition, and its own set of founding conditions. Moreover, each basic account exhibits real strengths and vulnerabilities in relation to past and present circumstance. Before wrapping up this chapter, we will take a moment to examine those strengths and vulnerabilities.

Complementarist Accounts and the Secularization of the Medieval Academy

The complementarist account has its roots in the Latin Middle Ages.[181] It works out of a deep reverence for the God-fashioned sturdiness of the cre-

179. Ibid., 46.

180. Ibid., 67–68.

181. I have described the grounding and figuring of the unity of scholarship implicit in the *Summa theologiae* of Thomas Aquinas in a book-length manuscript entitled *In Virtue of Glory: Thomas Aquinas and the Place of Science and Religion in the Shape of Human Flourishing*, that is being written under contract with the Pontifical Institute for Mediaeval Studies Publications.

ation. In that context, it embraces a relative autonomy of human rationality in its investigation of God, self, and world; the embrace expresses its founding confidence that God made the world well, gave it all that it needed to flourish, and therefore enabled it to withstand the ravages of sin divinely foreseen. It is this confidence that lies behind the notion of a sphere of nature that remains essentially unaltered by sin, a sphere that extends to embrace the human mind in its access to things (*ratio recta*). Of course, there is within this account a concomitant recognition of the Fall and of the spiritual struggle that permeates and makes difficult the contours of natural existence, a difficulty that would become an impossibility if it were not for divine mercy and the ubiquity of Grace that makes available to us a distinct and elevating sense of things, of otherwise hidden meaning that sets us in motion toward our and the world's perfection. Thus, there is recognition of the biblical pattern of creation-fall-redemption, a recognition that is given theoretical form via the categories, "Nature" and "Grace." But for the complementarist, the accent should never be placed on the Fall, for that would be to denigrate the original work of creation and the divine forethought that went into it. Rather, the accent rests properly on the intrinsic sturdiness of what God made and hence the continuity of the world's intelligibility and of a shared rationality, even across the devastation of the fall and ensuing spiritual struggle.

Such an account seems particularly apropos in the context of a culture wherein Christians dominate all cultural fields, or in which a given Christian community and academy are so isolated that they approximate in their isolation the conditions of Christian cultural domination. In such a context, the directive and regulative force of faith and its theological *intellectus* is acknowledged by scholars in the other disciplines. They acknowledge this force for a spectrum of reasons. On one extreme are those who are themselves Christians and, for that reason look to theology and the Church's magisterium (in the case of Protestants, replaced by authoritative confessions, fifteen fundamentals, and the like) for orientation in their thinking about the world. On the other extreme are those who operate in disciplines so dominated in body and spirit by Christian scholars of the first extreme that the disciplines themselves have been conformed to that theology and confession.

Such an account, of course, demands, as said, a teleological understanding of the world. It lives or dies with the meaningfulness and explanatory power of a thing's purpose, end, and perfection. However, remove the force of final causality and the account of the unity of scholarship that depends on that force is replaced by an intrinsic distinction into two: an emphasis which divides the faith-filled discipline of theology from the rest of the academic disciplines.

And, indeed, two hundred years of secularization, especially the much accelerated transformations of the last hundred, confirm this point, for they have had a dramatic effect upon the academy and its disciplines. The relative autonomy of the disciplines under the dual regulative direction of theology and the church magisterium has been replaced among the non-theological disciplines by what, at its most rhetorically vivid, can be termed a methodological atheism. Consequently, many disciplines have been reconstructed as profoundly naturalistic such that they function at crucial junctures in ways that conflict and compete with Christian theology and confession. The faith-antagonistic ethos that has thereby ensued has come to have its way even with Christian scholars. These scholars have been forced to accommodate their work to the methodological atheism and consequent naturalism of their discipline for that method and ethos has come to be identified *as essential* to the discipline itself.

Christian scholars, of course, also continue to be persons of faith. But it is only in the discipline of theology, where faith has remained unproblematically the very matter used by the scholar. As a result, the unity of the academic disciplines has come in fact to fray; theology has become increasingly isolated from—if not at war with—the other disciplines.[182] This is the situation that Catholic and Protestant academics have faced over the course of the nineteenth and twentieth centuries.[183]

Many latter-day exponents of the medieval Christian academy and its complementarist account of the unity of scholarship and the faith of the scholar have only tended to confirm the fragmenting division of the secularizing disciplines from theology. They have done so, because they have tended to respond defensively in the face of the expansive success of secularization. That is, they have tended to protect a field of human activity for Christians *as Christians*, namely, religion, including a beachhead in the academy—theology—against the corrosive force of methodological atheism and the concomitant scholarly naturalisms that have arisen in one

182. This story is brilliantly told in Milbank, *Theology and Social Theory*.

183. See in this regard Marsden, *The Soul of the American University*. For the Catholic academy in North America see Gleason, "American Catholic Higher Education," 15–53; Leahy, *Adapting to America*, and above Burtchael, *The Dying of the Light*.

discipline after another. They have legitimated this move by playing up the irreducible distinction they recognize between the faith-filled character of theology and its place within the church's magisterium, on the one hand, and the autonomous and merely faith-directed and regulated character of the other disciplines, on the other. But such a move has in effect constituted a retreat of Christian scholars *as Christian* from the non-theological disciplines. They have been forced thereby to view the resulting developments either as objectively providential and hence as appropriate to Christian understanding of God, self, and world, or as profoundly malignant and a spur to cultural "counter-revolution" or to a new disengagement and isolation.[184]

Integrationist Accounts and the Nineteenth-Century Rise of Ideology

The integrationist account emerged among Reformed scholars during the last decades of the nineteenth century in the context of and in response to the secularization of the academy and its impact upon Protestant scholarship in particular. It acknowledges that changes in the academy have worked against the force of a teleological understanding of Christian integrality. It also recognizes an important consequence of this acknowledgment. Complementarist accounts cannot effectively resist the fragmentation of the academy in ways that isolate theology and the Christian faith it mediates from the rest of the disciplines and so contributes to secularization. Indeed, in a world in which the non-theological disciplines have vastly greater cultural prestige than theology, complementarist vulnerability to secularization extends to theology itself, such that it comes to reconstruct itself as if it were a non-theological discipline and hence properly organized as a species of secularized, naturalistic understanding.

Consequently, the issue of spiritual struggle within scholarship comes to assume far greater emphasis. Indeed, the emphasis shifts from trust in the sturdiness of the divine Maker's creation, to a trust in the divine Redeemer's graciousness in the face of sin's ubiquitous spoiling of the creation.

184. For the optimistic pole of such responses in which secularization is itself understood in terms of the Christian notion of kenosis or the Self-Emptying of God, see Vattimo, *Belief*; Benedict XVI's musings on the need for a Re-Christianization of Europe can stand for the counter-revolutionary strand; while the widespread North American phenomenon of Catholic home schooling among Catholic believers whose distrust of culture has spread to Catholic educators and educational institutions themselves manifests the isolationist response.

That is, instead of emphasizing the sturdiness of the creation even in the face of sin, the integrationist views the world, including a significant section of the academy, in terms of an antithesis between sin and Grace played out with respect to the creation conceived as fallen nature. For the integrationist, secularization is to be greeted with suspicion and resisted. It is not providential; it belongs on the sin side of spiritual antithesis. Nevertheless, resistance does not take the form of retreat. Rather, resistance takes the form of a different understanding of Christian faith in its intersection with scholarship.

Integrationist accounts still speak of areas of life in which the spiritual antithesis between sin and Grace is barely to be noticed. They do so under the rubric of common Grace, a non-soteriological benizen poured out upon fallen nature in ways that heal and so provide the modicum of health necessary for other and greater spiritual transformations. Common Grace is available to the faithless as well as the faith-filled. It suffuses scholarly work in ways that tend to create the equivalent of the complementarist notion of *recta ratio*, though spiritual struggle is to be noted within the academy among a far wider spectrum of disciplines than theology. Indeed, one sees it operative in all disciplines in which one notes the productive and enduring presence of multiple perspectives (the humanities and the social sciences). Common Grace then allows the integrationist to concede that one need not be faith-filled in order to produce scholarship that furthers understanding of God, self, and world. Nevertheless, among faith-filled scholars, faith can and should play an added, productive role in their scholarship. Consequently, Christians can take their rightful place *as Christians* within the halls of the academy and produce scholarship that is self-consciously faith-inflected.

Such a position has the advantage of acknowledging that the dominant cultural ethos in the academy has been profoundly secularizing and of working creatively to conceive of a place that Christians can yet play in *that* world *as Christians*. It does so while avoiding a romantic nostalgia for a Christian culture now lost—the Christian Middle Ages of the Old World or the ethnic enclaves that resembled that lost Old World in the New. This position, however, does make religious identity an add-on to scholarship, albeit an addition that the Christian will *want* because the Christian wishes all that she does to be an expression of her faith in the God she meets revealed in the Scriptures. In other words, Christian identity will be an add-on to scholarship as scholarship, while being fully integral to the scholar as person.

Faith identity can inhere legitimately within scholarship even as it falls outside of the essence of scholarship per se.[185] But such a position implicitly assumes that in a secularizing academic culture the standard for judging whether faith has or has not contributed productively to scholarship lies with those whose office entails such judgments in the academy *as we find it*. This means inevitably, at least for the foreseeable future, an understanding of the judgment as a secularizing one. Moreover, since so many disciplines have been reconstructed by strictly naturalistic methods and assumptions, the Christian scholar is put in a difficult dilemma when facing those moments where Christian faith pulls the scholar in one direction but the naturalism of her discipline's guiding assumptions pulls her in another. When the final arbiter is secularizing, won't it necessarily be secularist?

Holist Accounts and the Twentieth-Century Search for a Radical Christian Critique

The holist account of Christian scholarly integrality has its roots in the ideological struggles of the first half of Europe's twentieth century. The account emerged definitively in The Netherlands during the decades of the 1920s and 1930s. It, like the integrationist account, has found its most articulate elaborators within the conservative or evangelically Reformed academy. It represents an intensification of the awareness of spiritual struggle in the academy at large at a time when ideological struggle was reaching its catastrophic apex in European culture and society. It places at the very center of Christian scholarship an awareness of all academic life as a schooled reflection upon the creation *within* the context of the spiritual antithesis of sin and Grace. The antithesis is not just restricted to disciplines in which the ineradicability of perspectival plurality is acknowledged. Rather, it so orients Christians to the ubiquity of ideological and ultimately religious struggle that the use of the doctrine of common Grace to create and approve a relatively neutral academic space, say, of logical functioning (Plantinga) or of historical consensus around technique (Marsden), is judged spiritually

185. This account has been elaborated within the Reformed and evangelical academy of North America, above all. Its sophistication and success has come to noticed in broader cultural circles in the last half-decade. See, above all, Wolfe, "The Opening of the Evangelical Mind."

fatal. Though such spaces will almost inevitably arise in an academy that has long been transformed by a secularizing ethos, in holist perspective they must be continually questioned until the implicit spiritual antithesis at play is brought to the surface.

Spiritual struggle between sin and Grace in the context of a shared creation marks out the fundamental spiritual orientation of this account, and it entails a number of virtues in the Christian scholar. In the first place, it entails a vigilant scholarly awareness of one's own religious depths and the religious depths of others. In the second place, it entails that the scholar be humble enough to be open to the possibility that her own scholarship too bespeaks a complex religious affiliation. In the third place, the Christian scholar must also be optimistic enough to think that such complexity will out; that one can always tell the difference (if only *post factum*) between what is theoretically God glorifying and what is not; that it is not the end of the world to be caught out and invited to adjust.

A holist account is critical to a degree that the first two are not. Indeed, it radicalizes the sensitivity to perspectival plurality and struggle by making such sensitivity a primary spiritual orientation to work in the scholarly disciplines. In so doing, it demands self-consciousness about the intrinsic connection between the religious mystery of our living even here and now before the face of God—and the scholarship we produce in our academic work—that is more intense than either of the other accounts. Such intensity has its dangers, as we shall see, but it also acknowledges in ways that the other accounts do not that many of our scholarly practices have been so transformed by the naturalism of the academy's secularizing ethos that the presence of spiritual antithesis has been hidden and can only be brought to the surface with great difficulty even within the community of Christian scholars.[186]

Of course, the account has weaknesses. Its constitutively critical moment can predispose scholars and scholarly communities to be unimaginatively and automatically antagonistic to scholarship that adopts a different language and makes claims it cannot immediately identify. Furthermore, some important versions of the account struggle against the mystification of their dependence upon claims and methods that come from outside of their religious origin and orientation. Finally, there are also versions of the

186. Good examples of what I am referring to here are provided by two small treatises of Vollenhoven. See his *De Noodzakelijkheid eener Christelijke Logica* and his *Hoofdlijnen der Logica*.

account that insist upon an *a priori* relationship between religious heart and the ideological starting points of scholarly engagement that in effect remove the religious heart from the scholarly process and its results and in so doing ensure (again *a priori*) the Christian character of the ideological starting points of scholarship. In doing this, however, these accounts succeed only in conflating religion and ideology, of turning religion into ideology. Nevertheless, these modulations of the holist account must be seen for what they are: authentic but flawed versions of the account, rather than the account itself. Indeed I wish to underscore as a strength of the account that it is in principle self-critical as well as critical of others, and it is this constitutive *self*-criticism that I value most.

Personally Appropriating an Account of Integrality as an Act of Creative Fidelity

Indeed, it is among scholars who work within a holist account of the integrality of Christian scholarship that I have chosen to make my scholarly home, though I freely acknowledge that the other accounts allow certain features of the integrality of faith and scholarship to come to the fore with great, and good, force. Complementarist accounts speak eloquently of the sturdiness of the Creation and the craft of the Creator. This is a profound religious good. Integrationist accounts speak eloquently of the graciousness of the Redeemer whose response to sin and the disruption of the creation is to dispense his common Grace hither and yon, letting it fall upon the faith-less and the faith-filled, refusing to see in sin a limit upon his love and care. This too is a great strength.

Moreover, I also acknowledge that holist accounts, because they radicalize the religious sensibility also present in integrationist accounts, share and indeed intensify some of the difficulties of integrationist accounts. In particular they do not always easily keep sight of the creation within their emphasis upon the struggle of sin and Grace. What I mean by that is that they struggle to give full value to the original craft of the Creator. Just one sin, one bad apple, and the whole of creation is threatened with rot and ruin, save for the swift outpouring of common Grace. Holist emphasis upon spiritual struggle, then, can lead to a substantialization of struggle between sin and Grace that comes to expression in a strong separatist tendency. Indeed, some versions of the account come close to dividing the human community into distinct species, its works into formally distinct labours such that all shared names and terms are merely equivocations.[187]

Nevertheless I have chosen, as said, to work within an academic community committed to a holist account of scholarly integrality. In so doing I too benefit from its strengths and struggle with its challenges. I do so for a very simple reason. I think that North American Christianity in all its works has become culturally flabby and slothful. It is so easy just to go along with what is happening. I am a North American Christian. Therefore, I *need* the discipline of an account of Christian integrality that primes one to struggle against the academic cultural flow, for such insistence militates against complacency. I am uneasy about the impulse to wield the account's highly developed tools for academic criticism as a cudgel to bash others over the head for a lack of religious attentiveness, though I do argue that there is a properly central place in Christian scholarship for mutual criticism. Nevertheless, I experience a positive vigilance resulting from understanding my own scholarly work as a religious battleground. My work, I confess it, is a site of profound religious antithesis, for it is the product of an unwillingly divided heart. Such self-critical vigilance is a healthy spiritual exercise in my own ceaseless struggle to think in line with the scriptures in their testimony to divine revelation.

So, I do not receive this holist account as superior absolutely, i.e., in any and every respect. Rather, I have appropriated it because I think that it does good work for me in the cultural context in which I find myself. It is relative to my needs that I make my choice, if choice it is. But this is already to work a change on the account as it has been generated and has functioned within the community of those who have received it as theirs. Indeed, the account was generated and developed within ongoing debate with representatives of the other basic accounts, and so was posited as superior to the other accounts without qualification.[188] But I have learned too much from scholars who embrace the other accounts to view my own account as superior, full stop.

There are two other important changes that I make to the account as I have received and appropriated it. First, I insist that the account's emphasis upon religious antithesis within scholarship be used as a means above all of self-critical reflection upon one's own scholarship rather than as a

187. See the discussion of Cornelius Van Til included in the next chapter.

188. See, for example, the account of rivalry included in Mouw, "Dutch Calvinist Philosophical Influences," 93–120.

way of distinguishing an "us" as opposed to a "them" via the scholarship that "we" and "they" produce. Second, I insist that there is a constant interaction between one's scholarly encounters and the shape of one's heart such that the spiritual risks inherent in scholarship or indeed any concrete socio-cultural endeavor remain visible, necessitating a culture of mutual correction within an ethos of mutual understanding, trust and forgiveness. I will return to these points in subsequent chapters. For now, it is enough to wonder whether the combination of fidelity and transformative creativity at work in my appropriation of a holist account of Christian scholarly integrality is a common, even an unavoidable feature of the process by which one appropriates accounts and traditions we receive and accept rather than create *de novo*?

I invite the reader to examine his or her appropriation of the account she or he is most at home in. Can she articulate for herself the pattern of her fidelity, the language she prefers as it points to one basic account or the other? Can he spot ways in which his language and arguments elaborate and develop one or another account in a creative direction? The suggestion encoded within these questions is simple. Could it be that we do well to think of our appropriation of basic accounts in all their creativity as well as fidelity? Can it be that appropriation of accounts of the integrality of Christian scholarship, like the Christian scholarship the accounts intend to illumine, are productively thought about via the metaphor of the folk recipe? Here too different concrete instances are properly different from each other while being recognizably the same; these differences too can be said to depend upon the "kitchen" and the predilections of the "cook."

In conclusion, then, each of the three accounts or faces of the integrality of religion, faith and scholarship that we have been examining have their strengths and weaknesses, which make better or worse sense in relation to each other. Each should lead, one would think, to a different account of the difference that marks out integral Christ-following across the scholarly disciplines, i.e., to what differentiates Christian scholarship from other kinds of scholarship to be found within the academy. But is this really the case? This question points us toward the next stage and new chapter of our analysis.

Chapter Four: The Lineaments of Christian Difference

No matter what account of Christian integrality one subscribes to, the intent is to craft scholarship to be a seamless piece of one's living with the scriptures and worship of the God revealed therein. This I take to be a given; Christian scholars are, as said above, all one at the level of intention. Differences result from the discourses developed to account for that intention. In particular, there are different accounts of the unity to which the term Christian scholarship refers and the consequent unifying dynamic Christian faith or religion introduces into scholarly life and production. These differences extend to how one properly views and deals with scholarship produced from, and as an expression of, a different set of founding hunches or principles. How, for example, was an early Christian like Justin Martyr or Augustine of Hippo to deal, *as Christian scholar*, with the wisdom of the Greeks and the Jews? How do contemporary Christian scholars deal with the scholarly products of positivists, post-structuralists, evolutionary biologists, pragmatists, empiricists, physicalists, and so on? What should one learn and how? What and how ought one to avoid learning?

Here is the rub and the source of a certain embarrassment: scholars who are intentionally *Christian* scholars disagree on what I have called "an account of Christian integrality across the scholarly disciplines." That may sound bland, but we do well to remind ourselves that it is through those accounts that we habitually construct and then negotiate the fraught relationship between a Christian "inside" and "outside."[1] It is in these negotiations

1. "Inside" and "outside," here, has to do not with the character of the Christian scholar or of her scholarly faith. Rather, it has to do with to what degree, the scholarship produced bears the mark of that scholar's Christ-following. Needless to say if such judgments are made outside of a context of mutual trust and love, the distinction between the latter judgment and judgments made about a person's Christian identity can become indistinct, to the sorrow and loss of all participants.

that one determines the extension and order of that scholarship one agrees to call Christian, and its rightful place in the academy at large.

Given the different accounts that have emerged to identify the integrality of Christian scholarship across the disciplines, one would think there would also emerge parallel accounts of the distinctive character of Christian scholarship in relation to other scholarly types. But that is not really the case. No matter which model of Christian integrality one adopts, scholars operating within the framework of all three of the models discussed in the previous chapter use remarkably similar terms and arguments in order to identify and circumscribe the difference that Christian identity makes to scholarship. I will illustrate my point in reference to one of the texts brought up in the preceding chapter. I am sure that in it and in subsequent analysis one will recognize terms and arguments that are very widely used among complementarists interested in questions of catholicity, as well as among integrationist and holist thinkers who ask what it is that makes scholarship Christian.

I have chosen to take up for a second time George Marsden's extended apology for Christian scholarship in his *The Outrageous Idea of Christian Scholarship* because his work brings the account of Christian difference I have in mind into clear focus. Indeed, he articulates an account of Christian difference that has heretofore monopolized Christian discussion around Christian scholarship.[2] In focusing on Marsden's way of writing, then, I examine him not in distinction from myself or from "our" way of speaking, but rather as speaking my and, in fact, our collective thoughts in such a way as to make their pattern particularly visible. Of course in using his way of writing our shared habits of thought and speech, we must be fair to him. Consequently, we do well to recall Marsden's project in the book whose language we will be examining. We remember that he wrote this book to argue that the mainstream secular academy should be open to explicitly faith-inflected learning and that faith-informed scholars should spend time and energy on the integration of faith and scholarship.

2. His articulation not only stands as metonym for the language and account developed by those attracted to the notion of Christian scholarship, but also for the language and account criticized by those who would jettison talk of Christian scholarship in favour of talk about scholarly faith or about the vocation of the faithful or Christian scholar. See in this regard, Jacobsen and Jacobsen, eds., *Scholarship and Christian Faith.*

Aristotle and the Christian "Difference"

If we boil Marsden's apologetic argument down to its essence, we render it as follows. Exclusion is unwarranted because explicitly faith-inflected scholarship is just like secular scholarship. In addition, exclusion impoverishes the academy as a whole, for it robs the academy of an irreproducible and generative scholarly voice capable of adding positively to the breadth and quality of the whole. In other words, explicitly faith-inflected scholarship is just like secular scholarship, but in its own unique or irreplaceable way. Faith-inflected scholarship is simultaneously the same as and different from other forms of scholarship.

I deliberately hone Marsden's position to a very fine point, because to do so brings to the fore an appearance of contradiction. How ought one to read this "contradiction?" One fairly jaundiced but impeccably holist way of interpreting it would be to deny *a priori* the possibility of common ground between Christian and any other kind of scholarship.[3] Since there is no common ground there can be no epistemologically justifiable basis for a claim of sameness. The fact that Marsden both denies and affirms a commonality or sameness must be seen as an antinomy, telltale sign of a divided scholarly heart.

Such an interpretation makes me uncomfortable. It seems to conflate common and neutral ground, and then to deny all common ground because there is no neutral ground. But I want to say that the creation is *precisely* common ground, though its investigation is in principle *never* religiously neutral.[4] If Marsden's sameness is a way of pointing to common ground while his difference is meant to deny neutral ground, then, I find myself thinking along similar lines. I need to ask how else we could understand the "contradiction" we have unearthed within Marsden's way of putting things?

3. Consider the following citation: "We conclude then that when both parties, the believer and the non-believer, are epistemologically self-conscious and as such engaged in the interpretative enterprise, they cannot be said to have any fact in common." Cornelius Van Til, *Common Grace*, 5. Of course it must be immediately added that Van Til goes on to affirm that in an objective and metaphysical sense "they have every fact in common."

4. The *never* in this sentence functions, as should be clear from the last section of the preceding chapter, as a spiritual exercise. It serves as an internal reminder to the writer and by extension the reader of the pervasiveness of the spiritual struggle of sin and Grace that extends beyond our limited vision, and therefore can be counted on to be present in places where we *see* no struggle at all. See for example the discussion of the role of spiritual exercise in chapter six below.

When I do ask this question, it seems to me that his way of putting things bespeaks the trace of a deeply ingrained rhetorical and conceptual figure. In the interests of making my point very clearly I will exaggerate the detail that can be read into the trace—though I will at least have the grace to let the reader in on my dirty secret and tell the reader when my exaggeration begins in earnest.

Marsden's way of putting things seems to presuppose that scholarship is a class or genus of being, a class or genus that is essentially different from all other classes or genera. Because scholarship is a general class or kind or genus of being, it is not sufficient in and of itself to account for what can be known or defined about a given instance of scholarship. Rather, it can itself be understood as constituted by a range of classes or kinds that are specific to the genus scholarship but are different from one another. Here I begin to make things far more precise than Marsden's language warrants, but I think that this exaggerated precision is in continuity with the trace I am highlighting—though not Marsden's position in all its historian's complexity and philosophical reticence.

Each of the species of scholarship can be indicated in a formal definition, a proposition constituted by a subject and its predicate, i.e., constituted by what is being defined and "the what" that defines. The predicate of such a definition has itself a precise form. It is constituted by two terms, one pointing to a general class of being to which the subject belongs, and another pointing to some formal difference that marks a specific group within that general class as irreducible to any other group. Genus and difference constitute the species to which the subject in question belongs; they together define *what* the subject is, at least when viewed from a certain distance.[5]

Such a conceptual figure arises from a recognizable quarter within the history of philosophy.[6] It owes its being to Aristotle and the Aristotelian tradition; it is an Aristotelian way of analyzing scholarship and its constitutive parts. What I am claiming then is that, when Marsden talks about Christian scholarship in its relationship to secular scholarship, he employs an Aristotelian mode of analysis and set of assumptions. And I think that

5. What is generic and what is specific will of course depend on the question asked and the angle of approach. They take on stable referents, however, when the species is assumed to be the smallest such group to which an individual instance of something can belong.

6. For a fine and refined introduction to the Aristotelian notions of genus, formal difference, species, and essence discussed here, see Aquinas, *Opusculum de ente et essentia*. An easily accessible English translation is Aquinas, *On Being and Essence*.

Marsden is representative on this score of all of us who find the notion of Christian scholarship to be meaningful, including those who prefer a holist account of Christian integrality to Marsden's own integrationist account or who find themselves more in John Paul II's complementarist account. Since I propose to criticize certain implications of this habitually Aristotelian way of putting things, Marsden might respond that I am like a pot calling the kettle black. And, he would be right. After all, earlier I spoke approvingly of identifying the essence of Marsden's position. Now an essence as I was using the term is more or less like what Aristotle meant when he used the term to denote the unifying conceptual intention that centers our understanding of the intelligible "what" we seek to know. Aristotelian habits of expression and conception have sunk deeply into the ordinary figures of schooled English. They operate so pervasively and at such an unconscious level that they are probably impossible to exorcise completely.

To say this is not, however, to counsel despair, even in the face of the important limitations we will shortly observe to inhere within Aristotelian ways of speaking about "the Christian difference" in scholarship. Even philosophical revolutionaries like Kant or Aristotle himself have only innovated within a strictly limited conceptual range.[7] They have remained for the most part dependent upon what they received from the scholarly and cultural traditions they have participated in or were formed to. The point is that, as Christian innovators in scholarship, we should not become obsessed with and paralysed by our dependencies. We should become sensitive to them and their half-perceived role in our thought. We should help each other identify them and the possible limitations they impose. But we should do so without the constant threat of scandal occasioned by insistence upon some impossible purity.

I would guess there is an "inner Aristotelian" tucked away in all of us. It is a ghost to be monitored, to be sure, but also to be examined with great care, for not all Aristotelian traces have been disastrous for the Christian community, though I hasten to add, only by the Grace of God.[8] In fact, though I want to point out an important limitation inherent within thinking of Christian scholarship in Aristotelian terms, such thinking has

7. The delimited range of Kantian revolution is well brought out in Vollenhoven, "Conservatisme en progressiviteit," 35–48. An English translation of the article has now been published. Vollenhoven, *The Problem-Historical Method*, 11–19.

8. Aristotle is not unique in inspiring pious haste; all theoretical traces that I know of including Christian ones are ambiguous enough in their effects to produce a parallel response.

also borne wheat as well as chaff. For many Christian scholars, it has been important to imagine that Christian scholarship is a form of scholarship like all other scholarship yet distinctive in some stable and scholastically identifiable way. It has been via this imaginative act that they have been enabled to think about and find ways to resist the practical "double truth" most if not all of us struggle against in a post-Christian academy. As we saw in the preceding chapter, most if not all of us Christian scholars have been formed as Christians within our spiritual community of faith and as "secularists" of one type or another as to our naturalized and methodologically atheist scholarly disciplines.

So, let us look at Marsden's way of putting things once more. To this point, I have claimed that his apologetic appears to presuppose that there is a genus of human cultural activity, scholarship, which is intelligible, more or less, on its own terms, and which is in and of itself indifferent to faith-identification. Christians and atheists—all can and do engage in scholarship, and just to the degree that they are engaged in scholarship, they are engaged in doing the same thing. Nevertheless, scholarship has many subdivisions. Most obviously there are the disciplinary divisions represented by college or university departments or faculties. Moreover, even within and across such disciplinary divisions there is another axis of division, a perspectival axis formed by a determinate set of ideological starting points that bespeak an ethos or orientation that grants to ideological starting points a specific color or character or spirit. One thinks in this context for example of Marxist, post-structuralist or feminist scholarship, to be sure, but also of a deeper sense of the world that lies behind and is expressed in their starting points.

It is along this second axis of subdivision within the genus scholarship that Marsden sees the distinction between explicitly faith-inflected scholarship and secular scholarship. And, of course, within the scholarship that is explicitly faith-inflected, Marsden sees Christian scholarship. To the degree that Christian scholarship is scholarship it is just like secular scholarship. But there is some difference that marks out Christian scholarship as Christian, some scholastically generative body of claims or characteristic methods Christian scholars formulate such that Christian scholarship adds something positive and recognizable to scholarship as a whole.

Of course, given the Aristotelian genealogy of this way of speaking, such claims would be most secure if the generative body of statements or methods employed by Christians were employed by Christians alone, though Marsden does not himself require such exclusivity. Indeed, he has thought productively about those dimensions of Christian scholarly identity that are intrisically and yet not exclusively Christian.[9] The question is, however, (for Marsden quite as much as it would be for a self-conscious and thorough-going Aristotelian) what the Christian difference might be.

The Embarrassments Entailed by Christian "Difference"

Marsden addressed the last third of *The Outrageous Idea of Christian Scholarship* to Christian scholars who are confused and embarrassed about the claim that there exists such a formal difference. He tried to identify for embarrassed Christian souls both what it is that makes Christian scholarship Christian and where they might look to encounter examples of Christian scholarship as he identified it. I turn for a moment to the embarrassment that Marsden sought to allay, for it says something important about our habitual attempts to understand the project of Christian scholarship in Aristotelian terms.

One form of embarrassment arises among Christian scholars who are uncomfortable with the notion of Christian scholarship, root and branch, scholars who champion focusing instead upon the vocation of the Christian scholar or the lineaments of scholarly faith. For such scholars, religion is one realm of culture, scholarship another. Each operates autonomously within its respective sphere, and the attempt to speak of a discrete species of Christian scholarship is a contradiction in terms. To be sure, those understandings of the world produced within the scholarly dimension of life should not contradict those proclaimed by Christian religion, and when they do we must assume that an error of some kind must be skewing the scholarly results. Nevertheless, it is dangerous nonsense to say that there can be a species of Christian scholarship.[10] This is not the embarrassment I am considering here.

I find that a much more instructive embarrassment arises in the breasts of those Christian scholars who accept in principle the meaningfulness and

9. See Marsden, "What Difference Might Christian Perspectives Make?" 11–22.

10. Those Catholic thinkers whom Etienne Gilson addressed himself to under the rubric of "Suarezians" in *Being and Some Philosophers* and under the rubric of "neo-scholastics" in *The Spirit of Mediaeval Philosophy* are good examples of those who exhibit this type of embarrassment. There are many Protestant thinkers who think along the same lines.

desirability of Christian scholarship, and understand that meaningfulness in an Aristotelian way. It arises in at least two different contexts.

In the first place, embarrassment arises because of the uncomfortable questions such a search opens up. Let me give you one rather famous example. Cornelius Van Til, long-time professor of Apologetics at Westminster Theological Seminary in Philadelphia[11] is said to have dealt with the issue of whether the Christian and the non-Christian mean the very same thing when they claim that 2 + 2 = 4. Staunch presuppositionalist that he was (and holist as to the integrality of Christian scholarship), he answered no, emphatically. Because the Christian principle is absolutely different from that of any non-Christian principle, no derived propositions such as 2 + 2 = 4 can possibly mean the same thing, for the two propositions 2 + 2 = 4 and 2 + 2 = 4, for all their terminological identity, derive from absolutely different starting points. They are in principle equivocal.

Now this is a very clever answer. But such a clever response is not in my judgment really satisfying, even when one believes that it is constructed from principles that are true. Even those of us, usually integrationist and holist thinkers, who insist on the distinction between Christian and non-Christian starting points are left feeling uneasy. We do not escape a sense that the Van Til of story is here engaged in a theoretical sleight of hand. It is a little like the description I once heard a former colleague give of trying to argue with Alvin Plantinga about one of his conclusions. Everything in Plantinga's argument was qua argument just perfect, my colleague conceded, and yet he remained unconvinced and indeed dimly suspicious that he had been taken in by a ruse or clever trick he had somehow failed to fathom. He acknowledged that Plantinga was smarter than he was and had talked circles around him—but was still wrong, of that he was sure.

I think my problem with this particular, stereotypical question and the answer ascribed to Cornelius Van Til radiates from a certain hyperbolic accentuation of the real difference in principle that I too would say can and does exist at the inception of scholarly understanding. This hyperbole calls attention to the non-neutrality of scholarship. If it is used as a universal first principle rather than like a wisdom saying, however, it does so in a way that effaces the creation-as-common-ground.

I can put things another way. Most of the distinctive claims of a tradition and account are, in my view, well seen as spiritual exercises. They

11. A large bibliography of his works and works about him and his thought is to be found online at http://www.vantil.info/

are exhortations, reminding the writer or speaker first and foremost of the spiritual conditions he acknowledges as a matter of religious or ultimate principle. They translate, one might say, something like the confession of the heart. In doing so, they operate powerfully in the scholarship of the writer or speaker and in the lives of those who receive the founding confession as true.

As exhortations, they function as calls to action. In particular they call one to view the world from *this* angle and to head in *that* direction. Their rhetorical form, thus, is not incidental to their meaning and proper use. They are not universal principles in the way in which an Aristotelian understands universal principles to be and function.[12] Rather, they function with respect to our understanding more in the mode of wisdom sayings. They open up understanding only when applied wisely or appropriately, that is, to address a conundrum to which they are fitting. Otherwise, they lead to foolishness.

Van Til's emphasis upon the absolute difference in starting point makes a fine example. I would want to say that there is nothing wrong with the emphasis as such; it can be a powerful tool in alerting scholars to the presence within one or another longstanding scholarly consensus of assumptions that are antithetical to founding Christian convictions about the world. Nevertheless, its application to determine the present problem makes me very nervous. While I am not averse to the assumption that here too one properly affirms the presence of the struggle of sin and Grace, I miss effective acknowledgement of the shared or common creation. As a result, no matter that I, a fellow holist, recognize much that I receive as true in the Van Til of story's clever response; I dislike the problematic that tempts me, following "him," to go there. The principle used in this way is ill-fitted to the conundrum. In other words, the process of searching for and testing the Christian difference in scholarship has led Christians into certain stock and sterile problematics.

It is not that the answers we give are illegitimate or indefensible, on some level; it is that some of the problems we feel forced to grapple with seem inappropriate. That is, when the difference that marks Christian scholarship as Christian is identified with its first principles, then, that difference constitutes a division that goes all the way down. The division

12. See Aristotle's discussion of the several meanings of principle, especially principles of thought and knowledge, and of elements, especially elements of demonstration and argument in *Metaphysics* 1013a24–1014b15.

creates equivocation whenever Christian and non-Christian scholarship use identically expressed terms, propositions and arguments. But then the term "scholarship" itself becomes an equivocation. The Aristotelian difference so identified destroys the very theoretical framework that gave it rise, for the shared genus turns out to be two formally distinct genera; the difference turns out to be an absolute difference in kind. So how is a proper recognition that Christian and, say, naturalistic starting points differ to be understood within an Aristotelian problematic without the embarrassment of self-referential incoherence?

There is also a second instructive embarrassment that I would like to consider. Some are embarrassed when they search for that body of claims or methods that is characteristic of Christian scholarship and only Christian scholarship. They feel that they have searched and searched and are still not convinced that they have found what they are looking for. They ask themselves what unique contribution Christians have made to the scholarly conversations they engage, and they mean (in good Aristotelian fashion) some contribution that can best be ascribed to the Christianity of these Christian contributors. While they find many scholarly claims that Christians have formulated, and methods that Christians have developed, they find themselves unable to convince themselves that these Christians' contributions have occurred directly because the contributors are Christians.

I cite an instructive example of the difficulty in a deeply honest attempt to work in this mode by the fine Sinologist Daniel Bays. In a paper given at Calvin College's Fall 2001 conference "Christian Scholarship: For What?" he asked himself the following question: *Is there anything we know or could know or any approach to knowledge about the history of the Christian church in nineteenth- and twentieth-century China that is demonstrably ascribable to a scholar's evangelical Christian faith?* Such a question asks for some Christian difference and its palpable effect. But he found such a question almost impossible to answer positively in a robust sense. We might, he thought, speak of an inclination impelling an evangelical Christian to "get there first." We might speak of certain methodological assumptions that, while not unique to Christians, yet prove attractive to Christians because of their faith commitments. We might speak of a Christian's ability to spot error in another historical understanding on the basis of an *a priori* faith commitment. The correspondence between Daniel Bays results and "the Christian difference" identified by Marsden in *The Outrageous Idea of Christian Scholarship* is remarkable. Marsden too spoke of faith-founded criticism of scholarship that proceeds on the basis of certain assumptions (reductionism or the humanistic, transcendent self), and of a faith-based impulse "to get there first" (a nose for the role of religion in people's lives).[13] Still, if this is "the Christian difference," it is a pretty limp affair.

The trouble as I see it is that theoretical results, when (and precisely because) they are articulated or disseminated, are open to all—at least in principle. Thus, there is no claim that a Christian scholar makes that cannot, once articulated, be made by a non-Christian; no method that cannot be assumed in principle by a non-Christian, and vice versa, of course. The best example of this from my own holist tradition comes from the world of information systems analysis. Andrew Basden is a professor and researcher attached to the Information Systems Institute of the University of Salford in the United Kingdom. He has found Dooyeweerdian ontology, i.e., the modal scale of creaturely aspects associated with the thought of Dooyeweerd and Runner presented above, extraordinarily helpful as a tool of analysis in his work, for it primes the analyst of concrete information systems to look to many discrete yet interlocking factors at play in any functioning system. His work has been picked up by scholars at the Lulea Technical University in Sweden. There are Christians among them but also others who are not. The non-Christians among his appropriators, have been attracted to his work, presumably, because they recognized something in it that they judged to be superior to the theoretical models they had been working with. So, now the world is treated to the spectre of secular Swedish scholars earnestly studying applied Dooyeweerdian ontology in pursuit of their scholarly ends.

The point is not that Andrew Basden and his non-Christian collaborators are engaged in scholarship that is religiously indifferent. It is rather to say that what makes Basden's Dooyeweerdian scholarship Christian is not to be lodged in unique claims and methods. Nor is what makes Basden's non-Christian collaborators' "Dooyeweerdian" scholarship secular to be found in their claims and methods. If Dooyeweerdian ontology could at one time be held up as marking out a "Christian difference" in the field Basden shares with his scholarly interlocutors, that difference disappeared once non-Christian interlocutors appropriated his work.

It is not just that a "Christian difference" is often hard to find (as in the examples of Bays and Marsden); it is that once one has found such a difference, it can in principle cease to be a "Christian difference" at any

13. See Marsden, *Outrageous Idea*, 70–100.

moment, precisely when it says something about the world that is received as helpful and so is appropriated by non-Christian scholars. But an Aristotelian inquiry into "the Christian difference" seeks to ground the claim to Christian scholarship in some stable set of claims and/or methods that are intrinsically if not uniquely Christian. A temporary Christian difference will hardly do. So if it is neither unique scholarly methods nor claims that constitute "the Christian difference" in our habitually Aristotelian way of thinking, *what* is it? Embarrassment deepens.

To recapitulate, the construal of Christian scholarship in an Aristotelian way demands the identification of some formal scholarly difference. But such a difference existing within the reach of the scholar *as scholar* seems hard to find. Indeed, as I see it, the search veers off in one of two directions. The sense of difference can be and is sometimes sought at the level of principles and starting points. When difference is located at the level of principles and starting points, however, it tends to call into question the assumption that Christians and non-Christians are engaged in the very same enterprise when they are engaged in what each calls "scholarship." On the other hand, if difference is sought at the level of claims generated and methods used to generate claims, a different tendency emerges. The search for such a difference proves endless. Despite generations of committed searchers it seems that such a difference has yet to be found, or at least posited with any confidence, or if confidently, with any wide success. The result of this seemingly endless deferral is that the Christian investigator becomes embarrassed and shy of suggesting such a difference at all. I am minded to say at this point that in the light of the embarrassments we have been examining, we might do well to leave our incipient Aristotelianism behind and look to some other way of identifying the difference of Christian scholarship.[14]

Before we do, however, we need to consider one last question: What has proven so attractive in the Aristotelian way of understanding Christian scholarship? Why have we persevered so stubbornly in our search for the elusive Christian scholarly difference? This is what I think. A formal Christian difference accessible within scholarly investigation and analysis promises the Christian academy a luminous and stable center; it offers Christian

14. I should say that to look for another way of understanding the difference of Christian scholarship is not to abandon what has been learned in and through the search for an Aristotelian difference. Rather it is to re-frame what we have learned so that the limitations of the prior and Aristotelian frame do not continue to burden Christian understanding as it does at present.

scholars the possibility of risk-free endeavor: *as long as you work from these claims and use these methods, your work will be God-fearing.* Deviate from these claims and these methods, however, and your work risks becoming God-despising. The matter so understood becomes clear and simple. Christian scholarship escapes thereby the universal difficulty of life.

Such a promise has undeniable allure; it is a powerful temptation. However, is there really such a thing as risk-free scholarship, or risk-free *anything* where cultural formation is at issue? If all the Creation is redolent of original blessing blighted by sin, then one could say (rather too grandly) that there is risk in just getting up in the morning. Blight is within and around us. The good we would do, we do not. We have all had the wrenching experience of observing language and concepts we love used by others to ends and conclusions that horrify us.[15] And this is hardly surprising; as the Gospels tell us, even the devil can quote scripture.

Cultural formation involves the realization here and now of determinate cultural potentials. This, in turn, necessitates the exercise of power by which such determinations are realized. And the persons and communities that have and employ power to these determinate effects are persons and communities whose hearts are riven, so that all such exercises of power have ambiguous effects. By implication, all scholarly traditions bear the traces of blight. Thank God that the operation of redemption is equally wide in scope. Thus, while all of our redemptive traditions carry the scars of blight, these scars do not preclude their being an edifying blessing to the community of faith and the world at large. It is to say, however, that when we and our scholarly traditions prove a blessing and do edify, it is in some mysterious way God's work.

So Christian scholars should acknowledge the presence of an "inner Aristotelian" and the way this presence limits thought about the difference Christian scholarship makes. And in view of these limits, Christian scholars should develop another, different way of speaking about how their scholarly lives and scholarship are Christian. The reason for doing so is this:

15. Those of us who come to the project of Christian scholarship out of the Reformed world, and in particular that part of the Reformed world that looks to Abraham Kuyper as founding voice, can cite the use of Kuyperian categories, language, and emphases to construct the social policy in South Africa that long went under the name of *apartheid*. There was no getting around the fact that a way of understanding the world that Kuyperians hold dear was being used in this instance to come to conclusions that were monstrous.

an approach becomes counterproductive if its terms make it impossible to say what needs to be said.

Christian Scholarship as Attunement to the Shape of the Christian Heart

What I am arguing for is an understanding of Christian scholarship that is self-consciously attuned to the shape of the Christian heart, individually and communally. I admit that this shape is a scholarly mystery. It can be named but it cannot be contained without remainder within a theoretical conception or field (even if the field is theology). And yet I will work in much of what follows to show that such a shape *can* be known and attended to. Lines of connection can be drawn from this shape to the pattern of our scholarly activity and results. Our scholarly activity and its results trace the scholarly implications we have managed to acknowledge of the mystery of our Christian hearts in their existence before the face of God.

In principle, Christian scholarship should be self-conscious enough to be able to account for these lines of connection. Surely this is what Herman Dooyeweerd was trying to say and exemplify in and through the now alien apparatus of a Kantian-style transcendental critique. It is what Alvin Plantinga was getting at with the formula, *if F then FS*. It was what Gilson was getting at with his profound meditation on the significance for philosophy of Exodus 3:14. In all of this I have been using my own language but invite the reader to use her equivalents, and my suggestion is simple: the shape of one's heart, *that* is the key, as well as the spirit it is gripped by. Such a shape will be contoured by what one can take in of divine self-revelation, of what one has been gifted and called to see. This gift and call is mediated by the scriptures, as they live, by God's grace, within the faith communities we inhabit and have been formed by. Of course, we inherit thereby and are forced to struggle with the blindness of our faith communities as well as profit from their acuity. In addition, my gift will differ from yours in terms of the configuration of self that I am and am ceaselessly becoming, that you are and are ceaselessly becoming.[16] Empowered to see, hear, and obey in ways that take meaning within our several communities and that are figured to our personal gift and call, our hearts, even in their obedience, will not have the exact same shape. One will be gifted with an eye for the

16. For a way of looking at and speaking about what it means to be human that I have used with gratitude, see Olthuis, *The Beautiful Risk*.

play of sameness and difference in our world, another for the intertwinement of universality and individuality, still others for the concatenation of structure and process. Some will see all of these things well and some none at all (although these latter will have trouble if they are determined to be scholars).[17] It is together in mutual support and loving correction that we forge incrementally a scholarship greater than the sum of its parts: that we forge, by the grace of God, a scholarship able to trace the lines from theoretical results and methods back to the mystery of the heart and its spiritual eye.

I am not being naïve here. In such a construction of Christian scholarship we will still argue, even about (theoretical) "first things." How can it be otherwise, for Christian scholars are formed by different communities with different emphases, different eyes for how to understand and order the world in terms of what they receive from the scriptures and their inspiring Spirit. The point is that we and our communities are finite, whereas the Spirit who speaks in the scriptures and our hearts is not. We take in what we can. The same is true of the faith communities and traditions that have formed us. And because that will always be a part of what there is to see, we will ever need each other to argue with, to correct, and to be corrected by.

Such argument and mutual correction can be a terrible thing, a striking out at one another in fear—and when it functions that way, it can have terrible consequences for the community, as well as shutting down important conversations. When it occurs in trust, however, it can be a joy, a perk of our academic calling. Such arguments are altogether worth having; such correction is an occasion for gratitude. When the lines are clear between heart and scholarly result, "faith speaks to faith" as Augustine said long ago. Then it no longer matters whether one's claims and methods are unique to the Christian since it is not in such difference that we see the difference that our Christian identity makes.

So the claim that will need to be imagined in greater detail and confirmed by argument and example in subsequent chapters is that there are lines to be seen that draw the eye back from the surface of scholarly result, of claim and method, back toward the deep recess of the human heart in and through which we face the Mystery of our lives.

17. For the issues raised here (sameness-difference, universality-individuality, structure-process) and the way of reading the "world of the text" in terms of the way in which these issues are handled see Seerveld, "Biblical Wisdom Underneath Vollenhoven's Categories," 127–143, and for the example of William of Ockham see my *Of Runners and Batons*, 11–12.

I admit that at present my claim is only a suggestion, one articulated in imprecise language. Nevertheless, this re-imagined root-metaphor already evinces certain strengths that are worth mentioning. It allows three things to happen that, in my view, take the conversation around Christian scholarship forward.

In the first place, though I frankly admit my acceptance and use of a holist account of the integrality of Christian scholarship, I do not think that the re-imagined account of Christian difference for which I am now arguing needs to be viewed as incompatible with any of the three accounts I have highlighted here. Rather, it could provide a framework for renewed conversation and understanding among all scholars who self-consciously seek to produce Christian scholarship.

In the second place, this re-imagined root-metaphor allows scholars to think articulately about their scholarship as Christian even if they work in a discipline where it would be nearly impossible to articulate any kind of Christian difference, if that difference is understood in an Aristotelian way. Christian mathematicians may find themselves silent in a conversation about Christian difference understood in an Aristotelian way. By contrast, they will be able to think and speak authentically and movingly about how their activity as a mathematician flows from their central intuitions about what it means for them to live before the face of God.

Finally, this way of re-imagining the integrality of Christian scholarship will facilitate participation in the conversation by Christian scholars who practice their discipline and profession in public (and thereby religiously and ideologically plural) institutions. Too often, the struggle to identify Christian difference in an Aristotelian mode has been restricted to disciplines such as philosophy, theology, or history where the range of methods allowable and the kind of claims deemed credible is sufficiently fluid. Equally too often, it has also taken place by and large among scholars working at explicitly faith-based institutions. This very piece of writing is a case in point. Nevertheless, I want to claim that my proposal invites the largest group of Christian scholars, those working at pluralist institutions as well, into the conversation in a way that can mean something to them. As such, it can foster a wider and more inclusive discussion than has been the case heretofore.

I am, of course, inviting a conversation. One does not do so if one already knows what claims and methods constitute the truth in its theoretical fullness *in saecula saeculorum*. But to invite conversation is not the same as saying that one joins the conversation as an empty slate. That too would be an Aristotelian moment and in this instance, a serious error. I myself have made a host of decisions about how I testify theoretically and via understanding of the world to the God whom I meet within the Christian community in its wrestling with the scriptures. A number of these have been on display already. These decisions are in my view matters of founding scholarly conviction. What I have been warning against, then, is a mis-identification of a Christian scholarly trace as the thing itself, Christian scholarship once and for all. I am claiming that because the difference constitutive of the Christian character of Christian scholarship is a matter of animating spirit,[18] and is thus an ever on-going achievement, it demands incarnation. Bodies being what they are, such incarnation must recur over and again in persons and communities, generation in and generation out. Though the breath of the self-same Spirit can be counted on to leave traces everywhere that one can identify, know, and think in accordance with, the breath itself remains unmarked.

Identification of the animating spirit of scholarship is much facilitated if the line from heart to theoretical result is self-consciously traced. The work of tracing, though, cannot itself be a purely scholarly act. Rather, it demands of the scholar a deeper capacity or discernment, and the opportunity to exercise the capacity of discernment in the company of other Christian scholars. Such discernment must be seen to be a communal virtue, a *mutual* discernment. We must consider what such discernment might look like as it operates within a scholarly community. To do so, however, we will also have to identify within many communities most open to the notion of Christian scholarship a widely prevalent attitude or posture that is not conducive to the mutual discernment I am calling for. Finally, we will conclude by exploring how Christian scholarship, thought about in the less Aristotelian way I have been pointing to, can be fruitfully inserted into the larger academy and its scholarly debates.

18. There is an ambiguity here that I must admit and so submit myself to possible correction. I want to say that it is finally the Holy Spirit that grounds the Christian identity of any bit of scholarship, but the Holy Spirit does so in a mediated way. Hence, there must be incarnation. But the mediation precedes incarnation within what I am calling the Christian trace of scholarly claims and methods. It already begins in the spiritual formation of the human scholar as person. In other words, the Spirit is mediated to scholarship by the spirit of the scholar not as scholar but as person. So one inevitably must speak of both the Spirit and the spirit of one's scholarship. The ambiguity is part of the very structure of the picture I am recommending for consideration.

Chapter Five: Crossing the Line

The suggestion is that Christian scholars interested in thinking about the Christian character of their scholarship think of its distinctiveness in terms of its animating spirit or ethos rather than scholastically determinate claims and methods. It means that the discernment of those lines of affiliation connecting our scholarly work to the shape of our hearts and the Spirit they are gripped by is a matter of perennial importance. It also demands that Christian scholars and the communities to which they belong assume an open and flexible posture or attitude. Christian scholarship, I am suggesting, is an ever on-going project of the community of Christian scholars. It is always in the making and never made, once and for all.

This necessitates that the community of Christian scholars learns to work in trust. It must trust first and foremost the creation and its Maker. Most importantly, that means trusting that the Creator is one who speaks to us of Self and the world Creator-made. Secondly, it means trusting that the creation is itself a site of meaning open to disclosure. In the third place, it means that the scholarly community must be one in which its members trust each other. It must maintain the discipline of patient allowance, even or rather especially, in the face of different vocabularies, spiritual formations or scholarly emphases that make it hard to recognize *prima facie* what is being said.

The kind of support I am talking about is not a matter of cheerleading, a vapid solidarity. Rather, I am imagining this support as centered upon mutual correction as we together struggle to keep transparent the lines between our daily work and our deepest scripture-inspired hunches about the world and its Creator-Redeemer-Sustainer. That is why Christian scholarship is never done, once and for all, but must be reconstructed ever anew in, as said above, a delicate balance of creativity and fidelity. Such a flowing or genetic enterprise is constitutively risky. It demands of its participants a profound sense of adventure. It can only really develop healthily among scholars who view their calling as something like a communal quest that they embrace with open arms, out of a willingness to fail, if need be, because they know in their bones that the effort is worth the risk.[1]

But here is the rub. Such an adventurous spirit is difficult to muster in many corners of the Christian world. This difficulty is one that pays careful consideration. I take as my example the corner of the Christian world that I know best: North American Protestant orthodoxy.[2] Catholic readers in particular operate under different conditions and so will have to work by analogy to sift what follows for what is helpful and what is not, though there is a Catholic equivalent to the ethos characteristic of what I am calling North American Protestant orthodoxy. Be that as it may, Catholic readers in particular may want to skip this chapter altogether or read it with a kind of anthropologist's fascination.

By Protestant orthodoxy, I do not mean Protestantism as a changeless doctrinal core that has remained the same since its emergence in the sixteenth century. I am sceptical that such a description is ever really useful except in certain infra-Protestant polemical contexts. I mean, by contrast, a stream of nineteenth- and twentieth-century Protestantism characterized by an attempt to resist implications of the nineteenth-century identification of historicity as an inexorable process productive of cultural difference.[3]

Protestant orthodoxy, as I understand it, reacted to modernist theological claims that historicity must be presumed to be present even in the very heart of our Christian foundations. This modernist claim of historicity was understood to posit an ineradicable difference separating us from our historical confessions, theological authorities, and—most damning of

1. I think it important to call attention to the fact that in moving away from an Aristotelian model of Christian scholarship toward a model of attunement one moves to look at the quality of scholarship produced in terms of the spirit of the scholar and the quality of her faith. This is a good example of a point made in passing in the very beginning of this volume, namely, that regardless of which term one centers attention upon in discussions of faith and the scholarly enterprise (i.e., scholarship, scholar or scholarly faith), one must eventually deal with the other terms as well if one's account is to have appropriate traction.

2. For the historiographical framework that follows see Sweetman ed., *In the Phrygian Mode*, 9–32.

3. Time can also produce cultural connections and continuities, of course. Tradition is one category developed to express time's production of a progressive continuity. The discovery of historicity however, perhaps because it inherited from the Enlightenment a deep suspicion of tradition, focused upon historicity's capacity to produce discontinuity and difference.

all—from the world of the scriptures to which we look to see God and the meaning of our lives revealed. Protestant orthodoxy has acknowledged, of course, the existence of historicity as a general phenomenon but has denied its ontological ubiquity. In particular, it has denied in several interesting and incompatible ways the historicity of the scriptures and of the central confessions of the Christian church.[4] Most often, it has tried to freeze Christian understanding by sanctifying a variously delimitable body of faith-formulations. In so doing, verbal formulae are taken together to forge a linguistic horizon in which Christian understanding is properly to be viewed. In addition, however, many adherents of Protestant orthodoxy have understood such formulations to have invariant conceptual content because propositions are posited to bear a changeless meaning no matter when and in what circumstances we articulate them. When the Council of Nicea (325) claimed, for example, that the God revealed in the scriptures is best understood as three *hypostases* or persons simultaneously and identically expressive of one divine *ousia* or substance, the intent of the Council is so captured in its verbal formulae that it remains available to anyone who comes to them in faith from whatever cultural and intellectual formation, without significant addition, loss or alteration of meaning.[5]

Such a position ignores authoritative acknowledgement of the pressure brought to bear on meaning in any act of cultural and lingual translation even within those authorities universally acknowledged to be shapers of orthodoxy itself. One thinks of Augustine's loving attention to just this sort of pressure in his exploration of Nicene meaning in the context of his own nearly contemporaneous Latin culture.[6] Can there in fact be a rigid

4. See in this regard my "Epilogue: The Future of Reformational Tears" *In the Phrygian Mode*, 287–309.

5. Such a notion, functioning as a founding assumption or orienting discipline, suffuses Benjamin Breckinridge Warfield's work in historical theology. See, for example, his *Studies in Tertullian and Augustine* (New York: Oxford University Press, 1930). Most Christian traditions will allow for the possibility of marginal differences in received meaning of authoritative faith formulae as confessed over time, but will insist on a core meaning that remains the same. Such a position would not however be fully satisfying to a thoroughgoing propositionalist. Since the proposition is properly the intelligible thing that the verbal formula refers to, there can be no additions, subtractions, or alterations of any kind because then the proposition in question is a new proposition and the faith a distinct faith.

6. The struggle to say what the Greeks say with the two terms *hypostasis* and *ousia* makes up one of the powerful theological motifs of Augustine's *De trinitate*. See, in particular, 5.2.3–5.10.11.

sameness of meaning across cultures and eras of the kind envisioned within a propositionalist understanding of orthodoxy? Granted the intention of such an understanding, namely, that meaningful Christian confessional continuity through time and across cultures is a central good, might this continuity not be better spoken of and argued for using a different language and set of assumptions?

We lay this question aside to note that Protestant orthodoxy has worked to limit the difference-producing effects of historicity with respect to scriptural meaning and the central confessions of the Christian church in order to defend what it presumed to have inherited from the past against the corrosive force of historicist modernism. The manner of this defence has been to remove authoritative texts and confessions from historicity understood in the modernist way. Biblical utterance and the authoritative confessional formulae of the churches somehow encompass or capture what they point to or reveal. The central mysteries of the Christian religion may be mysterious and so exceed our capacity to speak of them but somehow we know that they are, in and of themselves, like concepts and their propositional articulation. They function like reified units of intelligibility to which nothing essential could be added or taken away without changing their identity altogether. This is no less true when it is also recognized that they are inadequate to the reality they really grab hold of.

Defence of a concept-like immutability deemed to be characteristic of the central mysteries of the faith, however, induces a protective posture with respect to the constitutively processive, differentiating and provisional character of scholarly understanding. Such a posture does not live easily with a notion of Christian scholarship that acknowledges the ubiquity of risk, adventure, and failure. Rather the point seems ever to eradicate risk as much as possible, and to suspect anything or anyone that seems to gainsay the effort. This is an impulse already alluded to at the end of the preceding chapter. It is an impulse to be explored in what follows.

I am particularly struck by the importance of two qualities of orthodox Protestant culture. In the first place, Protestant orthodoxy takes very seriously the biblical theme and norm of holiness. It does so, however, in a way that conflates holiness with purity, which is itself linked to homogeneity. This latter association is crucial, because it directs reflection inexorably toward the question of origin. If holiness is a matter of purity understood via the metaphoric of the bloodline (homogeneity), then the origin becomes paradigmatic for all that descends from it. As a consequence, one judges holiness by looking ever back in time toward the origin. Such a reflex, in turn, predisposes one to the twin responses of nostalgia and the impulse to repristinate. In the second place, Protestant orthodoxy values above all the intellectual dimensions of faith. This has most often come to an expression in intellectualistic ways, as if those dimensions were in fact the very core of faith. The presence of intellectualistic faith[7] is clear whenever emphasis is laid upon the conceptual identity and hence upon the essential immutability of faith as understood.

These impulses emerge from Protestant orthodoxy's legitimate resistance to modern historicism's reduction of historicity to the production of cultural difference and distance. They constitute a shadow formed by the way in which Protestant orthodoxy chose to resist. Moreover, the combination, within the academic culture of Protestant orthodoxy, of these two qualities—the impulse to repristinate and to insist that the intellectual dimensions of faith stand for and norm the reality of faith as such—goes a long way toward accounting for its habitually combative suspiciousness in matters of faith, scripture, and scholarship.

Repristination and Reformation

Let us begin with repristination. There is a deep impulse to repristinate in all the historical movements of Christian renewal that I know. The sixteenth-century Protestant Reformation certainly had such an impulse. One thinks most spectacularly of the radical Reformers whom we group together under the label Anabaptists.[8] Whether one speaks of the radicals whom Zwingli opposed in Zurich, the millenarians who followed Jan van Leiden to disaster at Münster, or Meno Simons and his gentle disciples in the eastern Netherlands, they all shared a sense that the early church of the New Testament constituted a transparent and pure example of Church, an example to which they had immediate and full access despite the intervening centuries. Theirs was an access testified to by the pattern of their plain living and the simple worship of their believers' assemblies.

7. I do not mean a faith that is articulable in reflective ways that are precise and hang together. Rather I mean a faith that is fundamentally normed by reflective modes of thinking with their precision, definition, and self-consciously maintained logical consistency, such that it is or ought to be theoretically self-reflective by its very nature.

8. Cf. Williams, *The Radical Reformation*; Baylor, *The Radical Reformation*; and Hillerbrand, *Radical Tendencies in the Reformation*.

The sixteenth-century Reformers, however, did not appear out of nowhere. They were heirs of a long medieval tradition of renewal understood as repristinization. Carolingian reformers of the ninth century, for example, attempted to re-establish the Old Testament priestly and levitical orders in the Latin Church of their day.[9] The eleventh-century Gregorian reformers strove to re-establish the youthful vigor of the apostolic order within an aging and, in their view, deeply worldly communion of believers.[10] The twelfth-century Waldensians and Poor Catholics, and the thirteenth-century Dominicans and Franciscans sought to live a perfectly (i.e., literally) evangelical life to the pattern of Matthew and Luke 10: going out two by two, barefoot and penniless to preach repentance and the coming Kingdom of God.[11] Then there were the fourteenth-century exotically nudist Brethren and Sisters of the Free Spirit and their scandal-plagued efforts to establish a new Eden of so many figless Adams and Eves.[12] All of these reform movements and groups of reformers were set in motion, energized you might say, by their conviction that there existed a direct connection across the centuries between themselves and the scriptural communities of faith they held up as model. These biblical models were, in turn, conceived as perfect and accessible examples of communal purity. Thus, those communities directly connected, i.e., perfectly conformed, to their biblical models could be pronounced free of the rotting corruption which the reformers were convinced had come to cripple the community of faith in the centuries between their chosen biblical paradigm and themselves.

Moreover, the Protestant Reformation was hardly the last gasp of the Protestant impulse to repristinate. Pietists of the seventeenth and eighteenth centuries had a similar sensibility, if less sharply focused upon a specific biblical-historical paradigm, and more upon recuperating a now forgotten affective posture assumed to be in principle perennial.[13] The Protestant orthodox who split from the large established churches in the late

9. See McKitterick, *The Frankish Church*.

10. For a number of influential studies of the Gregorian Reform, see Blumenthal, *Papal Reform and Canon Law*. For a classic presentation, see Tellenbach, *Church, State and Christian Society*.

11. For a sense of this "evangelical revival" see Vicaire, *L'imitation des apôtres* and Chenu, "The Evangelical Revival," 239–269.

12. Important segments of their history are analyzed in Schmitt, *Mort d'une hérésie*.

13. I have been much helped in understanding pietism by Albrecht Ritschl's justly (in)famous theological study *Geschichte des Pietismus*; and Martin Schmidt's far more recent historical study *Pietismus*.

nineteenth and early twentieth century, such as Abraham Kuyper among Dutch Calvinists, fused their sense of the authoritative lessons to be learned from the Old and New Testament with a celebration of the purity of the Reformation churches and the confessional and theological formulations they generated. They thought of themselves as returning to the pristine purity of Reformation faith in the face of modern, educated apostasy.[14]

I do not dispute the legitimacy of receiving the scriptures or the *confessionalia* of one's community of faith as the authoritative starting points for understanding what it means for the community of faith and its members to live well in God's world. Rather my point is to highlight how thin the line is between a proper appeal to the scriptures or authoritative tradition and a repristinating understanding of them. That is, I am claiming that it is easy to cross a line between a properly reverent allegiance to the scriptural text or authoritative *confessionalia* and a romanticized attachment to the human communities they disclose.

In a repristinating perspective, communal identity comes to be forged around past moments of epiphany when the Kingdom seemed to edge so near that one could almost taste it. The effect is autumnal. One is predisposed to look bereft upon an era in which predecessors seemed to walk with God. Melancholy reigns. One sighs plaintively. It was different then.

Simple attachment to the continuing worth of the past is, however, not to be thought of as if it were synonymous with the repristinating impulse. Rather, a community becomes repristinating when a past expression of faith is held up *as pure, paradigmatic, and directly accessible*. The implication is that a past purity can and ought to exist again here and now; without significant loss, addition or alteration. Such a temporal stance is the exact analogue of the propositionalism we glanced at immediately above. Reestablishment of a past purity, in the present, is an end that can cover a multitude of sins. And so, to give a couple of true if outlandish examples, among Reformed theonomist social theorists, a repristinating approach to the Old Testament can lead to the conclusion that slavery is a biblically sanctioned institution with a current validity.[15] And polygamy can have a similar legitimacy for many conservative Mormons. When commitment to a past and paradigmatic example of communal purity combines with

14. See in this regard, the first two chapters of Robert Sweetman, ed., *In The Phrygian Mode*, 9–32.

15. For an overview of this school of Christian understanding, see Clauson, *The Idea of "God's Law."* A key text in the school is Rushdoony, *The Institutes of Biblical Law*. For a critical assessment from a sister tradition, see Barker, *Theonomy: A Reformed Critique*.

the founding conviction that that same purity ought and indeed can exist here and now, then any and all cultural difference or distance between then and now must be understood as a fall from original plenitude. But when the temporal process and its transformative dynamics are habitually experienced as Fall, the tendency is to want to freeze or reverse any consequent change. One becomes resistant to and suspicious of change as such.

Intellectualism and the Stability of Identity

Enter the second quality I mentioned, intellectualistic faith. I mean by intellectualistic faith, as said above, a pronounced tendency to identify faith with its cognitive dimension and content. Faith does have a conceptual side to it. It does, in my opinion, because human functioning, however diverse, is meant from the beginning to form an integral whole and concept formation is an irreducible dimension of human functioning. Nevertheless, faith is not comprehended by its conceptual side. To claim that it is so comprehended is to reduce it to one of its constitutive moments, and to distort it in the process. Such a reduction, such "robust intellectualism," can be found within Protestant orthodoxy, though it is not the dominant form. The more common form can be termed "soft intellectualism." In this version, adherents acknowledge that faith is bigger than its conceptual side while treating that side as if it were more important than its trust side, or its feeling side, its social side, aesthetic side and so forth. In this "soft" scenario, faith's conceptual side is still the single most important dimension when push comes to shove.

I think it is probably true that all orthodox Protestant scholars are intellectualists in this second or "soft" sense. At least, honesty requires me to admit as much about my own spiritual reflexes. Again I feel compelled to say that intellectualism, like the impulse to repristinate, is a risk inherent within the central choices and insights of Protestant orthodoxy as a whole. I want to expose certain problems inherent in the fusion of these two qualities. Nevertheless, I want simultaneously to reaffirm that a part of the glory of orthodox Protestantism, and of its scholarship, has been precisely its attentiveness to the conceptual side of religion and religious faith: its sensitivity to what conceptual formulations are healthy and what are profoundly unhealthy. I suppose one sees here yet another example of the truism that our strengths are at one and the same time our weaknesses. For it should be remembered that many people have felt deeply bruised or untouched by predominantly doctrine-focused communities of faith and so have left them for charismatic ones in part because they missed a parallel interest in and wisdom about the emotional or social sides of faith. Many others have left doctrine-focused communities for those that are centered upon the sacraments, and have done so in part because they missed a parallel interest in the aesthetic or symbolic sides.

An historical perspective helps us, I think, to understand the deep-seated intellectualism of Protestant orthodoxy. Protestant orthodoxy began as a response to the ascendancy of historicist modernism in theological institutions and within ecclesiastical clerical hierarchies. To be sure, orthodox elites moved quickly to ally themselves with other enemies of their common modernist foes. Nevertheless it emerged among Protestant theologians and clergy, first and foremost. As a result, it came into its own among people who had an intellectual vocation, i.e., among people for whom training centered upon careful analysis of language and conceptual formulations in preparation for a lifetime to be spent studying and expounding the scriptures. That they should come to have intellectualist reflexes is really hardly surprising. But we can legitimately ask whether their intellectualism should be normative for all people and times?

But perhaps I am moving too fast. Perhaps we need to ask first where the danger is in a soft intellectualist approach to religion and religious faith, particularly within the academy where intellectual activity in virtue of understanding can be said to mark out its very reason for being. Consider the following example: When we come to a scriptural invitation, say, to be of one heart and mind, an intellectualist understands such unanimity as rooted in conceptual unanimity. Conceptual unanimity in turn is conceived as understanding that uses identical or virtually identical verbal and conceptual formulations whenever it is expressed. Such a view most often supposes, in turn, that there is but one legitimate meaning or logical intention inherent within authoritative faith formulations—whether they are passages of the scriptures or authoritative confessions of one type or another—a meaning it is a faithful person's paramount duty to abstract and propagate. Any significant diversity in understanding the faith-formulations held up as authoritative or the meaning of the scriptures is suspect. Of course, intellectualists are far less sensitive to diversity on the aesthetic, social, economic, political and emotional sides of religion and faith. The ethical side is a grey area, since so many passages of the scriptures enjoin or proscribe concrete ethical behavior. In short, intellectualism will tend to orient the intellectualist to interpret stubborn, passionate and articulate diversity of understanding of the meaning of the scriptures or the central confessions of the church as a subversion of a proper unanimity of heart and mind. And when this intellectualist interpretation is fused with a repristinating impulse, one is impelled to see such subversions as a falling away from an original conceptual unity that constituted an original purity of the faith. Such diversity *must* be overcome. Salvation hangs in the balance, for one is potentially speaking of two distinct faiths. Is it any wonder that orthodox Protestantism has tended toward a combative and protectionist culture and academy?

My problem is not with an emphasis upon careful conceptual understanding of faith and religion. Certainly, such an emphasis must be part and parcel of the ethos of a properly Christian academy and of integral Christian scholarship. Rather, my problem with a repristinating intellectualism, including, or perhaps especially my own, starts when I and we live as if criticism and counter-criticism of faith-formulations is somehow the heart and soul of the Christian faith and religion. When all faith language and concepts come as a matter of course to be subjected to suspicious criticism, when suspicious criticism is seen as the very touchstone of our communal calling, legitimate resistance easily devolves into paranoia. Within such paranoia, only language and concepts identical to one's own become truly trustworthy. But the question then looms whether one can legitimately trust even one's own language and concepts? The spectre of checkmate lies in the air.[16]

In such a context, some intellectualists offer a possible way out of this dilemma. One can trust one's own language and concepts if that language and those concepts conform to language and concepts one receives as pure from a golden and pure source, say, the letter of the scriptures, or perhaps the framework of understanding established by Reformation era

16. One sees here the exact equivalent of the modernist use of critical skepticism, but whereas the modernist deploys skepticism against inherited ways of thinking and speaking, the orthodox use it against contemporary experiments with new thought and speech. The critical ethos is thoroughly modern in each case, though employed inversely. But where the critical spirit reigns unchecked the result will be death; only the instruments will differ. While the modernist will demythologize the central mysteries of faith until they have disappeared or been trivialized, the orthodox will perform the equally deadly operation of petrification—at any rate, that is what I suggest in the next couple of paragraphs.

confessionalia.[17] Here we see the orthodox fusion of the repristinating impulse and intellectualism offered in context as a potential way forward.

The sad fact however is that this way forward has tended to petrify language and concept formation. And what is petrified is no longer alive. "Dead orthodoxy" is a by-word among charismatic and evangelical believers quite as much as among modernist critics. Rightly so, I want to add. Protestant orthodoxy has often manifested itself as just that: a posture so stiff and self-protective, an attitude so dourly and resolutely suspicious that the notion of Christian scholarship as a great adventure in which scholars count on each other and on the presence of the Spirit to keep them from theoretical harm seems unimaginably naïve and dangerously flighty. It is almost as if it is forgotten that Christian scholarship too is saved and saving only by divine gift.

It is easy to see that rigidity and suspicion, springing from the fusion of the impulse to repristinate and intellectualism so widespread within Protestant orthodoxy should position orthodox Protestant scholars and scholarly communities to seek to minimize risk and forgo adventure.[18] And that means that orthodox Protestants like me need to unclench if we are to pursue Christian scholarship in the way I have been suggesting. But we need to unclench in a way that is faithful to ourselves as orthodox Protestants. My suggestion is this: let us see our orthodoxy too, not as the essentially identical reiteration of a body of formulae inherited from the past but as an on-going achievement that must be defined ever and anew in a living encounter with the cultural present by people who are interested in having the riches of the past speak afresh to the present and so are prepared to see the present enrich that same past. Such an orthodoxy will never be had once and for all.

This way of repositioning orthodoxy has the advantage that it, like Christian scholarship under my description, is conceived as a communal adventure born of mutual trust and correction. It is one that continues to refer itself gratefully to the language of the scriptures and the central

17. The role of the so-called Reformed principles of the Free University in providing a foundation for scholarship "built on Reformed foundations" is a fine case in point. See, in this regard, the chapter entitled "Om de macht en de beginselen" in Stellingwerff, *Dr. Abraham Kuyper en de Vrije Universiteit*, 185–226.

18. I would be remiss, however, not to acknowledge the role of financial stress and insecurity within the Christian academy and the vulnerability of scholars forced decade in and decade out to sell their wares, so to speak, in a buyer's market. Such vulnerability goes a long way towards producing an allergy to this sort of risk and adventure.

confessions of the church, but that leaves open, for ever-new communal discernment, the shape and exact meaning of that language in our Christian scholarly address of our world here and now. In the initial chapter of this book I summarized my suggestion as follows: we might try viewing our constitutive orthodoxy itself as at its deepest a faith-enabled and Spirit-guided, communal accrediting process rather than as a static, credible essence articulable in its core once and for all via propositions held as true by all, at all times, and in all places. Here too, then, I am calling attention to unity-in-difference; here too a site of folk recipe (*sensus fidelium*).

Chapter Six: Discerning the Scholarly Heart-lines

In chapter four, I suggested that those who find it meaningful to speak of and to pursue Christian scholarship attend to the embarrassments that result from insisting on an Aristotelian way of identifying the difference constitutive of Christian scholarship. Such embarrassments reveal two opposite tendencies that emerge from thinking in this way about the Christian difference in scholarship. The first tendency is to focus on difference at the generic level, hence at the level of scholarly starting points or principles, and to do so in such a way as to call into question the capacity of Christians and non-Christians to pursue a common enterprise under the shared name "scholarship." The second tendency is to focus on Christian scholarship at the specific level of claims or methods intrinsic to scholarship produced by Christian scholars by virtue of their being Christians. Such a tendency will move in a way that seems to deny the existence of any stable or meaningful Christian difference at all.

Each tendency questions its own starting point within an Aristotelian understanding of scholarly identity and difference; each tendency then suggests the possibility that the project itself is self-performatively incoherent. And still the drive to do scholarship that is of a piece with the life of faith, that is, the drive toward personal authenticity argued for at the very beginning of this volume, remains. Consequently, I suggested that Christian scholars try out a sense of Christian scholarship in terms of the spirit or ethos in which it is undertaken: as the scholarship produced by scholars who are attuned as scholars to the shape of their Christian hearts.

I went on in chapter five to explore some of the reasons such an imaginative leap would prove difficult for some, and how one might overcome the difficulty. It remains for me to begin to explore the implications of such a leap. I use the term "imaginative leap" advisedly. Imagination in this formulation stands for a variety of strategies used to halt the subterranean momentum of long intellectual habituation, of an old Christian *paideia*, if you will, a *paideia* that is so deeply ensconced as to form a subconsciously operative default position when thinking about Christian scholarship. If my proposal is to have a chance, one must be brought to other impulses than those rooted in the old Aristotelian way of thinking.

To begin: if we are to accept the risk and take the adventure of a scholarship attuned to our Christian hearts, we must explore two circumstances that such an adventure presents us. First, we need to attend to the process of discernment by which we are to keep open and transparent the lines of connection between our day-to-day scholarly production and our deep religious stance before God. Second, we need to attend to the processes by which we employ and deploy our cordially transparent scholarly efforts in the contemporary academy and in service of the world and its Creator.

The readership I address here legitimately includes those who account for Christian integrality across the curriculum in any of the three ways identified in the third chapter of this book. This is so, not only because all three accounts are at one in assuming an Aristotelian way of understanding the difference constitutive of *Christian* scholarship as opposed to other scholarly species. It is also so because each of the accounts flows from the same intuition about the human condition. That is, all three assume that there is a legitimate distinction to be drawn between human thinking and the thinker who thinks. Indeed, in none of the accounts is the human person to be identified with the *cogito* of modern philosophy since Descartes. Of course, one can distinguish between the thinker and her thought and still see thought as constitutive of or central to the identity of the thinker as person. In fact, the more Aristotelian one's habits of thought, the more likely this scenario is; in an Aristotelian perspective, to be human is to be a rational animal.

Consequently, it may seem surprising that such an anthropological identification is transformed in all the accounts presented in chapter three. This is especially surprising perhaps with respect to complementarist accounts. After all, their grateful deployment of Aristotelian tools to account for Christian integrality across the curriculum is explicit and heartfelt. Nevertheless, complementarist accounts such as Bonaventure's, Gilson's and John Paul II's, by the role they give to religion and theology in and through the category of finality or final causality, are themselves led to distinguish between the thinker qua thinker (a rational animal) and the thinker qua person (an incarnate spirit). Ultimately, what it means to be human is, for them too, to be a reflection of one's Exemplar, i.e. no one less than one's Creator. Moreover, even if one were to think about that Creator-God that human beings image as Meister Eckhart did—as that absolutely simple Existent (*esse*) who *is* his very act of understanding (*intelligere*) and who *is* precisely *because* he is his act of understanding—still one could not reduce human beings in their identity as God's images to their act of understanding, much less their act of thinking. There is necessarily a creaturely supplement to our imaging that must be acknowledged. Eckhart too, despite the depth of his intellectualism, insisted that we are images, not the Exemplar, creatures as well as divine likenesses, incarnate creatures who image the Creator-Spirit in a way appropriate to a world of bodies.[1]

So there is a distinction to be made not only between thought and thinker but also between a person as thinker and a person as person. To be sure, in all three accounts it is assumed that human personality includes as a constitutive moment a capacity to think. But it also includes much more. It includes all of what one brings to the business of imaging the One in whose image one has been made: in a word, everything one rightly is and has. And this insight, namely, that human personality or personhood exceeds the capacity for thought, underlies, as said, all three accounts. In fact, I would suggest that each account is an attempt to articulate Christian scholarly integrality in line with this intuition using the cultural and conceptual tools of the world in which the articulators acknowledge themselves to participate and that they hope to address.

As a consequence, all three accounts point toward the potential fruitfulness of spiritual-scholarly discernment as a starting point for a scholarship attuned to the shape of the heart, especially when one no longer grounds the identity of Christian scholarship in an Aristotelian or perennial and immobile difference intrinsic to the claims and methods of the Christian scholar. We would do well, then, to examine the nature of such spiritual-scholarly discernment in some detail.

1. See in this regard, Meister Eckhart, Questiones Parisienses, 1. in *Die Deutsche und Lateinische Werke.* For an accessible English translation, see Meister Eckhart, Parisian Questions. One of my master's students has provided an illuminating analysis of the necessity of the creaturely supplement in Eckhart's account of human personhood in Schulz-Wackerbarth, "Discovering Connection: The Dynamic Tension and a 'More-Than' in an Eckhartian Conception of the Soul." See especially 70–83.

Spiritual Scholarly Discernment

Since spiritual-scholarly discernment is necessitated by the complex excess of personhood with respect to a person's thinking and thought, it involves acknowledging that the excess of our personhood be mediated in our capacity for logical thought if we are to become conscious or aware of what lies deeper than that same capacity. Such mediation involves receiving world-orientation from outside of the things our thought can get a hold of *when focused reflexively upon itself.*

We have seen already in chapter two how Augustine acknowledged and tried to think about our thought-transcending being as persons. He spoke of the heart and its capacity to entwine intellect and affect in the act of love by which we experience within ourselves the opening up of a capacity for God. We saw how he used conceptual aporias to adjust the balance of intellect and affect, of thought and appropriate personal response. Under Augustine's tutoring we were asked to consider the paradox that we learn to love, truly, when we encounter the limits of thought to grasp and so resolve the fundamental mysteries of living. Thereby, we learn to receive these limits gratefully and with a perseverant determination to view such limits as opportunities, to refuse to accept thought's limits as marking out *our* very end.

The point is this: thought, or at least human thought, is not self-founding. Its roots pass beyond its ken and take their life from other soil. Scholarly discernment is that mediation of personhood to thought that allows one to become aware of those transcendent roots and their life giving soil. Such a practice of discernment also allows one to become aware of the relationship of our thought to its roots; to pick up, if I may stretch the metaphor, the direction from which the nutrients of their soil flow to our thought so as to enable us to arrange the germination of our thought in accord with that direction and flow.

Mediation can occur via a number of different strategies designed to stretch awareness in a number of different ways: imaginatively, emotionally, intuitively, etc. One of the things these ways all have in common is a certain interruptive capacity and function. What I mean is that scholarly thought, anchored by our logical functioning, because it is a ubiquitous presence in our scholarly life and activity, can easily come to seem somehow basic to that life and activity. That is, it can easily come to seem self-founding. It is not the only aspect of our life and activity that can seem that way, but its self-founding appearance is necessarily very strong since logical functioning gives to the academy its distinctive quality.

This appearance is only reinforced by a second feature of scholarly thought in its relation to persons. Human persons are always too late to be at the start of the scholarly conversation. We always join conversations in the middle. As a result, the lines of thought we have available to us and that we are invited to contribute to as scholars are older and deeper than we are, no matter how expansive or experienced our intellects. This concrete situation contributes to the scholarly sense that thought is somehow deeper than all other dimensions of human awareness and consequently that it must be thought of as if it were self-founding, or as if it unfolded by its nature in a continuous development from beginnings that cannot be conceived except as always already conceptual. What discernment does is to call such an appearance into question. It interrupts the unfolding of such apparent development and reminds scholarly persons that all thought is conditioned by what is deeper than and prior to it: the mystery of created selves that think, and the mysteries of creation and its self-revealing Creator that created selves gratefully receive to think about.

Discernment then has something like a genealogical function within Christian scholarship.[2] It is assigned the task of recalling scholarly persons to the deepest mysteries of their lives against the current, if need be, of contemporary scholarly expectation, so that they can reposition themselves to think in greater congruity with those mysteries even when the countervailing currents are powerful and swift. Discernment opens up the pos-

2. For genealogy as an approach to dominant lines of thought in scholarly culture see MacIntyre, *Three Rival Versions*. Genealogy as practiced by Nietzsche and Foucault is a form of critical analysis designed to subject naturalized and central categories of understanding to juxtapositions with their opposites in ways that expose them as nothing but forms of the culturally constructed, anti-authoritative categories they contrast to. In Nietzsche's case Christian love is "exposed" as a modality of self-interest, whereas in Foucault's case categories like humanity and humane, or madness and discipline, are "shown" to be not perennial and stable handles on reality but rather unstable ways of understanding that are historically and discursively generated. My students have often remarked on the parallels between Nietzschean and a variety of neo-Nietzschean genealogies and the critical work of Christian scholars. One thinks of the ground-motive analysis of Herman Dooyeweerd in his *Roots of Western Culture*; but one could also include Alvin Plantinga's analysis of what he called "perennial naturalism" and "creative anti-realism" in the pieces examined in chapter three, and even of Gilson's tellings of the history of western philosophy in his *Being and Some Philosophers*; and his *Recent Philosophy*, which he wrote together with Thomas Langan and Armand Maurer. In Gilson's case, however, such a reading could only occur against the grain of his own historiographical assumptions.

sibility of resistance, but more than that. It also opens up the possibility of redirection and transformation of the very currents themselves, for scholarly claims and methods that lead to flourishing can, as Andrew Basden's example illustrates, be appropriated by others to the benefit of all. It does not always work that way. When the cultural currents are strong and flowing away from encounter with the deep mysteries of life, redirection and transformation is at least as likely to take place the other way round.[3] Such are the risks of scholarship. But when it does work, there is heaven to pay.

World-Orientation and Spiritual Exercise

Christian discernment involves an orientation to or a way of approaching or looking at the world that is marked out by the phrase, "thinking in alignment with the scriptures." Such mediation allows the heart orientation to be translated, so to speak, into the discourse of scholarship, on the one hand. It also allows one to orient a discerning gaze toward the heart, on the other. This mediating condition of discernment and Christian scholarly world-orientation involves the creative presence of divine revelation. Of course, to think in alignment with the scriptures also involves a great deal of prior spiritual formation. Divine revelation is itself available to our thought in and through complex layers of mediation, and there is the mediation of the scriptures themselves. But there are also the communities in which the scriptures live. Thus, our encounter with the scriptures and the God revealed within them is also mediated by the spiritual formation of these communities. Their formation includes the socialization received in family upbringing, in schooling, in the church's formal catechesis, and in the informal mentors or spiritual directors we take on in the course of our lives. Of course that formation is always with respect to us and our configuration as persons. Our appropriation will condition that formation in significant ways and will do so whether self-consciously or not, whether the changes worked thereby are minimal or quite profound. In other words, the phrase—thinking in alignment with the scriptures—is a tag or handle by which to grasp onto and invoke a much more complex phenomenon. I am suggesting that this world-orienting alignment can in turn be pointed at using the phrase Creation-Fall-Redemption.[4]

3. For a description of transformative possibilities see Klapwijk, "Antithesis, Synthesis," 101–138.

4. Among those scholars who look to this phrase to name the biblical dynamic

Creation-Fall-Redemption as World Orientation

Creation-Fall-Redemption is a very common short form in Reformed and Evangelical discussions of Christian scholarship in its relation to the scriptures.[5] It is also to be found in important Catholic contexts.[6] The phrase is not used consistently. Rather, there are a range of uses and therefore it is well to be clear about the use I am employing here. I would also be clear about the spirit in which I distinguish my use from other possibilities. I am not interested in disputing the plausibility of other uses, or in implying that my use is incompatible with other uses. I highlight my particular use in distinction from others because it is neither the most common use encountered in the extant literature, nor is it the easiest to get a handle on, at least at first blush. So I do not mean by Creation-Fall-Redemption a summary of the organizing narrative of the scriptures. Even less do I mean to invoke the germ of a systematic, theological understanding constructed in the context of that summary narrative. I am referring to something else. As I am using the phrase, Creation-Fall-Redemption names a personal or spiritual orientation of one's thought toward the world, what might be termed a set of reflex-like expectations.

This set of reflex-like expectations—what I would also describe as that first impulse toward something one desires to understand—is an impulse in which one approaches something open to encountering it with indications of its original blessing, its marring and consequent ambiguity, and its reception of a new and redemptive meaning by which its original blessing

animating their thought there is a current debate about whether the phrase needs a fourth coordinate, consummation, in order to do justice to the scriptures in their eschatological moment. The thought is that redemption can easily be understood as a restoration of the original blessing of the creation without the openness to the newness claimed for Christ's work in the Gospels and spoken of in the language of prophesy or promise, especially in New Testament apocalyptic. I am indifferent about the outcome of the debate, for it seems to me that redemption cannot be reduced to a restorative function but must include a pointing to the newness of the future world-made-right. So whether one sees both the restoration and the futural openness included in redemption or whether one insists that redemption be restricted to restoration and that consummation be added to account for futural openness is a matter, in the end, for communal comfort and habituation, at least as far as I am concerned. I will stick with the older usage here but use it in such a way that it includes futural openness as well as restoration of the original blessing of creation within its field of meaning.

5. Cornelius Plantinga, Jr. provides a fluent example of a Reformed and Evangelical use of the motif in his *Engaging God's World*.

6. Cf., Alison, *Raising Abel*.

shines forth again and becomes redolent of new possibilities. One is open to, indeed, one *expects* to, find indications of all three moments present in every particle of the world one would understand: moments so intertwined as almost to seem simultaneous. That is, I do not mean by this orientation a kind of template, a category sieve or sorting device by which to assign the phenomena one would understand whether to the box labeled "original blessing" or "fall" or "redemptive openness to futural newness," though that is one of the ways in which the dynamic of Creation-Fall-Redemption has been used.

Perhaps I can put it this way: I am using Creation-Fall-Redemption to name a reflex impulse that sets one in motion toward the world *as if* signs of the complexity of this central biblical narrative were palpably present in every particle of it. I am not inventing a new Christian impulse here. In medieval theology and canonistic thought what I am calling the world-orienting dynamic of Creation-Fall-Redemption was called conscience (*conscientia*).[7] Conscience too points to something deep, something below the level of self-consciously assumed principles and premises; something that also orients its subject toward the world in a certain way, from a certain angle, even before one begins to think about things. But deep though conscience was thought to be, nevertheless it was assumed to exist articulately and thus at a penultimate level, for it was itself a product of enculturation; its patterns were understood to be inculcated in us by our families and churches, our schools and societies.

I say penultimate, for this enculturation of conscience was related to an even deeper and silent impulse that conscience could be said to educate or make articulate. This deepest impulse medieval theologians called *synderesis* and meant an absolutely pre-reflective or reflex response to the world in its original goodness, i.e., in its founding relation to the Creator-God, and by extension away from what taints that original goodness.[8] *Synderesis* was the medieval theologian's name for what is recognized, more or less, and named otherwise in other Christian contexts. I cite but two.

7. Still standard for the study of moral theology and philosophy in the 12th and 13th centuries is Lottin, *Psychologie et morale*. For conscience in particular however one should also consult Timothy C. Potts, *Conscience in Medieval Philosophy*; Saarinen, *Weakness of Will*; and Kent, *Virtues of the Will*.

8. For *synderesis* see all the literature cited in the previous note and in addition Kreis, "Origen, Plato and Conscience," 67–83; Trottmann, "La syndérèse selon Albert le Grand," 255–273; and Somme, "Infallibility, Impeccability and Indestructibility," 403–416.

In the biblical stories around the creation and fall of human beings it was termed "the knowledge of good and evil" (Gen. 3). John Calvin called it "the seed of religion" (*semen religionis*) that is planted in each of us and that germinates an "awareness of divinity" (*sensus divinitatis*) in all people.[9]

The world-orienting dynamic of Creation-Fall-Redemption as I am using the phrase, then, marks out a complex impulse toward the world, one that assumes the ubiquity of good and evil in each of its particles, but in which the good has both the first and the last word. This impulse understands things to have an identity rooted in their origination and an openness to newness, to heretofore unimagined possibilities, coming (as it were) from the future into our ambiguous here and now.[10] One might make the same point using other language. To think in alignment with the scriptures is to approach the whole world as if the self-revelation of God's active presence in his world is inscribed or written into every particle of that world.

It is clear that as I am using the phrase I am trading on intellectual content to point to a reflex response, a habit so deeply internalized as to have become "second nature." It is also clear, I think, that a Reformed catechetical and theological formation underlies my assumption of intellectual content. There is a disjunction then between the words I find myself needing to use and what I want those words to point to. In fact, I deliberately highlight the disjunction by explicitly differentiating the reflex I am pointing at from the content of biblical narrative and spiritual-theological traditions that are part and parcel of the particular process of formation behind *my* possession of the reflex. It is the reflex I am interested in, no matter what went into its process of formation as "second nature." I insist on this because I think that the shared scriptures and any number of Christian spiritual-theological traditions can and do work together to form the reflex, though I can only speak about it authentically using my own Reformed spiritual-theological language. Once again, the image of folk recipe is apropos.

The world-orientation I am calling "thinking in alignment with the scriptures" and am also identifying as thought animated by the spiritual dynamic of Creation-Fall-Redemption can also be named a nose for spiritual ambiguity. We can steal one of the rhetorical tricks of post-structuralist writers at this point and say that the world-orientation I have in mind

9. See Calvin, *Institutes Religionis Christianae* 1.3.1.

10. My colleague Nicholas John Ansell sees futural newness pervading creation as well as redemption. See his *The Annihilation of Hell*. Futural newness is also a powerful theme in Miroslav Volf's works *The Future of Hope* and *The End of Memory*.

involves a recognition that the world one would understand is un/trustworthy. Of course I do not mean that it is morally indeterminate.[11] Rather, the sense of the deep ambiguity of things I am imagining here is at the same time trusting, hopeful, and love-struck. What I mean, then, is that an orientation to the world animated by the dynamic of Creation-Fall-Redemption sensitizes one to the presence of moral complexity not only in the world generally but individually in each of its constituent elements.

Such an orienting awareness comes to expression in a posture of patient attention. If the world and its beings are complex and ambiguous, our attempts at understanding do well to enfold and express a feel for moral complexity: an eye for aboriginal goodness at play even in the presence of evil, an eye for the sorrows to be found even in life's relative bliss, an eye for the advent of surprise hidden even within our world's most stable and pedestrian features. Moreover, if the posture of patient attention is to be trusting, hopeful, and love-struck, flowing from a deep conviction that there is good to be found from beginning to end, that posture will be positive and constructive. On the other hand, if it is to avoid triumphalism it must enfold a critical moment within its constructive mien; there are sorrows aplenty to be described and mourned, indeed to be repented of.

Yes, complexity and ambiguity demand patient attention. They also entail the likelihood of competing accounts. One might think of it this way: the world one sees when animated by the dynamic of Creation-Fall-Redemption is common to all and yet by its very encompassing complexity is contested in its understanding. In such a world-orientation the sense of ambiguity and complexity and hence the need for an attentive posture will extend to the understandings that scholars generate of that world. That is, the understandings, like the world they claim to understand, can be counted on to reflect that world's ambiguity. This demands of the Christian scholar a discerning generosity, particularly with respect to the work of scholars who are not Christian or who are differently Christian, scholars who use a different vocabulary and set of categories to understand the shared world.

11. I use the adjective moral in this context as a synonym for normativity, or what might be called the direction or trajectory present within the movement of creaturely existence.

Generosity and the Cubist Painter's Eye

The figure I use to imagine this generosity is the Cubist painter's eye for and delight in multiple visual orderings, imaginings or understandings of the world of observation. If the world is really held in common, though in and through a contest about its proper understanding, then, one can approach the language and understanding of others expecting to find there the lineaments of the world as one sees it oneself, even when that language and understanding flows from a self-conscious attempt to re-order, re-imagine and re-understand that moves past the world of observation as was the case among Cubist artists. The world will doubtlessly be arranged in a different order, as are Picasso's cubist arrangements of human portraiture, and things will certainly circulate under different names, but underneath, if one looks attentively and patiently enough, one will be able to identify what in one's own understanding they are naming and understanding in their significantly different way.

Perhaps an example or two of what I mean will help. One of my students became very interested in writing his MA thesis on Bernard of Claivaux's "Discourses on the Song of Songs." He asked me about commentators he could read to help him come to terms with what he had in front of him when he was reading Bernard's Discourses. I listed a number of the standard explications of Bernard's surviving works, of the medieval tradition of commentary or meditation upon the Song of Songs, on the proliferation of forms of monasticism in the eleventh and twelfth century and where Bernard fit within this "new monasticism."

Many of the books I mentioned were written by historians of religious institutions and mentalities, historians who worked to establish the meaning of their primary sources "from the inside out." That is, they attempted to read *with* their chosen historical interlocutors in order to pick up their meaning via a sort of scholarly mimesis, what might be thought of as the scholarly equivalent of method acting. Their explications functioned, indeed were designed in some measure, to induct new readers into the same sympathetic mimesis or imitation, the same reading-with, the same respect, even reverence, as they exhibited themselves. But I also gave him the name of scholars who read Bernard in a very different spirit. They read *against* the text, testing its account of itself and of the world it brought to mind. Some of these commentators explicitly assumed the critical posture of the post-Enlightenment reader, tabling explicitly and precisely formulated late twentieth and twenty-first century concerns and attitudes. As a result, these readers saw and named the landmarks of Bernard's works and world in profoundly different and disturbing ways.

My student was confused by the latter recommendations. What was he supposed to learn from them? I asked the student what in particular he found unsettling. He spoke, for example, of Burcht Pranger's claim that monastic literature of the Middle Ages was a literature of despair and that the thematic of despair made up a central leitmotiv of Bernard's corpus.[12] My student didn't see it at all. I asked him what he would call what the scholar in question insisted one call "despair." After a silence, I asked whether the medieval Christian and monastic name for the modern scholar's "despair" might be "humility." As my student knew well, a *status humilitatis* or humble posture was normative for the monastic writer. In humility the monastic writer acknowledged that he lived and breathed and had his existence within the gift of his Lord God. This gift he received with gratitude. Whatever the reception of that gift entailed, be it suffering unto death, that he bore, trusting that the gracious Gift-Giver meant it all for his good. Then I asked my student to consider what this posture of humility would look like if one approached its literary witnesses from a modern sense of the human condition, from a normative sense of human autonomy, of human flourishing as the product of the human capacity and freedom to develop *as if* a rule unto him or herself. What would such a reader with such a sense of normativity and human flourishing call what the medieval monk called "humility?" I wondered whether the serene acceptance of heteronomy, or better, one's abject and unconditional dependence upon Another for one's least good, would not seem to be *in fact* a ceding of all hope for human flourishing, in a word, "despair?" In other words, I asked whether it were not possible to see a shared textual and spiritual phenomenon named "humility" by the medieval Christian monk and "despair" by the modernist theologian?

I offer a second example. Edwin Van Kley, long-time professor of history at Calvin College in Grand Rapids, MI, worked for many years on his assignment within the multi-volume series *Asia in the Making of Europe,* edited by his former supervisor Donald Lash, and published by the University of Chicago Press.[13] In the course of his research he ran across a number of seventeenth-century European, eye-witness descriptions of popular Taoism that made it back to and were circulated widely in Europe. They were

12. See in particular Pranger's *Bernard of Clairvaux.*

13. Lach and Van Kley, *Asia in the Making of Europe.*

filled with descriptions of devil worship and of rites of appeasement and the like. The spirit of the descriptions was one of revulsion, indeed, of cultural and religious superiority. Of course, the seventeenth-century discourse was not a wholly new invention. Rather, it employed ancient Christian habits of speaking forged already in the patristic period so as to account for the power of Graeco-Roman religions and their rites. As such the descriptions have long been dismissed as fabrications, as mere constructions of a fictive Other, an Orientalism one could say, perhaps.[14] But, said Edwin Van Kley, when China opened up in the 1980s and Western scholars were allowed into Chinese cities and universities to confer with their Chinese counterparts, new and sophisticated eye-witness descriptions of contemporary religious phenomena and rites began to show up in scholarly journals, including descriptions of popular Taoism and its rites. He could not help but think about the seventeenth-century descriptions, now so despised, that he had worked so hard to document. The modern scholarly descriptions, however sophisticated and different the discursive tools used, were recognizably about the same rites and notions that the seventeenth-century observers had witnessed and described in the patristic and medieval discourse they had at their disposal.[15] The point is this: there was a unity within the human phenomena under discussion that was recognizable in and through, as well as despite, the vastly different discourses used to name and understand it.

The sensitivity I was attempting to help my MA student work toward with respect to skeptical-critical analyses of medieval religious texts and that allowed Edwin Van Kley to see the shared world of popular Taoism in seventeenth-century travellers' descriptions and twentieth-century scholarly descriptions is what I am calling the Cubist painter's eye for and delight in the different names and orders we human beings give to our shared world. However, the delight I am speaking of is not a moral quietism. Not all accounts of the world are equal. One must sift and judge. And still on some deep level should there not also be wonder: amazement at the sheer

14. "Orientalism" is the term coined by Edward Said to invoke the tradition of scholarly discourse developed in the West to speak about non-Western peoples, especially those of the Middle East. See in this regard, Said, *Orientalism*.

15. Seventeenth-century Western accounts of popular Taoism are digested in Books 3 and 4 of *Asia in the Making of Europe*. 1285, 1657–1658, and 1725–1726. The description I have provided here of the connections to be made between seventeenth-century and twentieth-century accounts relates the gist of a fascinating monologue that Van Kley delivered impromptu in my presence in the faculty lounge of Calvin College's History Department during the Spring term of the academic year 1989 to 1990.

inventiveness of human understanding, an even deeper awe at the capacity of the world we would know to speak of itself in and through the most exotic inventions of human understanding? And perhaps deepest of all, a gob-smacked and worshipful silence before a Creator who made, watches over, and provides endlessly for a world able to bear such astonishing complexities, bliss, and sorrow in wild profusion?

Generous Humility, Right and Wrong

A Cubist's eye and delight is one way of imagining how the Christian scholar is to approach the riddle of a world understood in such a way that it is simultaneously shared and contested. There is a second way as well that I have been helped by. In the first chapter, I introduced this imaginative way in the following contrast. In a world in which a deep creational goodness and openness to redemption are ubiquitous, mistaken claims or understandings, whether made by a Christian or a non-Christian scholar, are more likely than not almost right. On the other hand, because of the ubiquity of the Fall and its effects, true claims and understandings, again, whether made by a Christian or a non-Christian scholar, are more likely than not almost mistaken.

I went on to distinguish this two-fold orientation to the claims and concepts of other scholars from considered judgments of such claims and concepts that result from subsequent, patient scholarly attention. Mistaken claims and their discursive contexts can be mistaken to a spectrum of effects, from the hellish to the trivial to the serendipitous. Moreover, true claims and the discourses in which they are generated are subject to a range of legitimate responses, including transformation, supplementation, recontextualization, re-articulation. But such judgments could only be made on the basis of patient attention, on the basis of scholarly assessment and study. What this imaginative way of speaking is designed to evoke is, as said, something different—a first movement toward, an expectation about, an impulse. What I am presenting for consideration is a way of viewing and shaping this first movement, expectation and/or impulse. I am suggesting that it is profitably viewed in terms of its humility as well as its generosity. I am suggesting that an approach to the work of other scholars from out of the Cubist painter's eye-for and delight-in the various languages and understandings they generate or work within be imagined as generous enough to find what is right (even when it is put in ways that seem profoundly wrong) and humble enough to know in one's bones that even those claims one is most sure about fall short of the reality toward which they point (and so are candidates for supplementation, even transformation).

A fine example of the generosity that I am thinking of is provided by Etienne Gilson in his profound reading of the history of Western metaphysical speculation in *Being and Some Philosophers*.[16] There he makes the claim that metaphysicians are rarely wrong about the things they insist on, including within their most basic metaphysical conceptions. Rather, they err most often in what they leave out.[17] He goes on to tell the story of Western metaphysics from out of the generosity generated by this seminal claim.

Again, there is no moral quietism, no relativism here. Gilson wrote as a partisan. He took on the current or post-Kantian slur of "dogmatic philosopher," that is, a philosopher ready and willing to insist upon ascribing intelligible reality to the various notions of being to be found in the pre-Kantian metaphysical tradition. In so doing, however, he refused to write the history of philosophy subsequent to the Kantian turn out of his story. Rather, contemporary post-metaphysical philosophy too could be seen within the same horizon. It too was right in some fundamental way about the things it saw and spoke about, but erred in what it left out. The frame of reference remained positive. As a result, the position he eventually argued for was to be thought of as true not because the other positions were false and it was the last position left standing. Rather, he argued for the truth of his position because it was expansive enough to include everything that other positions he identified within his story saw and insisted upon, but within a conception that also saw and included something deeper, more primordial, and indeed more expansive than its competitors.[18]

My guess is that his move was an Aristotelian one. He was looking at metaphysical and post-metaphysical accounts as if forms given in reality, forms that can be said to organize or order the same material. As such, they can be organized in a vertical relationship of lower and higher, in which the higher forms organize all that the lower forms organize and add to that a capacity to organize or enact something that escapes the lower forms.[19]

16. Gilson, *Being and Some Philosophers*.

17. This is the clear implication of the opening problematic of *Being and Some Philosophers*. See for example pp. 1–2. This position is put explicitly and given a historiographical/philosophical application in Gilson, *Christian Philosophy*, 52–53.

18. See the chapter, "Being and Existence," in Gilson, *Being and Some Philosophers*, 154–189.

19. See Aristotle, *De anima*, 2.3 414b29–33.

Surely, here one sees a scholar whose work breathes the sense that even those who err are achingly close to the brass ring. They too point to realities in ways that are luminous, even to those for whom their positive claims, or the horizons within which their claims take meaning, are problematic.

On the other hand, the spectre of humility is well represented by what may turn out to have been the crowning achievement of my late colleague at the Institute for Christian Studies in Toronto, George Vandervelde. For the long years of his tenure at ICS he worked as a theologian in the field of ecumenical theology. In that context, he developed a wide range of contacts within the Catholic world of theology.[20] The prominence of his work in this field recommended him to his Reformed denomination when it sought to strike a committee to examine the language of its beloved sixteenth-century Heidelberg Catechism regarding the Catholic understanding of the mystery or sacrament of the Lord's Supper. Indeed, its language was short and harsh. It urged its readers to condemn "the cursed idolatry of the Popish Mass."[21] He and his fellow committee members worked long and hard to evaluate that condemnation and to advise the denomination about what to do about it. That work led to an unexpected and gracious conclusion.

The committee of course was not dealing with just any sort of document. While the language of the Heidelberg Catechism is not to be identified with the language of the scriptures in Vandervelde's denomination, its language does assume an elevated status. It is to provide a context for healthy theological elaboration as well as the quotidian confession of the ordinary person in the pew. It was no small matter, then, to judge its language in error. Nevertheless, in an age in which Catholic and Protestant believers cooperate as Christians in any number of social and cultural causes and on all sides of the current "secular" divides, what was one to make of the harsh judgments of Reformation *confessionalia*? Did they not erect unnecessary barriers between Christ-confessors? Did they really need to be there?

20. One gains an appreciation of the warmth of his contacts by looking at the Catholic contributors to his recently published festschrift. Cf. O'Gara, "The Theological Significance of Friendship," 125–132.

21. The text of Question and Answer 80 is published in Bierma, "Confessions and Ecumenicity," 145–154 (HC80 is cited in full on 145–146). The account of the events also recalled in what follows picks up the story when the synodical committee Vandervelde served submitted its understanding of Catholic eucharistic theology to Catholic theologians. It is told from what might be called the official view of the committee as a whole rather than from the point of view of Vandervelde's role in the process, especially the informal part that preceded the focus of this article.

There was within the committee some feeling for defining a technical sense in which one could affirm the letter of the Heidelberg Catechism's condemnation while denying its obvious spirit, and by doing so avoiding the prospect of calling an authoritative confession into question. Vandervelde insisted, however, that such a position only perpetuated what he saw as a profound misunderstanding of the Mass and its role in Catholic spirituality as he had learned to see it in communion with Catholic participants in the project of ecumenical theology. He insisted that if the language of the Heidelberg Catechism were to be re-affirmed, it would be tantamount to claiming that Catholic Christians were idolators in the central communal act of their encounter with Jesus Christ. A serious mission to convert Catholics to true Christianity would have to be launched forthwith. At the very least, he argued, the committee should submit its understanding of the Catholic Mass to Catholic theologians to see if the committee's understanding was recognizable to them. What resulted was a process of encounter and transformation in which the whole committee became convinced that the Heidelberg Catechism's condemnation of the Catholic Mass was based on a misunderstanding of the Mass, and therefore that it should be repented of. Question and Answer 80 should no longer have any status within the *confessionalia* of the denomination (though it should, for historical reasons, continue to circulate with the Catechism with appropriate explanations and retractions). Henceforth, debate about the theology of the Lord's Supper should be restricted to how one best articulated the shared mystery of the sacrament in light of scripture as understood within the different traditions.

The willingness to reconsider one's most secure and authoritative understandings out of a sense that to be in right relationship (in the truth) with the world one seeks to understand is to receive that world as perduring mystery—this is the gracious humility that I am pointing to. It is the presence of that humility, the kind that submits to the discipline of mutual correction, (whether the correction of sisters and brothers in the faith, of fellow scholars in one's field, regardless of religious identity, or more metaphorically the correction of, say, the crystal one encounters through one's microscope) that I imagine as the impulse or posture to be fostered by the two phrases, *even to be right is to be almost wrong* and *even to be wrong is to be almost right*.

Discerning the Shape of the Christian Heart in the Concrete

Heretofore, I have been speaking of imaginative exercises that foster the right sort of posture to assume vis-à-vis the discernment by which one becomes attuned to the shape of the heart. But how does it work out in practice? I use my own experience to illustrate how it has worked out in the one instance I know from the inside. I present this practice bearing in mind the qualities introduced in the opening chapter of this volume, namely, that the shape of the heart is affected by scholarly investigation as well is effective of it, but that scholarship's affect is not such that it could *easily* change the shape of the heart in fundamental ways.

I begin with the shape of the process in general. Discernment as I understand it does not begin with an empty slate. Rather, I start out by assuming a formation to Christian religion within my Reformed faith community, and assume, even more deeply, the presence of divine Grace to which my faith bears witness despite its impurity. Additionally I assume a certain education, educational experience, and calling. All of these I cannot but bring to my Christian experience of the world, for they contribute to making that experience possible.

This experience of world becomes the field of investigation to be canvassed in determining the presence of persevering patterns of religious excitement and energy. Deep-seated religious excitement and energy that is sustained over the long haul, these are what I look for or seek to discern, for they point to the hidden shape of my heart. In other words, I look to identify what moves me to my core about belonging to the community that sees in the Jesus we meet in the scriptures the very hope and need of the world. That is what marks my hidden stance before God. I, then, try to make my scholarship a demonstrable contribution to the full and concrete realization of this heart's desire, a contribution in which the means are of a piece and are consistent with their heartfelt ends. So goes the story in general.

What gets me particularly excited about Christian faith is that the God whom we meet in Jesus of Nazareth is a peacemaker. Of course, that God is far more than can be named in the one term peacemaker, but it is his being a peacemaker that makes my heart flutter. Consequently, the topics I am interested in, the methods I employ and the claims I arrive at and articulate are those that flow from a would-be pacific understanding of Christian religion and the scholarship that properly flows from it.

In today's world such peacemaking involves, I think, reconsideration of the stark oppositions that we have used to map our understanding of the world and of our place in it. It involves questioning every either/or, recognizing the potential for violence implicit in any improper separation of this from that. Some of these stark oppositions will remain in place even after interrogation; stark oppositions are not problematic per se. Others will be transformed into other contrasts like contrariety or correlation or disappear altogether. But an understanding of the world that has sifted or criticized each habitual appeal to dichotomy will be a more pacific understanding of the world, or so I hope.

I have worked toward a practice of peacemaking throughout my graduate training and professoriate as historian of ancient and medieval thought. In particular, I have used my formation as a child of the Genevan Reformation to examine every feature of medieval Christian thought, life and piety that causes Genevan senses to tingle with offense. Thus, I have examined Marian theology and spirituality, the spiritual exegesis of the scriptures, the cult of the saints, the doctrine of purgatory, indulgences, and the like. Moreover, as an heir of the "Amsterdam School" of Christian philosophy,[22] I have done the same with the scholastic philosophical tradition: its concept of nature, its notions of being, its conception of authority, of science, story and argument, its negotiation of the correlation of universality and individuality in our experience of a world of concrete creaturely subjects.

In every case I have begun by asking what I want to call a pacific question. I want to know what it is that would make people of God-breathed faith imagine and think these things that I have been formed to imagine and think as troublesome. Moreover, the knowledge I strive for is not just a conceptual pattern. Rather I am after a deeper sense of knowing whereby I can acknowledge an authentically Christian sense of the world at play, and do so in my bones, i.e., in those inner recesses where Augustine says that "faith speaks to faith." "Peacemaker" and "pacific"—these terms mark for me the shape of my Christian heart. They set me in motion toward the world of scholarship I have been called to. They translate my heart's desire,

22. This is another way of indicating what is also known as Reformational philosophy and the community of philosophers who seek to work out of its central theses. This way of referring to Reformational philosophy seems to have started with its critics within sister Reformed and Presbyterian traditions. Cf. Nash, *Dooyeweerd and the Amsterdam Philosophy*; and Frame, *The Amsterdam Philosophy*.

i.e., how, at my best, I long to image the God I meet in scripture and worship in my scholarly service of his world.

Of course, my sense of peacemaking and of its divine Exemplar is not unaffected by scholarly and simple life experience. Thus, I have, at times, been brought up short with a sense of the limits of my own Christian heart. I have sometimes been forced to conclude that the kind of pacific questions I am most comfortable with are premature. Sometimes a pacific practice of scholarship first demands that one identify and seek to resist and rectify violence. Here, I have tried to do my bit to acknowledge, resist and rectify the effects of cultural violence against women by examining themes that foster a more adequate inclusion of women and women's experience within scholarly sense of the cultures whose philosophy I am responsible to understand. I have taken up patristic and medieval conceptions of marriage and family, women's spirituality, and the sexual division of sanctity. In philosophy proper, I have taken up medieval conceptions of sex and gender, gender and knowledge, gender and religion.

So peacemaking, constantly refined or challenged by new experience, scholarly and otherwise, continues to mark out for me the very shape of my heart; that Gospel flame that ignites my soul. And I have tried to honor the shape of my Christian heart by crafting a scholarly mode of production that leads to and is itself an expression of peacemaking. To the degree that I succeed, and that is a judgment that I cannot make on my own, to that degree I engage in integral Christian scholarship as I have been speaking of it here. But this does not mean that peacemaking is *the* scholarly master-key. Rather, in my understanding, there will be a wide range of such heart-filled identifications, for the Gospel is expansive enough to fill Christian hearts in many different ways. Here too I invite the reader to join in the fun, to identify for himself what moves him most about the God whom he worships, what he at his best lives to image. I invite the reader to ask herself if she can see a connection between the shape of her heart and her scholarly interests and methods of inquiry. I invite readers to examine their ongoing scholarly projects to see whether and how that shape has effected and been affected by subsequent experience whether scholarly or otherwise.

In all of this it will be noted that there is risk involved in Christian scholarship. Christian religion in its translated form, what I have called the shape of the heart, not only constitutes the framework within which Christian scholarship takes shape, it is also affected by subsequent scholarly experience and by the continuing circumstances of all concrete living. In and through such experience, the shape of the scholar's heart can be twisted and fractured as well as developed and deepened. As a result, it is important not only to discern the shape of the heart, but also to tend the heart so discerned.

Tending the Heart in Oceanic Movements

Moreover, this tending is not just an individual thing. By rights, such tending is a communal effort, just as the initial formation of the Christian heart is deeply and constitutively communal. Christian scholarly hearts are most effectively tended to within the context of Christian scholarly community. An active solidarity is called for, a solidarity of mutual criticism (testing or sifting) and correction. And, as said, such criticism and correction can only really be carried on healthily in an open spirit of mutual trust. Otherwise it degenerates into striking out at one another in suspicion and fear.

On the other hand, tending the heart can only ever be a means to an end. Discernment of the shape of one's Christian heart creates the transparency necessary to examine past and plan future scholarship that will be demonstrably consistent with that shape. Moreover, the scholarship itself is to be deployed in service of God's scholarly world, in all that world's original blessing and redemptive newness, to be sure, but also in all its insidious and malignant brokenness. And that means that one traces the shape of one's heart as part of a discipline of being open to the scholarly world in all its poignant ambiguity. In the ambiguity of the world that scholars are called to inhabit and the analogously ambiguous greater world that they are called to explore as scholars, Christian scholars encounter both danger and discovery.

In light of these considerations we see anew the mediating function of discernment. It allows us to see the posture we need to assume vis-à-vis the world we would study if we are to work in a manner consistent with our heart's shape. It also allows us to see the direction we ought to head in our study, i.e., what we ought to open ourselves up to. The health of Christian scholarship demands, then, movement back from scholarship to its animating heart and spirit on the one hand, and self-aware scholarly movement outward from that heart and in that spirit to God's world itself in all its ambiguity. How are we to imagine and order these movements?

It is at this point that I offer another imaginative analogy. One can think of the practice of Christian scholarship as oceanic, i.e., as having a natural ebb and flow. Since the end of both movements is healthy scholarship—a mode of service of and in God's world—scholarly movement into the world takes a certain precedence: the priority accorded, as we have seen, to relative final causes. Thus scholarly movement into the world is identified with flow in our analogy. Discernment of the shape of the heart, in turn, marks out an ebb, a movement away from the end in order to enable a subsequently more integral or sure-footed movement toward the end. This ebb and flow are equally constitutive of healthy Christian scholarly practice and are both to be prized and planned for.

Christian institutions of higher learning are, above all, natural centers for the ebb movements constitutive of healthy Christian scholarly practice. That is, these institutions have integral Christian scholarship as one of their defining ends. Consequently, they have a primary institutional interest in making sure that there exist the individual and communal discernment necessary to keep in sight, for mutual criticism and correction, the heart and spirit of Christian scholars and the scholarship they produce. These institutions should then provide resources and opportunities for such individual and communal discernment to take place and be rewarded.[23]

Moreover, because Christian hearts receive spiritual formation less in higher academic settings than in home, school and church, Christian institutions of higher learning should equally give serious thought to how they might help the Christian community with spiritual formation that can be taken up in its homes, in its parochial or parent-controlled schools, and in its churches. Indeed, in general, religious or spiritual formation should receive a great deal more thought and attention than is presently the case in most parts of the Christian world today.

Joining the Scholarly Conversation

The shape of the heart, once discerned, allows one to orient oneself toward the object of one's scholarly work in ways that are consistent with that shape. In other words, we who are energized by various intrinsic features

23. These sorts of initiatives are taken up by a significant number of Reformed and evangelical institutions of higher education. Moreover, there has been a significant reconsideration of the meaning of catholicity in many Catholic institutions. The point here is not to chronicle these efforts but to acknowledge that in creating this sort of opportunity for Christian scholars they are establishing an important condition for the development of Christian scholarship thought of as scholarship in attunement to the shape of the Christian heart.

of the Gospel will gravitate toward various scholarly conversations. On the other hand, because we live and work as scholars within a post-Christian scholarly culture, we will join conversations that are religiously heterogenous as well as ambiguous in their results. This heterogeneity and ambiguity, in turn, entails a two-pronged approach to the conversations we join.

In the first place, we should join the conversations open to learning from and being changed by what we encounter in the process. Furthermore, we must join these conversations in good faith, as participants prepared to take as well as give, to learn as well as teach. In other words, we should value the conversations we join as they are carried on when we join, even or perhaps especially when we also hope to transform them in important ways. There must be solidarity with the world we would serve, a solidarity that acknowledges that we all, Christian and non-Christian alike, participate in and contribute to both its blessings and its curses. Insisting that one stand outside of the conversation, that one maintain a marginal status vis-à-vis any and all conversations of a post-Christian academy cannot be *the* normative Christian stance. In such a mode, solidarity thins at the edges; one joins but only in ways that allow easy escape. Such reticence is too dispassionate, too careless to be deeply heartfelt. Conversations that we join in this edgy way remain somehow *their* conversations and do not become fully *ours*. And this remains so even when our marginal talk is of high academic virtuosity.

In the second place, however, we should join conversations sensitive to their spiritual heterogeneity and hence to the existence and location of sites of healthy transformation. While an appropriate solidarity or care will entail that we start where our interlocutors are, accepting their way of putting things, because we have much to learn, we will also be looking for ways in which we feel conversations can be profitably developed. As a result we will often move by inquiry and argument to redirect conversation in ways suggested by the dynamic or spirit of our Christian hearts.

Here again an example can help to illustrate what I mean. Janet Wesselius teaches philosophy at Augustana College in the University of Alberta. She did her graduate work at the Institute for Christian Studies and at the Vrije Universiteit te Amsterdam, in The Netherlands and so was trained academically to look at Christian integrality in scholarship in holist terms. I was involved in her program of study and, consequently, I know her example well. I cite it because her thesis project and subsequent research well illustrates the two-pronged approach I have been describing in the last few paragraphs.

Her interest was, from day one, to engage the community of feminist philosophers on an issue of real philosophical significance, in such a way as to insert her voice into the conversation as both feminist theorist and as Christian philosopher.[24] One could say that she was convinced that in feminist discussions were to be found a field of inquiry and scholarly endeavor that answered to the shape and call of her Christian heart. As a result, she self-consciously started where she found her feminist interlocutors starting. She also assumed their characteristic ways of putting things and of asking questions, and sought to contribute to the realization of their ends, not in contradistinction to her identity as Christian scholar but as its very expression.

In particular, she chose to engage a branch of Anglo-American feminist philosophy known as Feminist Epistemology, and to do so by engaging its most prominent philosophers in a discussion around one of the most vexing of their shared problems: the intersection of gender, political emancipation and scientific objectivity. She asked herself how the leading practitioners of Feminist Epistemology spoke about objectivity in their attempts to think about science or trustworthy knowledge in ways that would contribute to, rather than impede, the political emancipation of women. She engaged her interlocutors with a view to how they spoke about gender, emancipation and objectivity in the past; how they were speaking about them in the present; and how they ought to speak about them in the future in order to overcome demonstrable limitations of past and present discourse and so better accomplish the goals they had set themselves.

In the process, she presented a cogent analysis of the past and present limits of the conceptual framework developed by her interlocutors to name and analyze objectivity. She showed how each of them sought to resist a post-Kantian conceptualization of subjectivity and objectivity as dichotomously opposed (either/or), since that opposition was habitually mapped onto the distinctions male/female and valued/devalued in cultural discourse around science or secure knowing and its norms. That is, they sought to resist the identification of female in the dichotomistically conceived distinction male/female with the terms "subjectivity" and "devalued" of the subjectivity/objectivity and valued/devalued distinctions, respectively.[25] In the course

24. See Wesselius, "Points of Convergence," 54–68.

25. The point is put succinctly in Wesselius, *Objective Ambiguities,* 13–18.

of doing so, they manifested a consistent conceptual ambivalence in that they articulated equally powerful arguments both to abandon objectivity as a name for trustworthy knowledge and to maintain the term.[26] Wesselius accounted for this ambivalence via their willingness to maintain the post-Kantian dichotomy of subjectivity/objectivity on some deep subterranean level, even when attempting on other levels to transform the dichotomy into one or another modality of conceptual opposition.

Wesselius then drew on the tradition of Christian philosophy she had been trained in to recover in a post-Kantian language a way of speaking about knowledge as a form of intersubjectivity. One does not know objects but rather other subjects; and subjects, especially human subjects, are perduring mysteries, beings so full of meaning that they overwhelm even our most expansive conceptualizations. In such a framework, one might see knowers and the known as a correlation of two subjects-in-relation. In such a framework, objectivity, for example, might name subjects-in-relation when they are in right epistemic relationship with each other. Or one might want to give this normative relationship another name altogether. Wesselius herself has suggested using the word "contingency," for it bespeaks both being-in-contact or in-touch-with, and contiguousness, a being-right-next-to the subjects one would know.[27] Such a state, she would argue, expresses the intimacy required of trustworthy knowledge while preserving the sense of enduring mystery that *is* any subject one would know.

In the process of writing her thesis, Wesselius made contact with her interlocutors and submitted her analyses of their theories to them in order to solicit feedback. She heard from all three of her interlocutors. Two of them wrote back to say that they had read her material, that they

26. It should be noted that Wesselius' "conceptual ambivalence" shares features with what in the ancient world were called aporias, as discussed in chapter two. There is, however, one profound difference. The ancient skeptics and Augustine himself deliberately juxtaposed arguments and conclusions that were opposite and of the exact same logical texture and force, whereas Wesselius' interlocutors generated their arguments for opposite conclusions of the exact same conceptual force inadvertently. So it is perhaps better to identify Wesselius' "conceptual ambivalence" with the post-structuralist use of the term aporia as an inner contradiction brought to the surface by the process of deconstruction. See in this regard Caputo, *Deconstruction in a Nutshell.*

27. See Wesselius, *Objective Ambivalence*, 28–33. She has another piece prepared more recently and accepted for publication that addresses these matters in light of and as an elaboration on her thesis project entitled "Shared Marginalization and Negotiated Identities: Religion and Feminism in Philosophy," that is scheduled to appear in an interdisciplinary volume tentatively entitled *Meaningful Marginalities.*

recognized themselves and their work in her descriptions and that they needed to think about her positive and transformative proposals. I confess I do no know what has happened beyond these initial exchanges, but her intentions and its provisional effects well illustrate the pattern I am arguing constitutes the flow side of Christian scholarship.

Conclusion: What is Given Up and What is Gained in a Scholarship of the Heart

The kind of scholarship the exercises of this chapter presuppose is one that acknowledges risk as unavoidable in any human endeavor. Integral Christian scholarship, when imagined as scholarship attuned to the shape of one's Christian heart, is far more fragile and labile than would be a successfully conceived Christian scholarship in the Aristotelian mode. One of the intents of Christian scholarship that is given up in this proposal, then, is the task of making the world "safe" for Christian scholars. Christian scholarship, when it is built to serve as mental fortress in a scholarly world assumed to be at war, comes at too great a cost, for faith and its many works are living things that are robbed of their vitality when they are petrified so as to provide construction material for scholarly walls made of conceptual stone.

To be sure, Christian scholarship, even when it is imagined as attuned to the Christian heart, must come to concretion; it must receive careful conceptual determination. This conceptual determination is not for the purpose of plotting precisely the frontier between Christian ideas and methods and their non-Christian counterparts; rather it is a chance for the scholar to give a coherent account of the connections between scholarly results, on the one hand, and one's deepest sense of what it means to live before the face of God, on the other. One must be able to say what the connections are. In this framework too Christian scholarly results are tangible or open to being touched, to being observed. They are not transcendental conditions forever deferred within the sphere of concrete living. This model differs most strikingly from the model articulated in the Aristotelian mode in that the connections between heart and concrete scholarship can attach themselves to an indeterminate variety of scholarly methods and claims, as well as flow from differently configured Christian hearts. One can get at this character by adapting the words Etienne Gilson coined to capture the elusive yet accessible quality of philosophical Augustinianism. You can never predict beforehand what will count as integral Christian scholarship, but you will know it when you see it, for faith speaks to faith when the connections are visible between concrete scholarly work and the deepest shape of one's heart.

An increased awareness of risk and fragility is undeniable in this way of imagining things. Nevertheless, it too has its sources of confidence. It too lays claim to the self-revealing Creator Spirit who so moves within its creation and among its creatures to give meaning and direction to the faithful heart. By extension, that same Spirit is the ultimate source and guarantor of the Christian integrity of the scholarship we produce. Integral Christian scholarship in this telling is mysteriously God's work in and through our own.

Because one no longer looks to ascribe a stable essence to Christian scholarship, one must admit to the intrinsic presence of spiritual doubt. Doubt is the correlative of faith; a trustworthy sign of the presence of the faith that *can* be doubted. Consequently, there is no ground for the arrogance that says—"Now we have it, Christian scholarship, once and for all!" Nor are there grounds to withdraw from the religiously heterogenous academic world as if the Creator Spirit were not operative there but confined itself somehow to a world of Christian making. Rather, one must be humble enough to receive wisdom and knowledge from any and all of God's creatures, out of a sense that it is all meant for our good somehow. The question of what to learn and what not to learn is a matter for perennial and ongoing mutual discernment, but there is no good reason to say we have nothing to learn from "them," whoever "they" be.

On the other hand, a number of embarrassments resident within the conceptions of Christian scholarship understood within the old Aristotelian framework cease to seem so important. For example, the seemingly stubborn diversity of Christian conceptions about Christian scholarly integrity and difference ceases to be the burden it has sometimes been thought to be. There is no need to despair because Christians continue to differ on how properly to speak of Christian scholarship, or on what examples of scholarship radiate robust evidence of the mark of Christ, or the never ceasing need for mutual criticism and correction. This is just part of the ebb and flow of a real but limited scholarly faithfulness, a particular grace resident in each individual scholar, each scholarly community, and each generation. Christian scholars will ever need each other—the quick, the dead, and those yet to come—if the Christian community is to forge a Christian scholarship that manages to be greater than the sum of its parts.

In the end, though, these exercises too betray an Aristotelian trace and I would be churlish not to acknowledge as much and appreciate the delicate irony. That is, these exercises constantly work to help one imagine things from a middle position, a golden mean, so to speak. They foster seeing things from the middle between scholarship's self-reflective ebb and its world-transformative flow. They suggest a course between the too easy ascription of no discernable Christian character to the scholarship Christians produce and the perennially too difficult search for a determinate boundary in claim or in method that would allow an exhaustive and inerrant separation of Christian scholarship from any other. The former scenario denies the experience of discernable difference in those disciplines in which such difference is recognized as being productive as well as unavoidable. The latter scenario denies the experience of Christian scholars working in a way that is articulately or at least articulably connected to their Christian heart in fields that allow little or no difference at the level of method and range of claim, or in pluralistic scholarly settings that do not reward religious self-reflectiveness. These exercises imagine a middle way between the difficulty of a Christian formal or essential difference and the complacency of a denial of any difference. There is a mark but it is not indelible; rather it must be rediscovered ever and anew by scholars, scholarly communities, generation in and generation out. Finally, these exercises point to a middle ground in one last context. They point to a place between the separatistic Christian institutions of higher learning that would do their work over and against the work done in other sectors of the academy, and a Christian sense of solidarity with the greater academy that sees any effort at Christian self-reflection and difference as an unnecessary breach of scholarly community. They articulate a middle ground that is both articulately Christian (and hence, that demands places of Christian scholarly community in which mutual correction in love and trust can take place), and that is genuinely committed to the greater world of scholarship with its upbuilding work of understanding. Further, these exercises do so in the knowledge that Christians can be, and are, directed toward its opportunities and dangers by the very spiritual dynamic of their Christian hearts.

The End of the Line . . . ?

We arrive at the end of these tracings and exercises. I hope that they have been of service to a wide range of Christian scholars—Reformed, Evangelical, and Catholic—for whom the notion of Christian scholarship or of Catholicity across the curriculum has always made sense. I also hope that it has provided a less off-putting discussion of Christian scholarship for those scholars who come to matters of faith and scholarship from the other points of entry with which we began. Thirdly, I hope it has provided an imaginative stimulus to scholars who have heretofore paid little attention to discussions around integral Christian scholarship, whether because of the seeming hegemony of philosophically and theologically trained conversants, because the Aristotelian way in which the difference of Christian scholarship has been talked about has made it difficult to speak about one's scholarly production and one's faith in the same sentence, or because the conversation has seemed so obviously geared to scholars working at Christian institutions of higher education and not to the world that Christian scholars who live out their calling in pluralist universities, both public and private, inhabit.

It is my conviction, which I must now submit to the reader's criticism and correction, that imagining Christian scholarship as scholarship attuned to the shape of our Christian hearts offers something fresh for those who are already helped by the older language and conceptualizations, but also to groups heretofore unaffected by or averse to it. It speaks to the first and second groups by centering Christian integrity in spiritual formation and discernment rather than in a given scholarly discipline and its discursive tools. Christian mathematicians, for example, may feel constrained to silence if faced with defining those methods and claims that they make and use precisely and essentially because they are Christian. But they can be counted on to be able to articulate how their work as mathematician flows from their sense of what it means to live already here and now before the face of God. It speaks to the third group, by pointing to the finality or primacy of the flow movements of Christian scholarship. That is, while Christian scholarship's ebb movement *is* crucial to an ethos of spiritual self-consciousness or transparency and is best organized by Christian institutions of higher learning, the point of this ebb movement is to join the scholarly conversations extant in the academy and culture as we find it. Entry into the post-Christian conversations one is led to by the very dynamic of one's Christian heart can be easier for Christian scholars at work outside of explicitly Christian institutions of higher learning precisely because they are immersed in that world in a way that scholars working at religious institutions of higher learning sometimes are not.[1] Scholars thus immersed in a pluralist world have as a result a crucial role to play in the ongoing Christian scholarly response to the world and its challenges.

Throughout I have tried to view differences among the understanding of scholars committed to the project of Christian scholarship as unproblematic, even an opportunity. "Folk recipe" was the image I used to imagine the possibility of unity-in-difference that such an understanding demands. I have also spoken of that unity as thinking in alignment with the scriptures. I have argued that the posture toward the scholarly world at large that should characterize such thinking is a posture open to a complex moral ambivalence in that world. Such an open attitude betrays its connection to scripture in the phrase, Creation-Fall-Redemption. In such an open posture, we are to go to the world with a two-pronged approach. We go ready and willing to learn from it via the conversations we are directed to by the

1. I do not mean that scholars working at faith-based institutions avoid pressures that come from being full participants in the post-Christian academy. Indeed, just to the degree that we wish to join the broader conversation, we face all the same cultural and intellectual pressures as our colleagues in pluralist environments. But scholars at faith-based institutions also deal with questions and expectations that are unique to faith-based institutions and these supplementary concerns can be said to inflect their scholarly "voice." Consequently, scholars at faith-based institutions come in some ways to speak academically with a discernible accent, an accent their colleagues in pluralist institutions do not, as a rule, have. It is easier to be received as a credible voice when speaking without an accent. This is the line of thought my sense of "an advantage" flows from. Of course, the epistemic advantage of the margin must be put in the balance on the other side, an advantage that feminist and race theorists have been articulately sensitive to. Janet Wesselius indeed has seen here, in the epistemic implications of marginalization, a way of bringing feminist and Christian theory into fruitful conversation. So, the advantage of the margins might be said to provide a countervailing advantage on the other side, but I am speculating here; such musings demand far more thought and research than I can claim at present, even with Janet Wesselius' help.

very dynamic of our Christian hearts. And we go to it caring enough to be sensitive to its unredeemed moments, hoping to contribute our voices there where there is most need in ways that can transform conversation consonant with our deepest sense of what it means to live before the face of God.

In the end, however, these images and suggestions must remain just that: images and suggestions. They invite the reader to examine her own understanding and experience. In doing so, they invite conversation. In other words, here too I acknowledge unity-in-difference, folk recipe, and the mixing and matching that goes with a recipe recognizable even across constitutive diversity. The trick is to see the unity *within* the differences and to express it in one's own language, to be sure, but in a way that others can or might hear. Whether I have managed to do this is a matter for others to say. If conversations erupt as a result of this book, even if the conversations move in directions unforeseen in it, it will not have failed of its purpose. Conversation, real conversation, cannot be pre-programmed. Real conversation is the context in which mutual critical sifting and correction takes place, and it is this sifting and correction by which our hearts are strengthened to new scholarly efforts in service of, and marked by, our common Lord.

Bibliography

Alison, James. *Raising Abel: The Recovery of Eschatological Imagination*. New York: Crossroads, 1996.

Ansell, Nicholas John. *The Annihilation of Hell: Universal Salvation and the Redemption of Time in the Eschatology of Jürgen Moltmann*. Eugene: Cascade Books, 2013.

Aristotle. *The Complete Works of Aristotle Volume II*. Edited by Jonathon Barnes. Princeton: Princeton University Press, 1984.

Augustine. *The City of God Against the Pagans*. Translated by R.W. Dyson. Cambridge: Cambridge University Press, 1998.

Barker, William S. *Theonomy: A Reformed Critique*. Grand Rapids: Academie Books, 1990.

Baylor, Michael G. *The Radical Reformation*. Cambridge: Cambridge University Press, 1991.

Bierma, Lyle D. "Confessions and Ecumenicity: The Christian Reformed Church and the Heidelberg Catechism 80." In *That the World Might Believe: Essays on Mission and Unity in Honour of George Vandervelde*, edited by Michael W. Goheen and Margaret O'Gara, 145–154. Lanham: University Press of America, 2006.

Blumenthal, Ute Renata. *Papal Reform and Canon Law in the Eleventh and Twelfth Centuries*. Aldershot: Ashgate, 1998.

Bonaventure. *Breviloquium*. In *Opera Omnia (minor editio) V Opera Theologica Selecta*, 3–175. Florence: Quarrachi, 1964.

Burtchaell, James Tunstead. *The Dying of the Light: The Disengagement of Colleges and Universities from the Churches*. Grand Rapids: Eerdmans, 1998.

Calvin, John. *Institutes of the Christian Religion*. Edited by John T. McNeill and translated by Ford Lewis Battles. Louisville: Westminster John Knox Press, 2006.

Caputo, John D. *Deconstruction in a Nutshell: A Conversation with Jacques Derrida*. New York: Fordham University Press, 1997.

Clouson, Marc. *A History of the Idea of "God's Law" (Theonomy): Its Origin, Development and Place in Political and Legal Thought*. Lewiston: Edwin Mellen Press, 2006.

Conradie, A. L. *The Neo-Calvinist Concept of Philosophy: A Study in the Problem of Philosophical Communication*. Natal: University Press, 1960.

Coreth, Emerich, W.M. Neidl and G. Pfligersdorffer. *Christliche Philosophie im Katholischen Denken in 19. und 20. Jahrhunderts*. 3 Volumes. Graz: Styria, 1987–1990.

Dooyeweerd, Herman. *In the Twilight of Western Thought: Studies in the Pretended Autonomy of Philosophical Thought*. Philadelphia: The Presbyterian and Refomed Publishing Co., 1960.

———. *The Roots of Western Culture: Pagan, Secular and Christian Options*. Trans. John Kraay. Eds. Mark Vander Vennen and Bernard Zylstra. Toronto: Wedge Press, 1979.

Evans, E. P. *The Criminal Prosecution and Capital Punishment of Animals*. London: W. Heinemann, 1906.

Fish, Stanley. "Why We Can't All Just Get Along." *First Things* 60 (February 1996): 18–26.

Fortini, Arnoldo. *Francis of Assisi*. Translated by Helen Mouk. New York: Crossroads, 1981.

Frame, John M. *The Amsterdam Philosophy: A Preliminary Critique*. Phillipsburg: Harmony Press, 1972.

Geertsema, Henk. "The Inner Reformation of Philosophy and Science and the Dialogue of Christian Faith with a Secular Culture. A Critical Assessment of Dooyeweerd's Transcendental Critique of Theoretical Thought." In *Christian Philosophy at the Close of the Twentieth Century*, edited by Sander Griffioen and Bert Balk. Kampen: Kok, 1995. 11–28.

Gilson, Etienne. *Being and Some Philosophers*. Toronto: The Pontifical Institute for Mediaeval Studies Publications, 1952.

———. *Christian Philosophy*. Translated by Armand Maurer. Toronto: The Pontifical Institute for Mediaeval Studies Publications, 1993.

———. *The Spirit of Mediaeval Philosophy (Gifford Lectures 1931–1932)*. Translated by A. H. C. Downes. New York: Charles Scribner's and Sons, 1936.

Gilson, Etienne and Langan, Thomas. *Recent Philosophy: Hegel to the Present*. New York: Random House, 1966.

Gleason, Philip. "American Catholic Higher Education: A Historical Perspective." In *The Shape of Catholic Higher Education*, edited by Robert Hessenger. Chicago: University of Chicago Press, 1967.

Habig, Marion A., ed. *St. Francis of Assisi: Writings and Early Biographies, English Omnibus of the Sources for the Life of St. Francis*. Chicago: Franciscan Herald Press, 1972.

Hadot, Pierre. *Philosophy as a Way of Life: Spiritual Exercises from Socrates to Foucault*. Oxford: Wiley-Blackwell, 1995.

Heie, Harold and David L Wolfe. *The Reality of Christian Learning: Strategies for Faith-Discipline Integration*. Grand Rapids: Eerdmans, 1987.

Henderson, Roger. *Illuminating Law: the Construction of Herman Dooyeweerd's Philosophy, 1918–1928*. Amsterdam: Vrije Universiteit te Amsterdam, 1994.

Hillerbrand, Hans Joachim. *Radical Tendencies in the Reformation: Divergent Perspectives*. Kirksville: Sixteenth-Century Journal Publications, 1988.

Hoitenga, Dewey. *Faith and Reason From Plato to Plantinga: An Introduction to Reformed Epistemology*. Albany: State University of New York Press, 1991.

Jacobsen, Douglas and Rhonda Hustedt Jacobsen. *Scholarship and Christian Faith: Enlarging the Conversation*. New York: Oxford University Press, 2004.

John Paul II. *Fides et Ratio. Encyclical Letter Fides et Ratio of the Supreme Pontiff John Paul II on the Relationship Between Faith and Reason*. Sherbrooke QC: Médiaspaul, 1998.

Kalsbeek, L. *Contours of a Christian Philosophy: An Introduction to Herman Dooyeweerd's Thought*. Toronto: Wedge Press, 1975.

Kent, Bonnie. *Virtues of the Will: The Transformation of Ethics in the Late Thirteenth Century*. Washington D.C.: Catholic University of America Press, 1995.

Klapwijk, Jacob. "Antithesis, Synthesis and the Idea of Transformational Philosophy." *Philosophia Reformata* 51 (1986): 101–138.

Kok, John. *Vollenhoven: His Early Development*. Sioux Center: Dordt College Press, 1993.

Kupczak, Jarowslaw. *Destined for Liberty: The Human Person in the Philosophy of Karol Wojtya/John Paul II*. Washington D.C.: Catholic University Press of America, 2000.

Kreis, Douglas. "Origen, Plato and Conscience (Synderesis) in Jerome's Ezekiel Commentary," *Traditio* 57 (2002): 67–83.

Lach, Donald F. and Edwin J. Van Kley. *Asia in the Making of Europe. Volume III: A Century of Advance.* Chicago: University of Chicago Press, 1993.

Leahy, William P., SJ. *Adapting to America: Catholics, Jesuits and Higher Education in the Twentieth-Century.* Washington D.C.: Georgetown University Press, 1991.

Leclercq, Jean, OSB. *The Love of Learning and the Desire for God: A Study of Monastic Culture.* New York: Fordham University Press, 1974.

Lottin, O. *Psychologie et Morale aux XIIe et XIIIe Siècles.* Six Volumes. Glemboux: J. Duculet, 1942–1960.

McCool, Gerald S.J. *From Unity to Pluralism: The Internal Evolution of Thomism.* New York: Fordham University Press, 1989.

———. *The Neo-Thomists.* Milwaukee: Marquette University Press, 1994.

———. *Nineteenth-Century Scholasticism: The Search for a Unitary Method.* New York: Fordham University Press, 1989.

MacIntyre, Alisdair. *Three Rival Versions of Moral Enquiry: Encyclopedia, Genealogy and Tradition.* South Bend: University of Notre Dame Press, 1990.

McKitterick, Rosamond. *The Frankish Church and the Carolingian Reforms, 789–895.* London: London Historical Society, 1977.

Maritain, Jacques. *An Essay on Christian Philosophy.* Trans. Edward H. Flannery. New York: Philosophical Library, 1955.

Marsden, George. "What Difference Might Christian Perspectives Make?" In *History and the Christian Historian,* edited by Ronald A. Wells, 11–22. Grand Rapids: Eerdmans, 1998.

———. "Reformed Strategies in Christian Scholarship. A Response to Robert Sweetman." *Perspectives: A Journal of Reformed Thought* 16:7 (August-September 2001): 20–23.

———. *The Soul of the American University: From Protestant Establishment to Established Non-Belief.* New York: Oxford University Press, 1994.

———. *The Outrageous Idea of Christian Scholarship.* New York: Oxford University Press, 1997.

Meister Eckhart. *Parisian Questions.* Translated by Armand Maurer. Toronto: The Pontifical Institute for Mediaeval Studies Publications, 1974.

Milbank, John. *Theology and Social Theory: Beyond Secular Reason.* Oxford: Blackwell, 1990.

Moorman, J. R. H. *A History of the Franciscan Order From its Origins to the Year 1517.* Oxford: Oxford University Press, 1968.

Mouw, Richard. "Dutch Calvinist Philosophical Influences in North America." *Calvin Theological Journal* 24 (1989): 93–120.

Nash, Ronald. *Dooyeweerd and the Amsterdam Philosophy.* Grand Rapids: Eerdmans, 1962.

Nédoncelle, Maurice. *Is There a Christian Philosophy?* Translated by Illtyd Trethowan. New York: Hawthorn Books, 1960.

Nussbaum, Martha. *The Fragility of Goodness: Luck and Ethics in Greek Tragedy and Philosophy.* Cambridge: Cambridge University Press, 1986.

———. *The Therapy of Desire: Theory and Practice in Hellenistic Ethics.* Princeton: Princeton University Press, 1994.

O'Gara, Margaret. "The Theological Significance of Friendship in the Ecumenical Movement." In *That the World Might Believe: Essays on Mission and Unity in Honour of George Vandervelde*, edited by Michael W. Goheen and Margaret O'Gara. Lanham: University Press of America, 2006. 125–132.

Olthuis, James H. *The Beautiful Risk: A New Psychology of Loving and Being Loved*. Grand Rapids: Zondervan, 2001.

Owens, Joseph, ed. *Christian Philosophy.* A special issue of *The Monist* 75:3 (July 1992).

Palmer, Parker J. *To Know as We are Known: Education as Spiritual Journey*. San Francisco: Harper, 1993.

Pegis, Anton C. "Saint Bonaventure, St. Francis and Philosophy." *Mediaeval Studies* 15 (1953): 1–13.

Plantinga, Alvin. "Advice to Christian Philosophers." *Faith and Philosophy* 1 (1984): 253–271.

———. *The Analytic Theist: An Alvin Plantinga Reader*. Edited by James F. Sennet. Grand Rapids: Eerdmans, 1998.

———. "Christian Philosophy at the End of the Twentieth Century." In *Christian Philosophy at the Close of the Twentieth Century*, edited by Sander Griffioen and Bert Balk, 29–53. Kampen: Kok, 1995.

———. "The Twin Pillars of Christian Scholarship." In *Seeking Understanding: The Stob Lectures 1986-1998*, 121–161. Grand Rapids: Eerdmans, 2001.

Plantinga, Cornelius. *Engaging God's World: A Christian Vision of Faith, Learning and Living*. Grand Rapids: Eerdmans, 2002.

Plato. *Complete Works*. Edited by John M. Cooper. Indianapolis: Hackett, 1997.

Parks, Sharon Daloz. *Big Questions, Worthy Dreams: Mentoring Young Adults in Their Search for Meaning, Purpose and Faith*. San Francisco: Jossey-Bass, 2000.

Potts, Timothy C. *Conscience in Medieval Philosophy*. Cambridge: Cambridge University Press, 1980.

Pranger, Burcht. *Bernard of Clairvaux and the Shape of Monastic Thought: Broken Dreams*. Leiden: Brill, 1994.

Quinn, Joseph Francis. *The Historical Constitution of St. Bonaventure's Philosophy*. Toronto: The Pontifical Institute for Mediaeval Studies Publications, 1973.

Rabbow, Paul. *Seelenführung: Methodik der Exerzitiën der Antike*. Munich: Kösal Verlag, 1954.

Ritschl, Albrecht. *Geschichte des Pietismus*. Three Volumes. Bonn: Marcus, 1880–1886.

Runner, Howard Evan. *The Development of Aristotle Illustrated from the Earliest Books of the Physics*. Kampen: Kok, 1951.

———. *The Relation of the Bible to Learning*. Toronto: Wedge Press, 1972.

Rushdoony, Rousas John. *The Institutes of Biblical Law: A Chalcedon Study With Three Appendices by Gary North*. Nutley: Craig Press, 1973.

Saarinen, Risto. *Weakness of Will in Medieval Thought from Augustine to Buridan*. New York: Brill, 1994.

Said, Edward W. *Orientalism*. London: Routledge and Kegan Paul, 1978.

Schmidt, Martin. *Pietismus*. Berlin: W. Kohlhammer, 1972.

Schmitt, Jean-Claude. *Mort d'une Hérésie: L'Église et les Clercs Face aux Béguines et aux Beghards du Rhin Supérieur du XVe au XVe Siècle*. Paris: Mouton, 1978.

Schulz-Wackerbarth, Yorick. "Discovering Connection: The Dynamic Tension and a 'More-Than' in an Eckhartian Concept of the Soul." Unpublished M.Phil.F. Thesis. Institute for Christian Studies, 2003.

Schwehn, Mark R. *Exiles from Eden: Religion and the Academic Vocation*. New York: Oxford University Press, 1993.

Shook, Laurence K. *Etienne Gilson*. The Etienne Gilson Series 6. Toronto: The Pontifical Institute for Mediaeval Studies Publications, 1984.

Somme, Luc-Thomas O.P. "The Infallibility, Impeccability and Indestructibility of *Synderesis*." *Studies in Christian Ethics* 19 (2006): 403–416.

Stellingwerff, Johannes. *De VU na Kuyper: De Vrije Univesiteit van 1905–1955: een Halve Eeuw Geestesgeschiedenis van een Civitas Academica*. Kampen: Kok, 1987.

———. *D. H. Th. Vollenhoven, 1892–1978: Reformator der Wijsbegeerte*. Baarn: Ten Have, 1992.

———. *Dr. Abraham Kuyper en de Vrije Universiteit*. Kampen: Kok, 1987.

———. *Geschiedenis van de Reformatorische Wijsbegeerte*. Amersfoort: Stichting voor Reformatorische Wijsbegeerte, 2006.

Sweetman, Robert, ed. *In the Phrygian Mode: Neo-Calvinism, Antiquity and the Lamentations of Reformational Philosophy*. Lanham: University Press of America, 2007.

———. "Christian Scholarship: Two Reformed Perspectives." *Perspectives" A Journal of Reformed Thought* 16:6 (June/July 2001): 14–19.

———. "John Paul II's Account of the Unity of Scholarship in *Fides et Ratio*." In *That the World May Believe: Essays on Mission and Unity in Honour of George Vandervelde*, edited by Michael W. Goheen and Margaret O'Gara, 203–214. Lanham: University of America Press, 2006.

———.*Of Runners and Batons: Viewing the Marathon of Philosophy from the Cool of the Giant's Shade*. Toronto: Institute for Christian Studies, 2001.

Tellenbach, Gerd. *Church, State and Christian Society at the Time of the Investiture Contest*. Oxford: Oxford University Press, 1940.

Tol, Anthony. *Philosophy in the Making: D. H. Th. Vollenhoven and the Emergence of Reformed Philosophy*. Sioux Center: Dordt College Press, 2010.

Trottmann, C. "La Syndérèse selon Albert se Grand." In *Albertus Magnus zum Gedenken nach 800 Jahren: Neue Zugänge, Aspekten und* Perspektiven, edited by W. Sennen, 255–273. Berlin: Akademie Verlag, 2001.

Van Til, Cornelius. *Common Grace*. Philadelphia: The Presbyterian and Reformed Publishing Company, 1947.

Vattimo, Giani. *Belief*. Translated by Luca D'Isanto and David Webb. Stanford: Stanford University Press, 1999.

Verburg, Marcel E. *Herman Dooyeweerd: Leven en Werk van een Christen-Wijsgeer*. Baarn: Ten Have, 1989.

Vicaire, Marie-Humbert, OP. *L'Imitation des Apôtres: Moines, Chanoines et Mendiants (IVe–XIIIe Siècle)*. Paris: Éditions du CERF, 1963.

Volf, Miroslav. *The End of Memory: Remembering Rightly in a Violent World*. Grand Rapids MI: Eerdman's, 2006.

———. *The Future of Hope: Christian Tradition and Modernity and Postmodernity*. Grand Rapids: Eerdmans, 2004.

Vollenhoven, D. H. Th. "Conservatisme en Progressiviteit in de Wijsbegeerte." In *Conservatisme en Progressiviteit in de Wetenschap*, 35–48. Kampen: Kok, 1951.

———. *De Noodzakelijkheid eener Christelijke Logica*. Amsterdam: H.J. Paris, 1932.

———. *Hoofdlijnen der Logica*. Kampen: Kok, 1948.

Warfield, Benjamin Breckenridge. *Studies in Tertullian and Augustine*. New York: Oxford University Press, 1930.

Wesselius, Janet Catherine. *Objective Ambiguities: Feminist Negotiations in Epistemology*. Calgary: Glenn Mielka Design, 2001.

———. "Points of Convergence Between Dooyeweerdian and Feminist Views of the Philosophic Self." In *Knowing* Other-*wise: Philosophy on the Threshold of* Spirituality, edited by James H. Olthuis, 154–168. New York: Fordham University Press, 1997.

Willey, T. *Back To Kant: The Revival of Kantianism in German Social and Historical Thought, 1860–1914*. Detroit: Wayne State University Press, 1987.

Williams, George Huntston. *The Radical Reformation*. Kirksville: Sixteenth-Century Journal Publishers, 1992.

Wolfe, Alan. "The Opening of the Evangelical Mind." *Atlantic Monthly* October (2000): 55–76.

Wolterstorff, Nicholas. *Educating for Shalom: Essays on Christian Higher Education*. Edited by Clarence W. Joldersma and Gloria Goris Stronks. Grand Rapids: Eerdmans, 2004.

———. "Fifty Years Later." *Pro Rege* 34 (2005): 26–30.

———. "Public Theology or Christian Learning?" In Moltmann, Jürgen, Nicholas Wolterstorff, and Ellen T. Charry. *A Passion For God's Reign: Theology, Christian Learning and Christian Self*. Edited by Miroslav Volf, 65–87. Grand Rapids: Eerdmans, 1998.

Woudenberg, Rene van. *Gelovend Denken: Inleiding tot een Christelijke Filosofie*. Amsterdam: Buijten en Schipperheijn, 1992.

Index

Lightning Source UK Ltd.
Milton Keynes UK
UKOW05f1053150217
294459UK00021B/369/P